Human Ecological Issues
A Reader

Fergus M. Clydesdale
Frederick J. Francis
University of Massachusetts

K|H

KENDALL/HUNT PUBLISHING COMPANY
Dubuque, Iowa, USA   •   Toronto, Ontario, Canada

B   402197   01

Contents

Preface

The consumption of food is probably the most intense personal act that a human body entertains with its environment. In fact, during the act of eating the body and material from the environment become one. As a result many taboos, ethnic and religious laws, feasts, and ceremonies are centered around food.

In our society there has arisen a great emotional concern over the worth and safety of food along with a vague tendency to worship what we eat as a panacea for ill health and psychological depression.

Often this emotional concern is based on myth rather than fact and results in sensational extrapolations of science into the realm of fantasy.

One of the basic reasons for such extrapolations is the misuse of science and mistaken expectation of technology. Often science and technology seem to be given human attributes. That is, they are discussed in terms of moral values. How often have you heard technology spoken of as being bad? From a scientists point of view this is a ridiculous statement. Technology and/or science in and of itself cannot be bad. It simply reports a set of facts obtained from a controlled experiment or it carries out a function which has been programmed by a human being. It may be misused and certainly instances can be cited such as the abuse of chemicals for insect and weed control, pollution due to inadequate treatment systems and unethical medical experiments.

However, this does not change the basic fact that the science or technology itself does not have a moral value.

Science can tell us what will happen under a set of controlled conditions. Change the conditions and the results will change. This sometimes leads to a situation where frustration abounds because one absolute answer cannot be given for all circumstances. It is at this point that we leave the realm of science and begin a philosophical trip into extrapolation. The extrapolation of animal experiments to humans may provide correct or incorrect answers, there is no sure way to know. It is at this point that the science of statistics is applied which provides the probability of an event occuring, but again no absolute answers.

We can provide an estimate of risk but not an assurance of absolute safety.

This is the reason why scientists often disagree over the conclusions which a set of data provide from a given experiment. If scientists disagree then what are consumers to do?

Some years ago we began a course in Food Science and Nutrition at the Amherst campus of the University of Massachusetts. This course has enrolled over 20,000 non-science majors and it is from these students that we have learned about the frustrations which exist.

We wrote a textbook, *Food Nutrition, and You* published by Prentice-Hall but felt that it didn't provide enough viewpoints for the non-science student.

Therefore we decided to put together this compilation of readings. This book contains articles which a consumer can understand on many different sets of issues involving food, its safety, production and distribution. We have attempted to provide different viewpoints, where possible, so that readers might decide for themselves what science has to offer.

It is hoped that this book will show that food, although an extremely personal material, is not a drug, does not provide magic, is not good or bad, but is in fact a prerequisite for life that must be consumed with some knowledge based on scientific fact not magic or myth.

1

Who and What Do We Believe

Vitamin E increases the sex drive, processed foods are poisons, natural foods are toxic, synthetic foods are made from coal. How often do we see such assertions in the press, in journals, or in the media. Should we believe them? What is Vitamin E? What is a synthetic food?

These are questions that any reasonably intelligent consumer should ask.

It is for this reason that the following two papers have been selected. The first is a glossary of common terms which we come in contact with. Certainly the words must be understood and defined before a judgment can be made about the accuracy of a statement. The second paper is a chapter from a book entitled *Nutrition and Food Choices*. It is an excellent summary of how to evaluate food and nutrition information as well as how to decide on the accuracy of the author.

It is hoped that these two papers will provide a basis for evaluating much of the material to follow.

Food and Nutrition Terms

GENERAL NUTRITION TERMS

Additives: Substances or a mixture of substances other than a basic foodstuff which are present in food as the result of any aspect of production, processing, storing or packaging. Additives are categorized as intentional or incidental.

- **Intentional Additives:** Substances that are purposely added to food to perform a specific function—for example, to improve flavor, texture, consistency, nutritional value or keeping quality. Salt, sugar and spices are common examples.
- **Incidental Additives:** Substances which may be present in finished food in minute quantities as a result of some phase of production, processing, storing or packaging. For example, a substance could be present in food due to migration or transfer from the package or processing equipment.

Basal Metabolism: The amount of energy required by the body, in a state of complete rest, to maintain involuntary life processes such as respiration, heart beat, circulation and body temperature.

Biological Value: A method of rating proteins according to the percentage of absorbed nitrogen retained in the body for maintenance and growth. Egg protein has the highest biological value (100), and therefore is used as the standard for rating other protein foods. Other animal sources such as meat, fish, poultry, cheese and milk supply protein of high biological value.

Calorie: A measure of energy expressed in terms of heat. The word "calorie" is commonly used in non-technical publications, but the correct terms are "kilocalorie" or "Calorie." (Refer to the definition of "kilocalorie.")

Cell: The basic structural unit of which all tissues, organs, muscles, skin and bones are composed.

Cholesterol: A fat-like substance found in every animal cell. It is an essential constituent of blood, tissues, and bile, and is important in the synthesis of certain hormones.

Catalyst: A substance that influences chemical changes or reactions while remaining stable or intact.

Diet: The foods that a person or animal usually eats.

Dietary Standards: Quantitative recommendations of essential nutrients and kilocalories for the purpose of maintaining optimal nutritional status.

DNA (deoxyribonucleic acid): A chemical within living cells which contains the genetic code and transmits the hereditary pattern.

Digestion: The bodily process by which foods are converted into simple substances readily utilized by individual cells.

Enzyme: A substance that either speeds up or slows down a biological reaction without entering into the reaction.

Fiber: The indigestible component of food that aids in the passage of waste products through the intestines for elimination. Major sources of fiber in the diet are whole grains, nuts and vegetables. Fiber content varies according to the specific plant and its maturity.

- **Crude Fiber:** The component of food that remains after treatment with acid and alkali in laboratory analysis. Although this is a much more rigorous treatment than the digestive process in the body, food composition tables refer to crude fiber values.
- **Dietary Fiber:** The part of food that is not digested in the gastrointestinal tract of the human body. Dietary fiber includes crude fiber plus additional indigestible fiber. It is more important in analyzing diets, however the dietary fiber content of food has not been determined. Research has been initiated in this area.

Gras List: A list of about 600 substances which were exempted from the testing required by the Food Additives Amendment, because they were judged by experts to be "generally recognized as safe: (GRAS) under the conditions of their use in foods at that time. These substances are now under review by the Food and Drug Administration and contract laboratories to re-evaluate their GRAS approval.

Hunger: A strong desire for food. Hunger does not indicate malnutrition, but implies body energy depletion.

Inorganic: Not containing the element, carbon, or the qualities of living organisms. Minerals are an example of inorganic substances.

International Unit (I.U.): A standard unit of measure, used for vitamins A, D and E, upon which the actual biological activity of a vitamin can be measured.

Kilocalorie: A measure of body energy expressed in terms of heat. One kilocalorie is the amount of heat necessary to raise the temperature of one kilogram of water one degree Centigrade. Kilocalories or body energy are obtained from three nutrients: fat, carbohydrate, and protein. Energy is needed for physical activity and maintaining body processes.

Malnutrition: Undernourishment resulting from insufficient food, improper diet or physiological abnormalities.

Metabolism: The continuous chemical and physical processes by which living organisms and cells convert nutrients into energy, body structure and waste.

Minimum Daily Requirements (MDR): Amounts of various nutrients that are regarded as necessary to the diet for the prevention of deficiency diseases and are generally less than the RDA. These standards were established in 1941 by the Food and Drug Administration for labeling foods and pharmaceutical preparations for special dietary purposes. The MDR is now obsolete. The RDA and U.S. RDA are the current methods of expressing daily dietary needs.

Nutrient: A substance that is necessary for the functioning of the human body. Nutrients are used by the body in three ways: to provide growth and repair; to furnish energy and heat; and to regulate body processes.

- **Macronutrient:** Nutrients required by the body in relatively large amounts and constituting a large proportion of body weight. These include carbohydrates, fats, protein, calcium, phosphorus, magnesium, potassium and chloride.
- **Micronutrients:** Nutrients required by the human body in small or "trace" amounts. These include vitamins, iron, iodine and copper.

Nutrient Deficiency: A state in which a physical disorder occurs due to lack of a particular nutrient.

Nutrient Density: The ratio of a specific nutrient in a given amount of food to the total kilocalories.

Nutrition: The vital process by which the body converts the nutrients in food into energy and into the structural and regulatory substances of the human body.

Nutrition Science: A science that includes understanding the composition of foods and the knowledge of proper food selection to obtain an adequate diet.

Obesity: Weighing 20% or more above ideal body weight.

Optimum Nutrition: That which supplies the required amount of all essential nutrients needed by the body for maintaining good health.

Organism: Any living thing.

Organic: Having properties associated with living organisms or referring to a chemical containing carbon.

Overweight: Weighing 10% to 20% above ideal body weight.

Oxidation: The chemical process which occurs in the body as food is converted into body tissues, energy is produced and body tissue is broken down.

Recommended Dietary Allowances (RDA): Daily requirements of essential nutrients, established by the Food and Nutrition Board of the National Academy of Sciences, as adequate to meet the known nutritional needs of almost every healthy person. The RDA is categorized into seventeen classifications based on age and sex.

United States Recommended Dietary Allowances (U.S. RDA): Requirements of essential nutrients derived by the Food and Drug Administration from a composite of the RDA for use in nutrition labeling of food products. Generally, the highest value (that of an adult male) for each nutrient was selected. This, many normal healthy people may not need the full 100% of the U.S. RDA of a specific nutrient each day.

NUTRIENTS

Carbohydrates: A class of organic compounds composed of carbon, hydrogen and oxygen that supply energy (4 kilocalories per gram). Carbohydrates are synthesized by plants, with the aid of sunlight, from water and carbon dioxide in the air. They are classified as monosaccharides, disaccharides and polysaccharides on the basis of chemical structure.

Fats: A class of organic compounds known as lipids which are composed of carbon, hydrogen and oxygen, chiefly glyceride esters of fatty acids such as stearic, palmitic, oleic and butyric. Fats are soluble in organic solvents such as ether, but are insoluble in water. They are concentrated sources of energy (9 kilocalories per gram) and are widely distributed throughout the body, functioning as support and protection for vital organs and tissues.

- **Fatty Acid:** The component of fat that is responsible for the saturated or unsaturated quality.
- **Essential Fatty Acids:** Fatty acids that cannot be produced by the body.
- **Non-essential Fatty Acids:** Fatty acids that can be produced by the body.
- **Saturated Fat:** Fats that remain solid at room temperature and are generally of animal origin.
- **Polyunsaturated Fat:** Fats that tend to be liquid at room temperature. Vegetables are the most abundant sources.

Minerals: Inorganic components of foods. Essential minerals are part of the body structure or act as body regulators in hormones and enzymes.

- **Calcium (Ca):** The most plentiful mineral in the body which is important for: structure and growth of bones and teeth; blood clotting; and proper functioning of nerves, muscles and heart.
- **Chloride (Cl):** A macronutrient which combines with hydrogen to form hydrochloric acid secreted by the stomach for digestion.
- **Cobalt (Co):** A trace mineral which is necessary for the formation of vitamin B_{12} (cyanocobalamin).
- **Copper (Cu):** A trace mineral which acts as a catalyst in the synthesis of hemoglobin, the red substance in blood that carries oxygen from the lungs to all body tissue.

- **Iodine (I):** A trace mineral which is essential for the normal functioning of the thyroid gland and for the production of thyroid hormones.
- **Iron (Fe):** A trace mineral which is a vital component of hemoglobin.
- **Magnesium (Mg):** A trace mineral that is present in the bony structure of the body and is involved in basic cell processes.
- **Phosphorus (P):** A macronutrient which is found primarily in the bones and teeth but is also present in all cells and body fluids. It is necessary for calcium absorption and important in the metabolism of many nutrients.
- **Potassium (K):** A macronutrient which is instrumental in transmitting nerve impulses and maintaining the fluid balance in the body.
- **Sodium (Na):** A macronutrient which is instrumental in transmitting nerve impulses and maintaining balance in the body fluids outside of the cells.
- **Zinc (Zn):** A trace mineral which is a cofactor in many metabolic reactions and is essential to insulin activity. Zinc deficiency is rare. Toxicity due to excess zinc is a more serious problem.

Protein: Any class of naturally occurring compounds, composed of amino acids (containing carbon, hydrogen, nitrogen, oxygen and often sulfur) which are essential constituents of all living cells such as bone, muscle and blood. Protein makes up 15 to 20 percent of the human body. It also supplies energy (4 kilocalories per gram).

- **Amino Acids:** The smaller compounds of which proteins are composed. They are grouped according to essential and non-essential classification.
- **Essential Amino Acids:** Amino acids that cannot be synthesized by the body in amounts sufficient to support growth and repair, and therefore must be supplied by protein foods. There are nine essential amino acids required by humans: histidine, isoleucine, leucine, lysine, methionine, phenylalanine, theonine, tryptophan and valine.
- **Non-Essential Amino Acids:** Amino acids that can be synthesized by the human body. These include alanine, arginine, aspartic acid, cystine, cysteine, citruline, glutamic acid, glycine, hydroxyproline, proline, serine, tyrosine, norleucine, and hydroxyglutamic acid.
- **Complete Proteins:** Proteins that contain all of the essential amino acids in significant amounts and in the proportions necessary to maintain life and to support growth.
- **Incomplete Proteins:** Proteins that lack the amino acids that are essential to maintain life and support growth.
- **Partially Complete Proteins:** Proteins that contain amino acids in amounts and in proportions to maintain life but not support growth.

Vitamins: Complex organic compounds found in nature or scientifically synthesized in laboratories that act as catalysts, allowing the body to process and use food energy. They are essential to good health and cannot be synthesized by the body. Vitamins are categorized as water-soluble or fat-soluble. Excess fat-soluble vitamins can be retained by the body, whereas excess water-soluble vitamins are excreted. Overdoses of fat-soluble vitamins can have toxic effects.

- **Biotin:** A water-soluble B-vitamin involved in the formation of certain fatty acids and in the production of energy from the metabolism of glucose. It is essential for many chemical systems within the body.
- **Choline:** A water-soluble B-vitamin that is necessary for certain aspects of nerve functioning and fat metabolism.
- **Folic Acid:** A water-soluble B-vitamin that: assists in the synthesis of chemicals for the cell nucleus and amino acids; aids in the manufacture of red blood cells; and is essential in normal metabolism.
- **Niacin:** A water-soluble B-vitamin that is present in all body tissues and is involved in energy producing actions in cells. It promotes healthy skin, nerves, appetite and digestion.
- **Pantothenic Acid:** A water-soluble B-vitamin that is a key substance in body metabolism. It is involved in the conversion of carbohydrates, fats and proteins into the molecular forms needed by the body.
- **Vitamin A (Retinol):** A fat-soluble vitamin which is necessary to form and maintain healthy eyes, skin, hair, teeth, gums, and various glands. It is also involved in fat metabolism.
- **Vitamin B$_1$ (Thiamine):** A water-soluble vitamin which is necessary for normal digestion, growth, fertility and normal functioning of nerve tissue.
- **Vitamin B$_2$ (Riboflavin):** A water-soluble vitamin which functions in the body's use of carbohydrates, proteins and fats, particularly in the utilization of oxygen to produce energy. It is found in almost all body tissues.
- **Vitamin B$_6$ (Pyridoxine):** A water-soluble vitamin which acts as a co-enzyme, especially in the metabolism of amino acids and fats, and is essential for proper growth and maintenance of body functions.
- **Vitamin B$_{12}$ (Cyanocobalamin):** A water-soluble vitamin that aids in the building of vital genetic substances (nucleic acids) for the cell nucleus, the formation of red blood cells, and the functioning of the nervous system.
- **Vitamin C (Ascorbic Acid):** A water-soluble vitamin that is necessary for the formation of collagen, a protein that acts as a cementing substance in binding body cells together. Collagen is needed for tissue strength, bone and teeth formation, and wound healing. Vitamin C is also important in iron absorption.
- **Vitamin D (Calciferol):** A fat-soluble vitamin which aids in the absorption of calcium and phosphorus in the formation of bones and teeth.

- **Vitamin E (Tocopherol):** A fat-soluble vitamin which acts as an antioxidant in the body, protecting cell membranes, vitamin A, vitamin C and unsaturated fatty acids from destruction by oxygen.
- **Vitamin K:** A fat-soluble vitamin which is necessary for normal blood clotting.

Water: The most abundant nutrient in the body accounting for approximately 65% of the body weight. Water is needed to: carry nutrients to the cells and waste products from the cells; build tissues; regulate body temperature; aid in digestion; and replace water loss.

FOOD TERMS

Basic Four Daily Food Guide: A classification of common foods according to major nutrient contributions. It was established by the United States Department of Agriculture to facilitate the selection of foods for a nutritious diet. The basic food groups and the nutrients provided are:

- **Milk Group**—calcium, riboflavin (vitamin B_2), protein
- **Meat Group**—protein, niacin, iron, thiamine (vitamin B_1)
- **Fruit and Vegetable Group**—vitamins A and C
- **Bread and Cereal Group**—carbohydrate, thiamine (vitamin B_1), iron, niacin

Convenience Foods: Foods in which one or more steps of preparation have been completed before the product is offered for sale. They are designed to save time and labor. Examples are canned products, baking mixes, packaged dinners, frozen foods and soup bases.

Conventional Foods: Foods that man has learned to cultivate by gardening or by large scale agricultural methods.

Enriched Foods: Grain products, cornmeal and rice to which three B-vitamins (thiamine, niacin and riboflavin) and a mineral, iron, have been added to replace the amount lost during processing. The replacements are regulated by federal government standards. An example is enriched bread.

Fabricated Foods: New and unique forms of food or imitations of conventional foods manufactured from components derived from agricultural products with the intent of achieving specific characteristics. Examples are low-fat and snack food products.

Food: Any substance eaten or otherwise taken into the body to sustain life, provide energy and promote nutrition.

Food Analog: A fabricated food product designed to resemble a traditional food. Examples are meat-like products made with extruded soy protein concentrate.

Formulated Foods: Imitations of common foods or new types of food that have been developed in the laboratory. This is a more general classification than fabricated foods. Examples are foods designed for special needs such as infant formulas or hospital diets for total or supplemental feeding.

Fortified Foods: Foods to which one or more nutrients have been added, or in which the original nutrient levels have been increased. The intent is to provide additional amounts of nutrients to the diet. Foods are selected for fortification because they are appropriate carriers for specific nutrients such as the addition of vitamins A and D to margarine. In the cereal industry fortification refers only to the enhancement of the protein content.

Health Foods: In current vernacular, foods that are sold in health food stores or in other store departments labeled "Health Foods." In theory, these foods have undergone little or no processing; however, there are no government standards established for regulating the production and sale of health foods. In reality, all foods that supply nutrients and contribute to good health are health foods.

Textured Vegetable Protein (TVP): Products made from oil seed or cereal products which may contain binders, stabilizers, flavoring or coloring agents. Soy beans are a common source material. Textured items from soy come in cubes, chunks, chips, granules and rolls.

Expanding Nutrition Knowledge

by K.W. McNutt and D.R. McNutt

College courses are selected by students for a variety of reasons. Some are required for graduation, some are prerequisite for more advanced studies, and others offer knowledge basic to a chosen career. Elective courses are generally taken to provide background knowledge that can be expanded at leisure after graduation. For many students, nutrition courses fall into this latter category of learning experiences.

This book has presented concepts based on present scientific information and its application to questions of current interest, but the science of nutrition encompasses an ever-expanding body of knowledge. Future discoveries will affect the lives of all people. The goal of this chapter is to facilitate your ability to continue expanding your nutrition knowledge in the years to come.

NUTRITION RESOURCES

Many researchers who have spent a lifetime pursuing evasive vitamins and feeding various diets to rats are no doubt surprised that society has recently become very interested in the subject of food.

This public discovery of nutrition has had a variety of repercussions. Advertising agencies have capitalized on this interest in food commercials, the sales of diet-related paperback books have soared, and most astute political candidates include an anti-hunger plank in their campaign platforms. This atmosphere has created an excellent "environment for learning" (in educational terminology), but the climate is also ripe for the public to be misled.

Whom Can You Believe?

Almost every person who conveys nutrition information to the public (including your authors) has certain biases and perspectives. In most instances, these do not work against the best interests of the public, but sometimes, because of its presentation or its interpretation, the message is detrimental.

Expanding nutrition knowledge outside the classroom is made more difficult because of the communication gap between scientists and the press (who are primary sources of information for the general public). To make matters worse, the credibility of certain scientists is sometimes questioned because of

From NUTRITION AND FOOD CHOICES by Kristen W. McNutt and David R. McNutt. © 1978, Science Research Associates, Inc. Reprinted by permission of the publisher.

their professional affiliations with government, industry, or, at times, academia. This condemnation-by-association leads some people to disregard the statements of certain nutritionists before listening to and evaluating what is said.

The resultant dilemma is the natural product of our current social and political atmosphere. Depending upon your point of view:

1. Government may be viewed as conscientiously protecting the quality of the food supply or strangled by red tape to the detriment of both consumers and suppliers.
2. The food industry is seen as capitalistic exploitation or competitive free enterprise.
3. Consumerism is a long-overdue expression of society's rights or an opportunity for a vocal minority to impose its desires upon the broader society.
4. The free press is the strength of a democracy or license to purvey whatever news sells the most papers and advertising.

Researchers, teachers, and the general public all become entangled in these broad controversies.

Nonscientists are no doubt dismayed by conflicting information about nutrition that is reported from supposedly authoritative sources. Their confusion might be less if they realized that disagreements among scientists are the fodder for growth of nutrition knowledge. Differences of opinion regarding the methodology and design of an experiment or the interpretation of the significance and meaning of data from an experiment provide a check-and-balance that can be the best possible way of directing the application of science. This intellectually stimulating specific environment, however, often leaves the consumer confused because most people lack the background or interest to probe far below the surface of nutrition controversies. Under these circumstances, it is helpful to know where you can go for a reliable, balanced answer to questions of concern.

Organizations

"Nutrition" is rarely listed in the yellow pages of the telephone book, but the following suggestions may help locate a source of nutrition information.

Professional Societies.   Several disciplines related to food and nutrition have professional societies. Their membership is broad enough to take into account different points of view. Standards for membership vary among societies, but most members are currently working in the field and presumably must keep abreast of the latest information. Several of these societies joined together in 1974 to form the National Nutrition Consortium. These societies each maintain a staff and facilities for answering questions that fall within their own area of expertise.

Public Health Agencies.   Every state health department has a person who is the director or supervisor of nutrition services. Many county and city health departments also employ nutritionists. Community clinics, especially those for children, infants, and pregnant women, usually have nutritionists on their staffs. Programs for the elderly sponsored by the Administration on Aging also utilize nutritionists.

Colleges and Universities.   Nutritionists in colleges and universities may be located in several departments. Teachers may not be able to allot academic time to consumer inquiries, but most can suggest an appropriate source of information. Land grant institutions are staffed to answer questions from the general public related to food and nutrition.

Other Health-Related Groups.   Other groups, such as the American Heart Association, the National Foundation for the March of Dimes, the American Diabetes Association, and the Red Cross, often provide consumer services related to nutrition. Local chapters of such organizations may exist in your community.

Hospitals and Health Maintenance Organizations (HMO).   Hospitals and HMOs often have staff nutritionists. Consultations are usually given on a fee-for-service basis or as part of a prepaid medical plan.

Dental and Medical Associations.   State and local dental and medical associations (or societies) sometimes keep a roster of professionals qualified in nutrition. Occasionally these organizations can refer a physician to a dietitian who does fee-for-service patient consultations. However, such services should only be provided by dietitians who communicate with the physician regarding the total medical status of the patient.

Individuals

Because of their training and the nature of their work, nutritionists develop expertise of different types and differ in their ability to answer consumer questions.

The Meaning of Degrees.   A critical reader always checks the qualifications of a source of information. The string of letters behind an author's name is usually (but not always) an indication of the person's expertise in nutrition. However, a Ph.D., M.D., D.Sc., M.S., M.A., or M.P.H. is hardly a guarantee that the person is well informed on a specific topic.

Nutritionists are found in a variety of disciplines. The strength as well as the complexity, of this science is that it overlaps biochemistry, physiology, medicine, home economics, food technology, bacteriology, toxicology, and many other disciplines. No one person can possibly maintain an expertise in all these areas. For example, it is unrealistic to expect a food technologist to know the effect of sugar intake on diabetes, or to ask a physician how much vitamin C is destroyed by cooking asparagus. The inquirer, therefore, should ask a scientist what his or her major interest is before addressing specific questions. When an "expert" in the appropriate field is located, he or she should be asked whether there are other scientists who do not share the viewpoint expressed by this person. The response to this question may indicate how much confidence to place in that individual's opinion.

Specialist and Generalist.   Certain tradeoffs must be kept in mind when advice is sought from nutritionists. Some of the most brilliant nutritionists of necessity become so engrossed in their narrowly defined area of research that they are not aware of what consumers consider problems at the moment. Others who are more involved in applied nutrition, have a breadth of information in all areas but lack the depth. Society ultimately benefits from the contribution made by each group, but when seeking information, you should not expect from one what is the strength of the other.

Communication Tips.   Conversations with professional nutritionists can be frustrating if you are seeking brief, simple answers. Scientists are very precise in their thinking, and their conversations usually involve a lengthy clarification of the conditions under which any given statement is, and is not, valid. This is why most authoritative nutritionists are not popular on television talk shows, and why they communicate poorly, if at all, with the press. Their critical thinking pattern makes them less than sympathetic if you have not given serious thought and study, commensurate with what is easily available, before asking a question.

EVALUATION OF NUTRITION INFORMATION

Misinterpretation of nutrition information often occurs because people fail to read carefully or they overlook the real significance of numbers as they actually appear or are spoken.

Grammatical Rules

The following suggestions may uncover possible pitfalls in interpretation of nutrition information. These grammatical patterns may unintentionally slip into coversations or print, but they can be a warning that information should be examined critically. If a writer is careless about *how* something is said, the reader should be careful about *what* is said.

Multiple Subject-Multiple Object.   Sentences with multiple subjects and objects can mislead the reader. For instance:

"Sugar, fat, cholesterol, and salt cause diabetes, cancer, hypertension, and heart attacks."

You might assume that each dietary factor is required to cause all the diseases, that all the dietary factors must interact before causing any of the diseases, or many other permutations of these combinations of causes and effects.

Incomplete or Unquantified Comparatives.   Incomplete or unquantified comparatives leave the reader in the dark or open to make any implied—but not stated—assumptions:

"Fiber content is lower in the American diet."

Lower than what? It is important to know how much lower and also how much each diet contains before proceeding to evaluate other correlations.

Opinion.   Personal opinion is often subtly woven into nutrition articles, even those without by-lines. "In other words" is a phrase that should send up a red flag for a critical reader. "It is thought," "It is believed," "It appears," should make you immediately question "By whom?" "On what basis?"

Generalizations.   Generalizations are easily misinterpreted. "Many nutritionists recommend" may mean a majority of the professional nutritionists in this country or it may mean a much smaller group.

Qualifiers.   It may be helpful to mark qualifiers in an article to avoid being misled. "May," "seems to," "perhaps," "probably," and "assuming" should alert the reader that everything in that statement is a supposition and not a fact. Qualifiers can easily be forgotten if several pages of text go on to elaborate on a supposition.

Juxtaposition of Sentences.   The juxtaposition of two sentences can lead a reader to draw a correlation even though it was never stated by the author. For instance:

"The American diet in 1942 provided half as much meat as the diet in 1976. Many recruits in World War II were found to be in poor health."

The author never says that the recruits were in poor health because their diets contained half as much meat as the 1976 diet, but the reader has been led to make this correlation.

Undefined Terms.   Undefined terms plague the nutrition literature. The phrase "A nutritious food" is used too loosely by many people. It conveys no information about the nutrient content of the food or its relative contribution to meeting nutrient needs. "Harmful to health," "beneficial to your body," and "good for you" can be meaningful terms, but only if they are explained further.

Connotations.   Connotations of words can broaden the communication gap—intentionally or unintentionally. "Full of energy" has a different implication from "full of calories," but both mean about the same thing. "Gassing tomatoes" leaves a different impression from "tomatoes stored in a gaseous atmosphere." The following are pairs of words that have quite different connotations although their meanings are synonymous in many contexts.

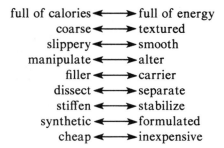

full of calories ◄────► full of energy
coarse ◄────► textured
slippery ◄────► smooth
manipulate ◄────► alter
filler ◄────► carrier
dissect ◄────► separate
stiffen ◄────► stabilize
synthetic ◄────► formulated
cheap ◄────► inexpensive

Mathematical Rules

Mathematics is considered such a precise science that numbers should not be misleading. They need not be—if you read carefully.

Reading Labels on Graphs. Understanding labels on graphs is important for correct interpretation of numbers. Often, a graph does not use zero as the lowest value. This saves space and allows the reader to visualize small, but significant, changes. However, it places a responsibility on the reader to know what degree of change corresponds with a significant deviation from normal.

Graphs that present changes compared to 100 percent of a certain index clearly indicate trends, but unless you understand the meaning of the 100 percent standard, it is difficult to interpret the significance of fluctuations from this initial value. In graphs of nutrient consumption trends, check whether the values refer to the weights of nutrients eaten, the amount eaten as a percentage of the amount eaten earlier (for instance, in 1978 compared to 1913), or the energy provided by that nutrient as a percentage of total energy intake. All three of these types of graphs are useful, but each conveys different information.

Dosages of Nutrients. Dosages of nutrients are often cited in nutrition literature, and it is helpful to compare these values to the RDA. Few people keep a table of RDA values at their fingertips and most of the exact numbers memorized for this course will probably be beyond your recall six months from now. It is rarely necessary to know the RDA to the last decimal point, but it would help to recall whether a nutrient is needed in milligram or gram quantities, maybe even a bit closer than that.

Students are better or than teachers at devising easy ways to memorize lists of names and numbers. The best method we know is a senseless string of syllables and rounded-off numbers that approximate the RDA in milligrams—perhaps Table 1 will help you in the future. Vitamin B_{12}, the micronutrient with the lowest RDA (3 micrograms), and protein, the nutrient with the highest RDA (46 to 56 grams), are not included in Table 1.

Toxicity Calculations. Toxicity calculations are difficult unless you are familiar with certain mathematical conversions, but occasionally such efforts

TABLE 1. Guide to Remembering Approximate RDA Values

Approximate Adult RDA	Nutrients	Initials of Nutrients Needed in Approximately the Same Amount
Less than 1 mg	Iodine Folacin	IF
1–2 mg	Thiamin Riboflavin Pyridoxine	TRiP
10–20 mg	Zinc Iron Niacin	ZIN
50 mg	Ascorbic acid (vitamin C)	A
1,000 mg	CAlcium Phosphorus	CAP

may be worthwhile. . . . The questions that should be posed are the same when trying to put into perspective the hazard of any noxious substance—whether it occurs naturally, is produced by a bacterium or fungus, or is added during food processing.

Many writers do not try to help their readers through these calculations. They may state ill effects without also stating toxic doses and the amount of toxin in food. The reader is often left without an answer to the question that applies to everyday life.

Anecdotes

Anecdotes fill the pages of many books that bear nutrition-related titles. These stories tell of people with a broad array of disorders—warts, infertility, dandruff, recurrent crying spells, upset stomach, irritability, terminal cancer—who have been miraculously cured by taking nutrient supplements or making a dietary change. These stories provide a glimmer of hope for people who feel they have no other recourse; they also sell thousands of books and trillions of vitamin and mineral capsules.

Such books must be read very carefully. Earlier chapters of this book have pointed out the need to consider all variables that may affect a physiological change and the importance of carrying out well-controlled studies that compare the effects of a placebo and a nutrient. The interpretation of anecdotes is further limited because the abnormal condition is frequently self-diagnosed by people who have no way of knowing what other diseases (psychological or physiological) can cause the same disorder.

It is incorrect to say that ingestion of nutrient supplements never coincides with remission of symptoms or disease. However, we can say that, with few exceptions, there is no evidence that vitamins or minerals in excess of recommended nutrient needs cause reversal of these conditions. In some conditions, the progress of some patients coincides with changes in their psychological state. Some people call it faith or the will of God; others claim it is mere coincidence; some call it positive thinking; still others, more scientifically oriented, try to monitor fluctuations in brain waves and coincidental changes in physiologically measurable indexes.

The study of these phenomena borders on another frontier of medical knowledge. The untapped potential of the human brain has not been thoroughly explored. The influences of the mind on physiological function (psychosomatic effects) have been recognized, but these effects have not yet been explained through carefully controlled research. Until these correlations are understood and harnessed for the benefit of humanity, you can only keep in mind that a possible explanation of "vitamin cures" may be linked to the fact that people believe the cure will work.

Usually, it is a waste of time to try to convince a person who has been cured that his or her micronutrient supplement was not the cause of the cure. It may be worthwhile, however, to know how to discuss such stories with other people—those who are curious and might be easily persuaded to believe in the cure, yet not so emotionally involved that they lose sight of reason. The following questions will not apply to every situation or story, but they may lead a discussion toward patterns of thought that will be helpful for people who have not studied nutrition.

1. Was the person's diet adequate or inadequate before the cure?
2. Was the cure measurable or was it just a change in the way the person feels? Who measured the effect?
3. Was the cure part of a controlled test of the effect of the micronutrient?
4. What else might have caused the cure?

USING FOOD LABELS

Compared to full-color advertisements for miracle diet books, fascinating true-life stories of nutrient cures, and entertaining television celebrities who are self-proclaimed nutrition experts, it seems terribly boring to turn to the label on a can of beans to expand your nutrition knowledge. This is not the only way to learn, but it offers certain advantages:

• It is easily accessible information.
• Its validity is carefully controlled.

Much of the print on food packages is not there by chance or fancy, but because of government regulations. These regulations are always being expanded and revised, depending upon consumer needs and use and upon the growth of knowledge in the field. Nutrition-related information that currently appears on many food packages includes the categories described below.

Ingredient Labeling

The part of the label that lists the ingredients of the product in order of their predominance can be helpful in estimating nutrient content. Order of predominance can be misleading, however, unless you read carefully. For example, enriched flour may be listed as the predominant ingredient of a pastry; since enriched flour has a relatively high nutrient density for several micronutrients, you might assume this to be true for the pastry also. However, if the ingredients listed after the enriched flour include sugar, molasses, and corn syrup, it is quite possible that the sum of these foods that supply only energy is greater than the amount of enriched flour in the pastry. Similar confusion regarding the significance of the listing sequence arises when a food contains several types of flour of several sources of fat. Knowledge of the nutrient similarities of various types of foods helps to put ingredient labeling information into perspective. Another way to guess how much of an ingredient is present is to find a spice or condiment in the list (such as salt); any ingredient listed after the condiment is present in relatively small amounts—probably less than a gram per serving.

Nutrition Quality Guidelines

The FDA has developed standards of nutrients and ingredient composition for certain groups of foods. Products are not required to meet these criteria, but only the foods that measure up to these standards can bear the following statement:

"This product provides nutrients in amounts appropriate for this class of foods as determined by the U.S. Government."

The minimum levels of nutrients for frozen heat-and-serve dinners are shown in Table 2. Few consumers will ever even wonder about how much thiamin is in a TV dinner, but if they look for—and find—the quality guideline statement, they have some assurance that the dinner has a relatively high nutrient density, as shown in Table 2.

Standardized Foods

The labels of certain foods do not list all ingredients. Instead, laws require that the product meet carefully defined standards if it bears a specific commonly used name (such as mayonnaise). The details of these regulations are

TABLE 2. Minimum levels of Nutrients for Frozen Heat-and Serve Dinners

Nutrient	Minimum Levels	
	For each 100 Cal of the Total Components	For the Total Components
Protein, g	4.60	16.0
Vitamin A, IU	150.00	520.0
Thiamin, mg	0.05	0.2
Riboflavin, mg	0.06	0.2
Niacin, mg	0.99	3.4
Pantothenic acid mg	0.32	1.1
Vitamin B_6, mg	0.15	0.5
Vitamin B_{12}, mcg	0.33	1.1
Iron, mg	0.62	2.2

quite complex, but in many ways they guard against the consumer's being misled while shopping. The standards for standardized foods can be obtained by writing to the FDA.

Nutrition Information Panel

The nutrition information panel, which became a mandatory part of the food labeling regulation in 1975, is required only if (1) a nutrient is added to a food, or (2) a claim is made in advertising or on the package that in any way conveys a message related to nutrition.

This panel may be used voluntarily by the manufacturer on any other product, but if it is used, it must comply in every way to the regulation. For instance, a label cannot state protein content without also providing information about energy value and the other nutrients that must be listed on the label. Consumer awareness of the nutrition information panel is gradually increasing, but the information given is not always understood.

Standard Information.   The first point that must be understood is that the values on the label (Table 3) refer to the amount of nutrients in one serving of the food. People who eat more or less than the serving size amount must adjust all other values accordingly. The amounts of energy (in Calories) and macronutrients (in grams) per serving are listed below the serving size description.

The bottom part of the label tells the percentage of the U.S. RDA of protein and seven other nutrients (calcium, iron, vitamin A, vitamin C, thiamin, riboflavin, and niacin) provided by one serving of the food. The protein value at the bottom of the label takes into account the quality of the protein,

TABLE 3. Nutrition Information Panel on a Food Label

Serving size	1 cup
Servings per container	10
Calories	110
Protein	3 g
Carbohydrate	22 g
Fat	1 g

Percentage of U.S. Recommended Daily Allowance (U.S. RDA)

Protein	4
Vitamin A	25
Vitamin C	4
Thiamin	25
Riboflavin	6
Niacin	20
Calcium	4
Iron	10

as well as its weight. For foods with a PER equal to casein, 45 grams of protein is equal to 100 percent of the U.S. RDA. Foods with a PER less than casein must contain more protein—65 grams—in order to be labeled as containing 100 percent of the U.S. RDA for protein.

Optional Information. U.S. RDA values have been established for twelve other vitamins and minerals. The manufacturer may list any of these with no requirement of listing the other optional nutrients.

Manufacturers may also elect to provide on the label the content of cholesterol, saturated and polyunsaturated fat, and/or sodium. This type of labeling must include a statement that the information is provided for persons whose physician has recommended dietary modifications.

Potential Problems. Appropriate use of nutrition labeling information requires an understanding of several points.

1. The values given are a measure of nutrients present after processing, but they do not make any allowances for nutrient losses caused by the consumer who overcooks or repeatedly reheats food.

2. The percentage U.S. RDA values are rounded off at various intervals. (Values less than 10 percent are rounded to the nearest 2 percent, 10 to 50 percent are rounded to the nearest 5 percent, and over 50 percent are rounded to the nearest 10 percent.) This treatment of numbers is important when a comparison of the nutrient content of two products is being made. Nutrition labels do not convey useful information about small differences in nutrient content.

3. The greatest potential hazard of nutrition labeling is that the consumer may assume that only the nutrients listed on the label are needed.

The third problem seems to be unavoidable because information is not currently available to establish U.S. RDA values for many nutrients. Also, if too many nutrients were listed, the consumer would be so overwhelmed that the information would rarely be used.

The problem is partially alleviated by the fact that in a particular food, the amounts of some of the nutrients required to be on all information panels often parallels the amounts of some other nutrients not required on the label. The presence of one nutrient therefore often indicates the presence of another. This principle is not applicable, however, when foods are fortified with an "indicator nutrient." For instance, foods that are good sources of iron usually also provide other trace elements that travel into the food supply along with the iron. However, if a food is fortified with iron, the value for iron on the label does not indicate a comparable increase in trace element content.

Advantages of the Label

Nutrition labeling information cannot currently be used to assess total daily intake because many fresh and processed products are not labeled. The usefulness of the label, therefore, is mainly for:

- Learning which foods are better sources of each nutrient
- Learning the energy value of food
- Approximating nutrient density
- Determining relative macronutrient composition of a food

Although the label does not provide sufficient information to answer all consumer questions, teaching people to use the values that are available remains an enormous challenge to nutrition educators.

STUDY QUESTIONS

1. Where in your community (besides at your college or university) might you be able to find a person to answer questions about nutrition?
2. How can you determine whether a person is qualified to provide the type of nutrition information you seek?
3. What grammatical patterns might be misleading in the context of nutrition discussions?
4. How much bread must you eat daily to consume a toxic dose of potassium bromate if this additive is present in bread at a level of 75 milligrams of potassium bromate per kilogram of bread and if a toxid dose is 75 milligrams of potassium bromate per kilogram of body weight?
5. How can anecdotes about vitamin cures be misleading?
6. What information is available on food labels?

SUGGESTED READING

1. K.W. McNutt, "Public understanding of nutrition: Implications for education programs," *Contemporary Nutrition* (March 1977).
2. P.L. White, "The perfect environment for nonsense," *Nutrition News* National Dairy Council (October 1973).
3. "Nutrition misinformation and food faddism," *Nutrition Reviews Supplement* 32(1974):1–74.
4. "Standards of identity," *Nutrition Reviews* 32(1974):29–31.
5. J. Mayer, "How to find the facts about good nutrition," *Family Health* 9(1977):32, 66.
6. O.C. Johnson, "The Food and Drug Administration and labeling," *Journal of the American Dietetic Association* 64(1974):471.
7. M.L. Ross, "What's happening to food labeling?" *Journal of the American Dietetic Association* 64(1974):262.
8. *Nutrition Labeling: How It Can Work for You.* Bethesda: The National Nutrition Consortium, Inc., 1975.
9. L.M. Henderson, "Programs to combat nutritional quackery," *Journal of the American Dietetic Association* 64(1974):372.
10. R.N. Podell et al, "The public seminar as a nutrition education approach," *Journal of the American Dietetic Association* 64(1975):460–63.
11. "Nutrition beliefs: More fashion than fact," *FDA Consumer* 10(1976):24–27.
12. E. Newman, *Strictly Speaking* New York: Bobbs-Merrill Publishing Co., 1974.

2

When Were the Good Old Days

We live in a fast paced, bewildering, frustrating world. We are beset by a lack of confidence in our leaders, a mistrust of big industry, and a general cynicism towards our fellow humans.

Understandably, this has led to the desire for a simpler, slower moving, more honest and basic life style.

It has led to a belief by many that there was a time in history when utopian conditions existed and people lived in harmony with each other and with the land around them.

We see great merit in the desire for a more harmonious life style but from a historical point of view we are unable to find a time when utopia existed.

The feeling of many that they wish to go back to nature is often unrealistic. How far back do they want to go? Back to outhouses and no running water? Back to the melting of ice in the winter and the collection of rain water in the summer in order to survive? Back to pestilence and disease and an average life span of 40 years? Back to salt cod and beans as the total diet in the winter?

We don't believe so. The drive to lead a simpler life may have great benefits but such a life may be lived in "the to-day" not in "yesterday."

This chapter provides three readings on this topic, quite variable in content.

One recommends the natural way, the other takes a realistic look at the good old days, and the third provides some insight into where we have been and where we are to-day.

No one enjoys stress. However, if the effort to reduce stress causes us to deal with fantasy then perhaps it is time to view reality and reduce stress within its confines.

Your New Style in Eating

by Beatrice Trum Hunter

Are you a newcomer to the idea of natural foods? If you are, welcome to the rapidly expanding club! You probably joined up because you were alarmed by many stories in the news. Although it was reported that mercury-contaminated fish was seized, you were assured that it was "perfectly safe to eat." Yet pregnant women were warned against it. Then, there was l'affaire cyclamate. The safety of this artificial sweetener was cleared several times, but ultimately it was banned. USDA officials have admitted that cancerous organs of meat are cut out, while the rest of the carcass passes inspection. The same agency was willing to allow chickens with a cancer virus to be sold on the market, provided the birds "do not look too repugnant." This agency considers pesticide contamination of food "no imminent hazard"—that is, the food is safe if you don't drop dead five minutes after eating it.

Recent news items may have made you distrustful of repeated assurances that our foods are nourishing. You may recall the one about the rats that were fed white bread—the bread that most Americans eat—and how the animals starved to death because of a dearth of vital nutrients. This evidence fortified the recent testimony that most breakfast cereals are so low nutritionally that they constitute a threat of "empty calories." The national nutrition surveys showed disturbing dietary deficiencies, affecting not just the poor but also the middle class and the affluent. How can this happen if our foods are nourishing?

Or maybe you have joined the revolt against many of the tasteless, overprocessed fabrications that now pass for food. You have become a label reader and are shocked to find that many present-day foodstuffs seem to be more appropriate for a chemical laboratory than a kitchen. Possibly you are hip, anti-Establishment, and *Man!* natural foods are the in thing! Or you have long felt a dragged-down, knocked-out feeling of chronic fatigue, and some energetic friend has suggested that improved eating habits may make you feel better.

Whatever your reasons, as a novice you probably have lots of unanswered questions about natural foods. How do you begin? What changes will you have to make in your marketing habits? Where will you find natural foods?

Aren't they costly? What changes will you have to make in your meal planning? Doesn't it take more time to prepare natural foods? What kitchen utensils and equipment will you need? If you are an experienced cook, how can you adapt your favorite recipes? How can you substitute more nutritious ingredients and make certain that the rest of your family will not revolt? These are some of the questions beginners ask repeatedly. Many mass-media articles have ridiculed natural food partisans with epithets such as cultists, faddists, crackpots, and a few less kindly. The beginner is apt to think that natural foods consist of concoctions such as marinated seaweed laced with blackstrap molasses and topped with a dollop of yogurt. Not so! Many, if not most of the ingredients, are already known to you. If you are an adventurous cook, you may enjoy experimenting with new ingredients and creating new and better ways of using the old familiar ones.

WHAT IS MEANT BY NATURAL FOODS?

Let's start at the beginning. Aren't all foods natural? The simplest one-sentence definition that I've ever heard was expressed by a homemaker, who said, "The shopper, really informed, and looking for a plain food with nothing added or taken away, is like Diogenes with a lantern unable to find an honest man."

A food with nothing added? This means that there will be no added perservative, color, flavor, antioxidant, emulsifier, extender, modifier, bleach, acidifier, clarifier, or any of the other thousands of additives now being used in food processing. It also implies that the food has not been treated with or does not contain any residue of pesticide, hormone, antibiotic, or other chemical, drug or serum that is now commonly used in food production. Nor will the food have unintentional additives, such as transferred wax, phenol, chemical, or other substances from the wrapper or packaging material.

A food with nothing taken away? This means that the food will not be stripped of its essential nutrients, either in the way it is grown, produced, or processed. Produce grown on fertile, well-mineralized soil may be far richer in nutrients than that grown on impoverished soil. Melons, for example, picked unripe, never develop their full mineral, vitamin, or enzyme content, nor do they taste as sweet as those that ripen on the vine. This is also true of other fruits and vegetables. Refining foodstuffs strips them of essential nutrients. If you know what happens in the milling of flour or the refining of sugar, you realize that many vital nutrients are removed or destroyed, and you, the consumer, are short-changed. For this reason you will learn to choose brown rice rather than white, and shun refined sugars.

WHAT WILL NATURAL FOODS DO FOR YOU?

You will discover, or rediscover, the good taste of foods when eaten in their natural state and free of chemicals. Taste a vine-ripened tomato and you'll never again buy the boxed unripe green ones that are merely gassed to redness.

When day by day you eat balanced meals, composed of a variety of foods, you are attempting to supply your body with the necessary nutrients. The rewards of such daily practice should be reflected in a feeling and appearance of well-being, mental alertness, energy, and high resistance to infection. For children especially, good eating habits and wise food selections, started early, may result in lifetime benefits. Natural foods, rich in minerals, vitamins, proteins, enzymes, and other essential elements, help build healthy bodies and promote normal growth for children; an over-consumption of starchy and sugary foods does not.

We have become increasingly aware of the biochemical uniqueness of each individual. Natural foods seem to be "normalizers" of weight. The elimination of rich sauces and gooey desserts helps trim obese figures, while those painfully thin may lose their gauntness with an improved metabolic balance.

Foods, however, should not be regarded as panaceas. There are no "miracle foods." Natural foods should be looked upon as tasty, nourishing, satisfying, and as sensible ingredients in sane life styles.

How Natural Is the
Science of Brewing?

Very unnatural, says the Miller company

by Eliot Marshall

Natural purity, though an imprecise concept, has fascinated people for ages—formerly as a trait of character, now more often as an attribute of food, drink, and other tangibles. It is a serious matter these days to claim that one's product is natural, as the war between the beer makers illustrates.

The two largest beer companies in America find themselves locked in a confrontation over which of them makes the purer beer, or to put it differently, over which uses the more noxious chemicals. The latest development came on February 1, when Miller Brewing Company, the second largest in the nation, accused Anheuser-Busch, the largest, of perpetrating a "campaign designed to mislead consumers into believing that its beers are natural products—which they are not." The charge came in a formal complaint (about an inch thick) filed this month at the Federal Trade Commission (FTC), which regulates advertising.

Miller specifically seeks to have the FTC stop Anheuser-Busch from using the words "natural" and "naturally" in its advertisements because, according to the complaint, the beers are "highly processed, complex products, made with chemical additives and other components not in their natural form." The brief cites earlier rulings and a staff report which sided against claims of naturalness by other companies, and it argues that it is inherently deceptive to call something "natural" when it contains ingredients that are more than minimally processed. One reason the ads are deceptive, Miller claims, is that they may be used to induce buyers to pay more for the product.

More interesting than the legal challenge, however, is Miller's intimate description of what it believes to be the unnatural techniques its competitor uses in brewing its beers—brands such as Budweiser, Busch, Anheuser-Busch Natural Light, and Michelob. The description, spread abroad in a Miller press release handed out simultaneously with the filing of the brief, takes two vicious swipes at the Anheuser-Busch (AB) beers. One goes right for the jugular.

As far as Budweiser is concerned, the jugular is something described on its labels as "beechwood ageing" (sic), a unique brewing process whose name

From *Science*, Vol. 203, pp. 731–732, February 23, 1979. Copyright 1979 by the American Association for the Advancement of Science.

evokes an image of wooden casks resting in an unhurried, tradition-bound brewing cellar. As the label says, this method creates a taste "you will find in no other beer." Miller's lawyers would like to spike the image: "We seriously doubt," they wrote, "that consumers understand that 'beechwood aging' consists of dumping chemically treated lumber into a glass-lined or stainless steel beer storage tank." Miller's "understanding" is that its competitor boils beechwood slats (18 by 2 by ¼ inches) in baking soda and then drops them in the brewing vat for hours at a time to create the effect it calls beechwood aging.

Miller's other accusation was more alarming but less justified than the description of the lumber. Raising the specter of toxic contamination, Miller's attorneys wrote: "AB uses tannic acid as an additive in its beers. . . . Residues of this additive remain in the final packaged product sold to consumers." It sounds awful, especially when the contaminant is described as "a processed chemical . . . pentadigalloyl glucoside, with the empirical formula usually given as $C_{76}H_{52}O_{46}$." Although the Food and Drug Administration (FDA) regards tannic acid as safe, Miller's lawyers wrote, "its classification is now under review by FDA and some question has been raised with respect to possible health hazards associated with a significant increase in consumption of this additive above current levels." Miller appended to its statement a table of tannic acid concentrations found in AB beers sampled around the country, showing a range from about 1 to 6 parts per million. Miller mentioned parenthetically that it does not use tannic acid. (It uses other chemicals.)

On closer examination, the Miller brief reveals that tannic acid in beer may not be so poisonous an additive as a quick reading might suggest. It does not say that the concentration of tannic acid in AB beers in higher than in other beers, nor that it has increased over the years. The report cited by Miller in raising the health alarm is informative in this matter. It states: "There is no evidence in the available information on tannic acid . . . that demonstrates or suggests reasonable grounds to suspect a hazard to the public when it is used at levels that are now current and in the manner now practiced [1977]."

George Irving, Jr., chairman of the committee at the Federation of American Sciences for Experimental Biology which wrote this report for the FDA, said that the conclusions on tannic acid were written in the "standard boilerplate" used on such occasions. In this instance, tannic acid was given the rating known as "number two," slightly less than the perfect bill of health—number one—which implies that no future health risks are envisioned. Examples of additives that have received the lowest rating—number four—are salt and caffeine, both considered more hazardous than tannic acid. Incidentally, a mug of tea is likely to contain much more tannic acid than a glass of beer.

Miller's brief goes into great detail on the chemistry of brewing, the doctoring done to adjust the acidity of water with calcium sulfate and sulfuric acid, and the use of heavy machinery to prepare and cook the brew. All this detail is meant to demonstrate that beer making is industrial and not a natural process.

At first, AB issued a terse response, calling the Miller complaint a "publicity ploy without substance." About a week later, AB sent wholesalers a pamphlet titled, *Beer, the Natural Question,* in which it attempted to refute Miller's charges in detail. In this propaganda booklet, AB claims that the tannic acid used in its beers is a "natural material," that its beechwood "chips" are not a marketing gimmick but a "generations-old and extremely costly" natural catalyst used in the fermentation process, and that the chemicals added to the brewing water are the same as those used by municipal water companies. "Anheuser-Busch generally brews with the same water that comes from the tap in people's homes," the pamphlet says, but in some plants AB "further purifies and adjusts its water" using the "same materials and methods" used by water companies. Next, the pamphlet offers a sharp critique of the competition, including a list of "man-made" compounds allegedly found in Miller beers.

Like all good quarrels, this one has a long history. It was preceded more than a year ago by a similar attack on Miller in a brief filed at the FTC by Anheuser-Busch. In this challenge of November 1977, AB accused Miller of deceiving the public by packaging its American-made Lowenbrau beer in containers that were virtually indistinguishable from those used for the German beer called Lowenbrau. Miller bought the right to use the German name, the labels, and the recipe, but it marketed a beer that many consider to be a distinctly inferior doppelgänger of the European beer. Anheuser thought consumers were being tricked into believing that Lowenbrau was German, and it asked the FTC to investigate.

In its petition, AB pointed out that the American Lowenbrau was artificially carbonated, produced from a malt of 28 percent corn grits, and doctored with "at least two non-natural additives" to produce clarity and good foam. The original beer is made of 100 percent barley malt, contains no additives, and is carbonated by natural fermentation, according to AB. The FTC declined to investigate these charges, but the petition had its desired effect. Miller suffered a bout of bad publicity and modified its advertising to make it plain that Lowenbrau is made in America.

The FTC thus far has shown no interest in becoming the referee in this name-calling contest because disputes over labeling of alcoholic beverages falls within the jurisdiction of the Treasury Department's Bureau of Alcohol, Tobacco, and Firearms. But the FTC may be compelled to take an active role. Miller spokesman Guy Smith said it is a "very serious matter," and "not at all a reprisal" for the earlier AB brief against Lowenbrau. Since the FTC has ruled on naturalness in other products, it may have no alternative but to define, once and for all, what is natural and unnatural in brewing.

Food and Drink

by O.L. Bettman

There is a Benign nostalgia for the food of the Gilded Age, reinforced no doubt by the proliferation of old-fashioned cookbooks crammed with mouth-watering recipes. The cornucopia comes to mind as neatly symbolizing America's blessed fertility which lured the half-starved Irishman across the Ocean. Culinarily speaking, America appeared to be one gigantic, groaning board.

But the board in reality groaned only for a small minority of Americans. The country's fertility notwithstanding, the masses were forced to subsist on a crude and scanty diet of which tea and bread were staples, supplemented now and then by a soup or stew of questionable origin. Ragpickers and fellow paupers ate what they could find in trash cans, and many people shopped for their dinner at the secondhand food market—a feature of large cities—where they could select from leftover groceries and castoff trimmings and bones from butcher shops.

With lack of hygienic standards, the established purveyors in the slum districts—from street vendor to corner grocer—sold food that would not today be considered fit for human consumption.

Nostalgia even for the food of most rural Americans cannot survive the light of truth. While to a degree substantial, their diet was very simple, monotonous and often far from healthful.

CHILDREN'S FOOD

Reflecting upon what it had to endure, one is impressed by the ruggedness of the Victorian stomach. But what of the children—especially the poor children—and their tender insides? Many of them "had not ever eaten a mouthful of wholesome food." Pushed onto the streets to beg and pick rags, they foraged for the rotten discards from groceries and restaurants. And whatever few cents they did make were spent on foods that played havoc with their stomachs.

Many children developed a strange hunger for pickles, generated, Robert Spargo believed, by chronic underfeeding that caused a nervous craving for some stimulant—much like the craving of an alcoholic for liquor. But the deterioration went further. "It is a horrible fact that many children whose diet is so unwholesome cannot eat decent food even when they are hungry." Slum children at times refused to touch passable food offered them during outings arranged by charitable groups. Some of them had to be taught to eat: it took days before they could be induced to touch eggs and drink milk and give up their pickles.

EATING HABITS

In the preparation and eating of food, American custom in the late nineteenth century kept faithful pace with the crudity and haste of industry. Except in rarefied circles, people did not practice artful cuisine or etiquette, which were regarded as incompatable with the no-nonsense sentiments of a bullish nation. *Harper's Magazine* observed of contemporary cooking habits ". . . we are indifferent to a degree that is almost criminal . . . If you pass out of the narrow range of millionaires, you find a superabundance of bad, hasty cooking, indigestible hot bread, tough beefsteaks, greasy potatoes."

BEWARE

Before the rise of the meat-packing industry, beef reached the cities "on the hoof," shipped live from the West in slow trains. The cattle that survived the journey in the packed rail cars arrived so emaciated and maimed that their drovers had to prod them with pointed steel rods to keep them on their feet. The final stop was the slaughterhouse—an extravagant formality, it seemed, for beasts that were about to succumb to starvation.

These conditions made it difficult even for the rich to buy fresh viands. *Harper's Weekly* complained in 1869: "The city people are in constant danger of buying unwholesome meat; the dealers are unscrupulous, the public uneducated." The poor, meanwhile, had to settle for the cheapest cuts, which often were decayed.

In the absence of electric refrigeration, perishable goods were subject to the whims of the weather. Meat and fowl for sale were simply hung on racks or placed on market counters. The New York Council of Hygiene reported in 1869 that the foods thus displayed "undergo spontaneous deterioration . . . becoming absolutely poisonous . . . One is tempted to believe that with meat and fish so unreliable the urban Victorians sustained themselves by consuming an abundance of fruit. But that was not the case. They had a lingering suspicion of fruit—and vegetables—that had its origins in a cholera epidemic of 1832 which was believed to have been caused by fruit. In fact, following the epidemic, the New York City Council had forbidden the sale of all fruits, and though the ban had been lifted some years later the mistrust was to remain.

Bought by the grocers in green condition so that it would remain salable for a longer period, the fruit—instead of ripening attractively as they had hoped—rotted on the counters. *Harper's Weekly* in 1872 complained that in markets throughout the city there were carloads of decayed fruit such as bruised oranges and rotten bananas "to partake of which was almost certain death."

MILK

It was common knowledge to New Yorkers that their milk was diluted. And the dealers were neither subtle nor timid about it; all they required was a water pump to boost two quarts of milk to a gallon. Nor was that the end of the mischief: to improve the color of milk from diseased cattle they frequently added molasses, chalk or plaster of Paris.

No wonder, that in 1889 New York's public health commissioner reported seeing in certain districts a "decidedly suspicious-looking fluid bearing the name of milk."

Bacteria-infected milk held lethal possibilities of which people were unaware. The root of this problem was in the dairy farms, invariably dirty, where the milk cows were improperly fed and housed.

It was not unusual for a city administration to sell its garbage to a farmer, who promptly fed it to his cows. Or for a distillery to keep cows and feed them distillery wastes, producing what was called "swill milk." This particular liquid, which purportedly made babies tipsy, caused a scandal in the New York of 1870 when it was revealed that some of the cows cooped up for years in filthy stables were so enfeebled from tuberculosis that they had to be raised on cranes to remain "milkable" until they died.

When in 1902 the city's Health Commission tested 3970 milk samples it was found that 2095, or 52.77 percent, were adulterated.

BUTTER

Dairy by-products, it appeared to the Victorian manufacturers, provided a fine opportunity to improvise; here imagination was needed, not scruples. And the butter they produced demonstrated a remarkable talent—not for making butter but for making money. Selling in the 1880's for a respectable average of 19 cents a pound, it was often rancid, and either a mixture of casein and water or of calcium, gypsum, gelatin fat and mashed potatoes.

The alternative was "bogus butter," and the ingredients of this concoction were so wildly incongruous as to generate several investigations by city and state. Fat from hogs along with every conceivable animal part that the slaughterhouses could not turn to cash were picked up by the oleo makers and processed in filthy worksheds. Bleaches were blended into the mix to give the product the appearance of real butter.

A margarine factory employee in 1889 told New York State investigators that his work had made "his hands so sore . . . his nails came off, his hair dropped out and he had to be confined to Bellevue Hospital for general debility." That customers frequently bought this pestilent muck and fed it to their families was due to the artfulness of the grocers, who scraped off the real labels and relettered the boxes "Western butter" or "best creamery butter."

ADULTERATION

Adulteration of foodstuffs was conventional practice among the bakers and grocers of the 1880's, who met the growing food demands of city residents by extending their raw materials with a variety of questionable additives. The bakers—never noted for cleanliness, and historically obdurate to public criticism—stretched and preserved their dough with doses of alum and sulfur of copper. Customers were continually enraged to discover chunks of foreign matter in their loaves, such as oven ash and grit from the baker's machinery.

The national craving for a cup of really good coffee was just as intense as it is today, though the chances of brewing one were incalculably smaller. A report of the 1870's suggests why. "How complacently we receive from the hands of the grocer a package of 'pure Java'—which is not Java at all but only a mixture of roasted beans and peas, flavored with the ever-present chicory and rye."

When it came to candy, to which adults were addicted almost as much as children, the ingredients were notably harmful.

Candy could not be made attractively colorful without the addition of strongly toxic substances. The resultant sweets "on which the children nibble all day long" contained elements that were markedly dangerous—the degree of harm depending on the health of the consumer and the amount eaten.

The expansion of food canning raised hopes that spoilage—which caused uncountable deaths—would be conquered. But the side effects of canning should have been predictable. Only the cheapest varieties of foodstuffs were canned, and chemicals added to prevent decay didn't always work: "The jar of pickles upon your table contains an acid so powerful and so fatal to health the pickle becomes a soft mess that crumbles to the touch." At least in the "fresh" food market one could smell a fish. But who could smell beforehand what was inside a can?

The widespread distrust of "tinned food" was vindicated in later years by the Embalmed Beef Scandal, which revealed that U.S. soldiers during the Spanish-American War were fed from tin cans containing decayed meat. There were even claims that cans had been left over from the Civil War.

Consider, too, that this fare was eaten at flank speed, whether at home or in a restaurant. Americans, it was noted, "take their food as if it was part of their work," displaying great impatience to get it over with. In an 1856 article, "Why We Get Sick," *Harper's* described a businessman rushing through dinner "where ten to one he is clinching a bargain . . . between bolted beef and bolted pudding." Waiters loyal to ritual often served all dinner courses simultaneously, goading the diner to speed up his "wolfing," so he could finish his soup before the entrée went cold.

Foreigners were greatly amused by the American office sign, "Out for lunch—back in five minutes," which neatly suggests the atmosphere of the standard eating place: "The clatter of plates and knives, the slamming of doors, the bellowing of waiters are mingled in a wild chaos—everybody talks at once, orders at once, eats at once."

The same circuslike scramble prevailed in the boarding houses, where a long reached increased the inmate's chances of survival. Dickens described the reduction in ten minutes of a heap of food to a few scraps "as if a famine were to set in tomorrow morning."

The Hungarian writer Vay de Vaya held the opinion that for a regimen calculated to injure the stomach, teeth and general health, no one could surpass the Americans. Whatever the clinical definition of stomach distress, it provided a gold mine for the patent-medicine makers, who might as well have advertised: "We will help your stomach digest any food properly. You do the eating—we'll do the rest!" Despite criticism, the market burgeoned. It appeared that the dyspeptic was here to stay, "growling and groaning by turns through life, a burden to himself and a bore to his friends."

THE WESTERN DIET

The staff of life in the West can be described with laudable brevity: corn. Easily cultivated on the frontier, corn kept the pioneers from starving and enabled them to push onward; without it the Great Migration, some believe, would have taken a hundred years. But although it yielded sustenance, corn did not provide an adequate diet, even if more than thirty-two ways were contrived to prepare it in the form of bread, hominy cake, pudding—whether it was boiled, roasted, mashed or popped. Eaten three times a day, seven days a week, the frontier family's diet would cause a riot in today's penitentiaries. The children, especially, suffered from the lack of fruits and vegetables, except for seasonal greens like dandelion, pigweed, buffalo peas and sheep sorrel, which did not add up to a sufficient amount of vitamins to promote growth or prevent scurvy.

During her stay in the South, Harriet Martineau compared corn to gold: "The man who has it has everything; he can sow the land with it, and for the rest everything eats corn, from slave to chick." Corn also helped raise the second mainstay of frontier life: hogs. They provided meat the year round, and their fat was used as a substitute for butter. But apart from its desolate monotony, the pork and biscuit diet often was injurious to health, as 6.3 percent of all pigs were infected with trichinosis.

DRINKING

The drinking habits of Americans in the good old days paralleled their eating habits: both were frenzied and excessive. Although never a notably sober people, their drinking developed during the period to become a national menace, the per capita consumption of alcohol rising from 8 gallons in 1878 to 17 gallons in 1898, reaching in that year the staggering total of 1.25 billion gallons. The temperance movement grew correspongingly, and its zealous crusade compelled a number of states to go dry. But its influence was more theatrical than actual, as it made no noticeable impact on the upward curve in the statistics of drunkenness.

The causes of heavy drinking were both ethnic and social. Each successive group of immigrants appearing in the cities carried its own bottled tradition, whether it was the German addiction to beer or the Irish fondness for malt liquor. Dismal living conditions and loneliness magnified their thirst, and the liquor that was a gratifying indulgence for the rich became for them an inescapable crutch. To the poor the downtown saloon, no matter how squalid, was a warm refuge from habitations that the *New York Graphic* in 1874 described as "unfit for horses or swine."

The flourishing bar trade in the slum districts of every major city was a model example of the supply-and-demand theory in practice. In New York, Chicago, Philadelphia and Boston, "dram-shops yawned at every step." It was estimated in 1880 that for every hundred of its male inhabitants, New York contained one saloon. (The national average in the same year was 1:735.) They outnumbered churches ten to one and schools twenty to one. Jacob Riis counted 111 Protestant churches below 14th Street against 4065 saloons, and in the neighborhood of Jane Addams' Hull House there were 9 churches and 250 saloons; the Chicago average was 1:300. Judging by these odds, the maxim "Wherever God builds the devil builds next door" paid an unintended tribute to Satan's propensities.

However, the devil's success was in no small measure due to his alliance with the politicians, who allowed saloons to proliferate in gross violation of the licensing laws. For here was the fulcrum of their power—the simple exchange of booze for votes—indeed the direct route from barroom politician to alderman or state senator. For the same reasons, closing-hour ordinances existed only on paper. George Ade tells us there were saloons in Chicago that had not closed their doors for years.

With few exceptions the oldtime taverns could be graded only in degrees of squalor. Jacob Riis noticed in the worst of them that dogs were unable to stand the atmosphere and fled into the street. George Ade describes a typical saloon, a mill-town shack in Pennsylvania where a halfnaked iron-puddler gulps down—after a 12-hour shift—an enormous hooker of straight rye, "each heroic wallop followed by a tall glass of beer as a chaser."

A repeated symbol of the Gilded Age is the elegant bar of New York's Hoffman House. But a more accurate symbol would be Demon Rum and its dispensaries.

BIBULOUS BACK COUNTRY

For the city dweller who visited his country relatives, the bleak prospect of forced abstinence did not exist. Whether New England farmers, Western settlers or nomadic cowhands, they were sure to have a supply of liquor, or at least to be in close proximity to one. Nor was alcoholism an epidemic peculiar to cities alone; when it came to strong liquor, country folk proved just as susceptible.

On the frontier, the indispensable fixture of a town was the saloon, where drunken brawls and gunfights were far more savage than in Eastern cities. Notable among our Western heroes was an alcoholic murderer—Doc Holiday—hired to clean up Tombstone, Ariz., by Wyatt Earp, himself a former bar bouncer. The importance of alcohol on the frontier may be gauged by the number of "whiskey towns" that grew around liquor stores. Often located close to Indian reservations, where alcohol was outlawed, these towns flourished, as in the case of Lexington, Okla., aroung a single trade—drinking.

Even the Western farmer, often pictured as the very model of virtue and temperance, was subject to heavy drinking, the victim of his own mash. With corn and rye in abundance and markets far removed, he found it considerably cheaper to convert the grain into liquor—at a cost of 20 cents a barrel—and transport it in reduced bulk. His temptation to imbibe was sharpened by a lonely, hostile environment and, in the brutal winters, to have an attractive confederate against the cold.

Everyone indulged: "men, women and children, preachers and church members as well as the ungodly." Besides Scripture, liquor was a source of inspiration for some Baptist ministers, whose sermons often were nothing but alcoholic tirades. New Englanders, like other rural Americans distilling their liquor from the most abundant local crop, ineluctably became addicted to cider, and to its more potent essence, applejack. Horace Greeley, a teetotaler, maintained that in New Hampshire a family of six or eight consumed a barrel of cider a week. At this rate the graduation, or descent, to alcoholism was simplified: "The transition from cider to more potent stimulants was easy and natural, so that whole families died drunkards and vagabond paupers. . . ."

THE SALOON

The effect of alcoholism on both the victim and his family is well known, but in the Victorian period it had an even more profound, more hopeless impact. There were no social agencies or privately sponsored clinics to help the alcoholic; there was no real understanding of his compulsion. He could turn to only one place for commiseration, for relief, even for food: the saloon.

The drunkard's wife was an object of deepest tragedy. Cast into despair by a lack of love and seeing her husband's earnings disappear, her suffering was increased by fears—often realized—that in their poverty and demoralization the children would follow in their father's path. A woman in the slums of Chicago told Jane Addams: "You might say it's a disgrace to have your son beat you up for the sake of a bit of money you've earned scrubbing, but I haven't the heart to blame the boy for doing what he's seen his father do all his life; his father forever went wild when the drink was in him and struck me to the very day of his death."

Child alcoholics were not uncommon, having developed an early taste for drink as the result of constant trips to the bar to have a pitcher filled with "beer for Father." From her bed in New York's Presbyterian Hospital, young Lucie Zucheriechi lisped, "Give me whiskey, a little drop of whiskey, and I will give you a kiss." Carried thence from a slum, she was an alcoholic, dying of cirrhosis of the liver.

When it came to the quality of his drinks, the alcoholic got less—or more perhaps—than he paid for. Liquor was "in its majority a vile compound," often pure alcohol with some coloring added and a fancy label, sold as genuine whiskey, brandy or rum. Beer was spiced with adulterants and had a high alcoholic content to keep it fresh, causing, it was observed, riotous scenes "as if murder was about to be committed." Many saloons offered free lunches, making their foods "saltier than the seven seas" to ensure that the drunks would remain thirsty—and inside.

Ultimately, the human wreckage caused by alcohol ended either in the hospitals, where the victims died in a rage of delirium tremens, in reformatories such as Ward's Island, N.Y., or in prison. In 1870, 60 percent of New York City's prison inmates were found to be drunks. The committee of Fifty, a group of citizens studying the effects of alcoholism, were alarmed to find that out of 13,402 convicts they examined, 50 percent were alcoholics, and that liquor was at least a determining factor, if not always the "sole cause of their crime."

Summarizing the problems of alcohol during the Gilded Age, it is startling to note that the per capita consumption was somewhat less than it is today. But several factors render the comparison largely invalid, among them the social drinking of modern women; the rigid supervision of distilleries, breweries, and the bar and package trades; the widespread partiality toward moderate use; the successful rehabilitation programs for alcoholics. In the old days such an enlightened climate did not exist, and the result was liquor abuse of unmitigated horror.

The Reality of Change
in Illusionary Society

by Fergus Clydesdale

Historically *homo sapiens* have found that it was dangerous, if not deadly, to place their survival solely upon the products of nature without some kind of intervention to circumvent periods of hunger and starvation, when the land did not produce and the forest did not provide. This became evident thousands of years ago, when preservation of food began. The survival of the human species has occurred through a constant battle with famine.

All of us are familiar with the biblical story of Joseph, who placed grain in storage for seven fat years to prevent famine against seven lean years. This concept was simply one of attempting to accumulate food material to ward off death and starvation due to hunger.

In a very literal sense—this in simple terms—is the aim of processed foods. To ward off death due to starvation by lengthening the life-span of crops, such that they may be utilized by humans rather than rotting in the fields, or being consumed by rodents, insects and pests. When this aim is

TABLE 1
LONG-TERM TRENDS IN NUTRIENT DISAPPEARANCE

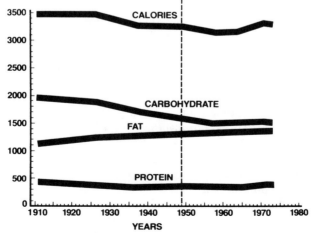

From *Processed Prepared Food, 147* (6) 63–9, by permission of Gorman Publishing Company.

considered, it becomes evident that the manipulation of foods satisfies a basic need, and in so doing, creates the foods, which ultimately will be consumed.

Thus, the response of technology to changes in society will directly affect food usage. Again, if we view this manipulation historically, its sole function was to provide enough food to prevent starvation and, therefore, the types of food were not questioned only the amount available.

At that time, any process which produced more food was viewed as a blessing. And there was no question as to the type of food—starvation was considered a vital risk and food a vital benefit—a perception which has changed in the development of society and which has fostered some very real problems in today's environment.

In fact, with some of the negative views expounded today, we have the paradox of knowing nature cannot provide enough, yet the refusal to accept the concept of technology in order that there may be enough. This feeling has not been lessened by certain types of advertising which have been deemed to be essential in satisfying perceived consumer needs, whether actual or not.

In neolithic times, societal changes did not alter food usage greatly. Food preparation was a home industry with the major thrust being the production of enough food. Nevertheless, towards the end of this period, and in the beginning of the Copper, Bronze and Iron Ages, such techniques as sieving, salting, seasoning, pressing, alcoholic fermentation, acetification and bread making were developed.

Interestingly, in what is now Iraq and Iran, a great dependence on beer began to develop around 3000 B.C. with as much as 40 percent of the cereals being converted to beer. This is a societal demand which both then and now seems to take precedence over many food needs, although the first McGovern report failed to recognize it.

Ingenuity and invention were the keys to further changes in food usage in early times. It must be remembered that a variety of foods had to be available prior to a widespread change in usage. Movable type allowed inventions to be dispersed. And the industrial Revolution provided power sources which could be applied to food production, making food availability and variety greater.

These events are, at times, ignored and people point to a certain "food usage" as a sign of the times. For instance, our affluent technological society is sometimes accused of being the sole reason for over-eating. The gorging that took place in Roman times and Stuart's England is often forgotten. During this latter period, an ordinary dinner for the upper class might have had as many as 30 different dishes.

War has had a dramatic impact on food usage. Not only does scarcity develop on the home front, but there is generally a critical need for innovations in the field. The Napeolonic Wars stimulated the search which ended in

Nicolas Appert's discovery of canning. The U.S. Civil War expanded the canning industry about six fold, thus making available a choice in the matter of food usage. World War II saw the development of improved dehydration procedures and the national goal of fortification of foods.

These are non-subtle events which caused great upheaval in society and part of their overall result was a change in food usage patterns. However, lest the historical approach of gigantic upheavals produce boredom rather than insight, it might be wise to skip further details and leap to the more immediate era of the last 50 to 100 years, looking at more subtle events than war, but events which, nonetheless, have had a profound effect on food usage.

First, it would be of value to consider food usage or consumption on a macroscopic scale. That is, how have our major energy sources changed, prior to looking at the societal events which have created such changes. It should be pointed out that I will use the term "food consumption" rather freely, knowing fully that we do not have an accurate measure of food consumption.

The data which I will be referring to are U.S. Department of Agriculture statistics of food disappearance at retail. It seems to be the best we have. Yet it doesn't consider spoilage, cooking waste, plate waste or other sources.

The average daily per capita disappearance of calories has changed very little for the past 65 years. This isn't that surprising. We exercise less. But physiologically, our stomachs are probably about the same size. Also, although types of food have changed, the total calorie intake is roughly balanced by substitution. The major sources of calories, protein, fat and carbohydrate (excluding alcohol) have changed somewhat, with protein remaining constant, and an apparent shift of 10 percent of the total calories from carbohydrate sources to fat sources.

It is apparent that consumers have chosen carbohydrates and fat as their major sources of calories, and still do. Also, more specific consumption figures show that the consumption of fats and oils has not changed appreciably in the past 50 years. However, there has been a change in the types of fats and oils consumed, such as the substitution of margarine for butter.

This, along with other figures, seems to indicate that consumers in general, consciously or subconsciously, substitute similar types of foods when changes are made. Based on these facts, it becomes obvious that the increase in fat consumption must be due to the consumption of fat-containing foods, and not fats and oils themselves. Indeed, this is the case. And one of the major reasons for this increase may be explained by a shift in the type of protein being consumed which has some economic overtones.

The proportion of protein from animal and plant sources has undergone a major change in the last 65 years. From a 50-50 split, we have gradually shifted to where approximately 68 percent of our protein is animal based and only 32 percent is plant based.

TABLE 2
BREAKDOWN OF FOOD ENERGY

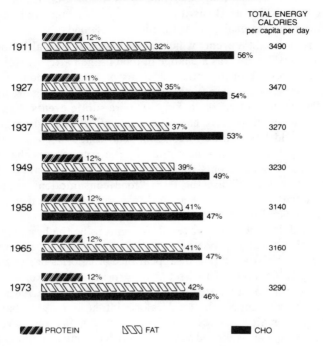

TOTAL ENERGY
CALORIES
per capita per day

Year		Calories
1911	12% / 32% / 56%	3490
1927	11% / 35% / 54%	3470
1937	11% / 37% / 53%	3270
1949	12% / 39% / 49%	3230
1958	12% / 41% / 47%	3140
1965	12% / 41% / 47%	3160
1973	12% / 42% / 46%	3290

PROTEIN   FAT   CHO

Having very briefly examined the macroscopic changes in food consumption, it is now necessary to examine not only how and why these have occurred, but also to examine the apparent degree of satisfaction that the consumer has with such changes. This latter point is unfortunately often ignored. But it must be examined, if we are to consider societal changes which are often derived from demands for perceived satisfaction.

Without writing volumes, it would be impossible to consider all the factors that have produced changes in food usage. Therefore, although limiting my scope somewhat, I am going to consider only a few general factors which society currently demands in the food it consumes.

Today we are often told that the primary concern of the consumer is nutrition. This is true to some extent. Certainly in many cases it is true right up to the point of purchase. But, at that time, other factors such as cost, quality, convenience and safety become pre-eminent.

It is interesting to note that if a product fails on the marketplace, it is generally because some of these factors have been ignored in order to magnify others. For instance, a product that answers a nutritional need to the exclusion

TABLE 3
SOURCE OF PROTEIN

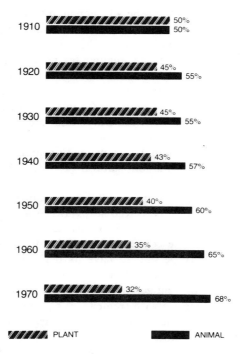

| | PLANT | | ANIMAL |

of cost and quality considerations will likely fail. This is a simple fact, which many people fail to realize.

Therefore, it might be of interest to consider these factors in terms of their development in a changing society and how technology has attempted to fulfill their demands.

In early history nutrition meant food. As time progressed, nutrition meant the prevention of gross deficiency diseases such as scurvy, rickets, beriberi and pellagra. Today the consumer in the U.S. does not view nutrition as solving these problems, since most of them have disappeared.

They view nutrition more as a panacea for health and are concerned with such things as "suboptimal and marginal intakes" and "suboptimal functioning." These terms are difficult for the scientist to come to grips with and are virtually impossible for the consumer to articulate.

As a result, society has come to expect food to have a therapeutic effect— a concept that is most difficult to correct, but is essential to correct, if the consumer is to be educated. For instance, in a recent survey on the public's knowledge, attitudes, beliefs and behavior, conducted by the Food and Drug

Administration, it was found that 51 percent of all shoppers are not well informed. Eighty-one percent believed that all food from the supermarket was not good for you.

What a difference from the time when enough food meant nutrition to a current rejection of many of the 10,000 items in a supermarket. This change in perception is really radical and has occurred within the past 20 years. Consider that as recently as 1955 a Canadian textbook stated: "In many parts of Canada one child in every nine shows evidence of having had rickets."

Obviously, the major reason for the occurrence is that there is more than enough food for the average American. Couple this with the Woodward-Bernstein phenomena and some of the truly remarkable nonsense, both published and aired on television, and you have a problem.

This nonsense, which emanates from many sources including the food industry and its advertisements for "natural" foods which imply (never directly stated because of the legal aspects) that "natural" food is a panacea, ignores the tremendous success of technology in meeting society's actual nutritional needs (as opposed to perceived needs) over the years.

Fortification of food is an area which has had a great impact upon the health of the consumer. The concept of fortifying food and/or water with nutritional chemicals may be said to have its beginning in 1833 in South America, when the French chemist Boussingault recommended the addition of iodine to table salt to prevent goiter. This practice has been adopted widely in Europe and North America with tremendous success.

The history of fortification is impressive. Margarine fortification with Vitamin A, Vitamin D fortification in milk and the enrichment of bakery-produced white bread and family-used white flour by the addition of thiamine, riboflavin, niacin and iron are only some of the examples. The enrichment of degerminated corn meal, corn grits, whole grain corn meal, rice, pasta products and, of course, fortification of cereals.

Not only is there a need for products which the head of the household can prepare, but there is as great a need for products which the head of the household can trust children to prepare in safety. This is an area which is still open for product development.

In general, the food industry has responded well to this demand. However, it might be safe to state that technological improvements can and should be made.

One of the few basic certainties that nature promises is that change will occur. Along with that change both perceived and actual needs will arise. Perhaps one of the keys to the promising future is to attempt to meet actual needs rather than perceived needs. Prior to this commitment, however, it is essential to discover methodology to measure actual food and nutrition needs of the consumer. Our current survey techniques and measurement of food consumption are inadequate.

As well, industry, legislators, scientists and the consumer must be made aware that they are producing, recommending and buying food on the basis of not one, but many factors. Studies should be conducted in order to better define the importance of each of the factors discussed in relation to the others, so that new products which meet actual needs will be recommended purchased and eaten. A commitment in this cause would be justified under any set of moral or economic standards.

In terms of technology, it is to be hoped that we will not only improve on current techniques, but also realize innovations undreamed of before. It is interesting that canning is a rather new type of processing, when it is ranked chronologically with the others. Enzyme technology shows great promise as a vehicle for new processing systems. But aside from that, the list is limited.

New plant and animal varieties and hybrids are always looming on the horizon and will, undoubtedly, produce changes in food usage and perhaps in food production and distribution.

The food industry has a right to be proud of its response to needs. But it cannot always take a defensive stance on the basis of its record. It must look more closely at communications with the public, at an increasing role in providing information, as well as food, and as an innovator of new research and development.

3

What Should We Eat

Chemicals in food, cancer, DES, Red No. 2, food additives, natural toxicants, aflotoxins, increased prices, consumer rip-offs and the list goes on.

The consumer is awash in a sea of accusations and denials all seeming to come from well meaning, dedicated and highly trained individuals.

The authors of this book cannot give absolute answers to these questions, nor do they wish to try, for absolute answers cannot be guaranteed by a scientist who is being honest and following the dictates of science.

There are different viewpoints which can arise from the same evidence, however, most of the material which seems to reach the public from the press and media is negative in nature.

Such material promises in general that if one avoids certain foods and eats only others, that health and happiness is sure to follow. Since the other, more positive viewpoint is rarely heard we have decided to include two papers which give another view. We do not necessarily agree with this view but it is our belief that truth can only be arrived at by presenting all sides of an argument, not just one.

The third paper in this chapter deals with an issue which is of key importance to feeding our country. That is the issue of cost. Often consumers are told to let government pay for it or to let industry pay for it. Unfortunately, they do not realize that in either of these cases the consumer ultimately pays for it in increased taxes or increased cost of product. Therefore, the third paper presents some facts about the cost of regulation which consumer dollars will pay for. This is a vital consideration in determining just how much regulation we want in our food supply system.

The last paper presents an interesting discussion on the one-molecule theory of cancer and specifically how it relates to saccharin.

Consumers must be aware of these issues so that they may have a responsible voice in determining the destiny of their food supply.

Cost of Federal Rules
to Firms Detailed

In 1977, 48 large U.S. companies spent $2.6 billion in incremental costs to comply with the regulations of six federal agencies, the Business Roundtable told the Senate Governmental Affairs Committee last week. The largest segment of the incremental costs, $2 billion, was spent to comply with the regulations of only one federal agency—the Environmental Protection Agency.

The two agencies imposing the next highest costs were the Equal Employment Opportunity Commission and the Occupational Safety & Health Administration, at $217 million and $184 million, respectively. These were followed by the Department of Energy with $116 million in incremental costs; compliance with the Employee Retirement Income Security Act provisions with $61 million; and the Federal Trade Commission with $26 million.

Of particular concern, Business Roundtable representatives told the committee, is the fact that operating and administrative costs, which recur each year, accounted for 42% of the total $2.6 billion. Incremental capital expenditures accounted for 33% of the total, extra product costs for 21%, and R&D costs for 4%.

Business Roundtable is an association of chief executive officers from 192 companies and was established to examine public policy issues. The 48 companies participating voluntarily in the study represent a wide variety of products and services. They included banks, oil companies, and utilities, appliance and computer manufacturers. Chemical firms participating were Allied Chemical, Dow Chemical, Du Pont, Eastman Kodak, Monsanto, and Stauffer Chemical.

The study found certain regulations to be especially burdensome for companies. For example, two EPA regulations accounted for $900 million of 1977 incremental costs—Control of Air Pollution from New Motor Vehicles and the National Ambient Air Quality Standard for Particulates. And as expected, the impact of regulation showed a wide variation among industries. The incremental cost of OSHA rules averaged only $6.00 per worker per year in the banking industry, but $220 per worker per year in the chemical industry.

Business Roundtable believes its study is unique because it is concerned with identifying the costs of a specific group of regulations, not the total costs of all regulations. In addition, the study concentrates on incremental costs, which for the purpose of the survey were defined "as that expenditure by the companies which in their judgment would not have been made in the absence of regulation."

In addition to listing costs by agency, the study also identifies the cost of complying with specific rules enforced by each agency. The breakdown of costs for complying with OSHA regulations shows that 33% of $60 million was spent on existing and proposed toxic and hazardous substances regulations. Noise and ventilation control accounted for 16% or $30 million; general administration and knowledge of the regulations 12% or $22 million; machinery and guards for machines, 7% or $12 million; walking-working surfaces, 5% or $9 million; materials handling and storage 4% or $8 million. Compliance with all other areas of OSHA regulations (all less than 4% each) cost $43 million.

One result of the study that may be particularly valuable to the committee and others interested in reducing the costs of government regulation, the Business Roundtable believes, is the identification of nine attributes that are almost invariably associated with high-incremental-cost regulations. These are: continuous monitoring, forcing new technology, capital intensity, recurring costs, retrofitting, specific compliance action, inadequate risk assessment, engineering solutions, and changing requirements.

Chemical companies have been watching the Business Roundtable study. For example, in its latest annual report to stockholders, Dow Chemical refers to preliminary results of the survey. Dow says that these results indicate that its experience with regulatory costs has been repeated broadly across the U.S.

Dow has been measuring its own regulatory costs since 1975. In 1976 and 1977 the company found increases of 27% and 44% in the cost of complying with federal regulations. The bill for 1977 came to $268 million or about 7% of U.S. sales. Reminding readers that this is "money that our customers and the consumer ultimately must pay," Dow says regulation is its fastest-rising cost.

Citing one example of regulatory overkill, Dow says that its moderate-sized Pittsburg, Calif., plant must file each year 563 separate permit applications to meet requirements of the Bay Area Air Quality Maintenance District outside San Francisco. The plant actually has 124 points in its 250 acres where emissions may occur. However, permits must be filed for each of these points, for 69 abatement devices at these points, and for 370 "sources" for the emissions escaping through these points. The source permits require information on products, rate of throughput, per cent of annual use, and other subjects that, in Dow's view, create an issue on exposing proprietary information.

The Politics of Health Nonsense

by Stephen J. Barrett

Promoters of pseudoscience characteristically misinterpret scientific data for personal gain. Their motive may be financial, but quite often they believe in themselves and seek primarily the satisfaction of gaining converts to their ideas. They speak to emotions, offering better health to those who buy their ideas or products. They oppose consumer protection laws, especially those which forbid unfounded health claims.

Currently, the leading promoters of health nonsense appear to be Adelle Davis,* Rodale Press, the National Health Federation, and chiropractic. Their public following is growing, and with it, so is their ability to influence legislation.

Adelle Davis is a familiar figure on TV talk shows. She has an alert, confident manner. Her books have sold by the million. She has been trained in nutrition but, unfortunately, she has strayed from scientific thought. She has promoted hundreds of ideas which have no scientific basis, such as the use of beet juice to treat cancer (1972, p. 299). She opposes pasteurization of milk and fluoridation of water. She recommends dangerously high doses of vitamins A and D. Her books refer to thousands of scientific articles that she claims support her theories. Investigators find, however, that most of her references are irrelevant and misquoted (Rynearson 1973).

Rodale Press, Emmaus, Pa., publishes *Prevention* magazine, *Organic Gardening* magazine, the *Organic Food Marketing* newsletter, and many "health" books. According to its 1973 marketing survey, Rodale Press claims that *Prevention* readers spend 267 million dollars per year on "vitamins, supplements and health foods." *Prevention* is a device which permits sellers to get around existing laws prohibiting false sales claims. Shielded by freedom

Reprinted from *The American Biology Teacher,* Vol. 36, No. 8, November 1974; courtesy of the National Association of Biology Teachers, Inc., 11250 Roger Bacon Drive, Reston, VA 22090.

Stephen J. Barrett, M.D., graduated from Columbia University's College of Physicians and Surgeons in 1957 and he completed his psychiatric residency at Temple University Hospital in 1961. A vigorous crusader against health quackery, Barrett has, since 1969, served as board chairman of the Lehigh Valley Committee Against Health Fraud, Inc., a lay and professional consumer protection group. He is also a member of the Pennsylvania Medical Society Committee on Quackery and the Pennsylvania Health Council Committee on Health Fraud. This paper is based on a speech Barrett made to the American Association for the Advancement of Science in February 1974. Address correspondence to the author at Lehigh Valley Committee Against Health Fraud, Inc., Box 1602, Allentown, PA, 18105.

*Adelle Davis died in May 1974, after this speech was given.

of the press, *Prevention* articles and editorials promote all manner of unproven ideas about health, many of which boost products of its advertisers. The advertisements (which cost about $5,000 per page!) contain no health claims. If the claims in the articles were made in the ads, sellers could be prosecuted for fraud or misbranding. *Prevention* contains some useful information, but its readers are left to their own resources to separate facts from nonsense.

The "health food" approach is one which gives people false hopes and false feelings of security in return for their money. Often, the people who are most influenced are the ones who can least afford the luxury of unnecessary supplements. Many people make a religion out of health faddism. The late J.I. Rodale seemed to understand how gullible people can be when he wrote in 1954, "Man has been a creature of fallacy ever since time began. It seems inherent in his make-up to believe in false things. Straight, unvarnished facts seem too dull. Better an interesting fallacy than a stupid truth. There is overwhelming evidence that man likes to be hoaxed. In the field of medicine, especially, man seems to delight in being completely taken in . . . ."

Two years ago, J.I.'s son Robert began a syndicated column called *Organic Living*. To promote the column, notices in *Prevention* ask readers to write letters to the editors of their local newspapers. So far, about 40 papers carry the column.

The National Health Federation (NHF) is a unique alliance of promoters and victims of pseudoscience. Founded in 1955, and based in Monrovia, Calif., NHF supports the gamut of unproven health theories and "treatments" and opposes such proven public health measures as fluoridation and vaccination. Although its stated aim is "freedom of choice" by health consumers, most NHF activity promotes quackery and opposes governmental control of deception by quack promoters. The backgrounds of its leaders suggest why this is so. Many of them have been in serious legal difficulty for promoting "health" products with false sales claims (Anon, 1973a).

Most NHF followers apparently hold sincere beliefs that they can achieve superior health by following methods espoused by NHF leaders. Many exhibit a paranoid outlook, fearing that government is thoroughly failing to protect them from "poisons" in their food and from exploitation by the medical and drug industries. For the privilege of believing they support a wholesome cause, followers pay from $5 per year for regular membership to a lump sum of $1,000 for "perpetual" membership. Many chiropractors and health food marketers are found among the major contributors. Although contributions are not tax-deductible, NHF advertisements and letters welcoming new members have stated otherwise. In 1972, the Internal Revenue Service ordered NHF to stop misrepresenting its tax status.

Chiropractic is based on the theory that all diseases can be traced to misaligned spinal bones. Since chiropractors are unable to render appropriate treatment (Cohen 1968), they must maintain intense political activity to remain licensed. Chiropractors tend to encourage patients to take unnecessary nutrients and many sell high-priced supplements in their offices. Their political activities coordinate with those of other promoters of pseudoscience.

Chiropractic supports the National Health Federation and vice versa. Chiropractic journals regard Adelle Davis and *Prevention* as authoritative. They also carry many nutritional supplement ads, some of which contain misleading information. Adelle Davis speaks at NHF conventions, gives testimonials for chiropractic, and writes for *Prevention*. *Prevention* is pro-chiropractic, and its executive editor, Harald Taub, is a member of the NHF board of directors. Thus, Adelle Davis, Rodale Press, the National Health Federation, and chiropractic form a mutually supportive network.

"Health" Foods and Nutritional Supplements.   Nutritionists know that in the absence of special dietary situations, people can get all the nourishment they need from a balanced variety of foods. Yet most Americans worry that their food supply may be deficient as a result of "worn out" soil, food processing, and food marketing. Many who believe these myths seek correction with extra vitamins or "special" foods. Families which subscribe to *Prevention* spend an average of $190 per year for such products (Anon. 1973b).

Federal and state laws prohibit false claims in advertising or labeling. Enforcement is easiest where such claims falsely exaggerate benefits, for example, that "Wheat germ oil prevents heart stress." Enforcement has been most difficult where claims take the form of misleading generalizations which imply that food supplements are needed by most people. To counteract this problem, the U.S. Food and Drug Administration has issued regulations (cited in Belovian 1973) forbidding labels to say or imply (i) that a food can prevent, cure, mitigate, or treat any disease or symptom; (ii) that a balanced diet of ordinary foods cannot supply adequate amounts of nutrients; (iii) that a lack of optimal nutritive quality of a food, because of the soil on which that food was grown, is or may be responsible for an inadequacy or deficiency in the daily diet; (iv) that storage, transportation, processing, or cooking of a food is or may be responsible for an inadequacy or deficiency in the daily diet; (v) that a natural vitamin is superior to an added or synthetic vitamin; or (vi) that a food contains certain nutrients when such substances are of no known need or significant value in human nutrition. (This prohibition is aimed at rutin, other bioflavinoids, para-aminobenzoic acid, inositol, and similar substances.) Such unproven ingredients may continue to be marketed as food items, but they may not be combined with essential nutrients in products labeled for dietary supplementation.

The new FDA rules limit nonprescription dosages of vitamin A to 10,000 and vitamin D to 400 international units, on the grounds that greater amounts of these fat-soluble vitamins are of no benefit and can be harmful. Other supplements which contain more than one and a half times the U.S. recommended daily allowance will now be classified as drugs subject to FDA regulations. The National Health Federation, which has always opposed government regulation of nutritional supplement claims, responded to the new rules with an unprecedented barrage of political activity. H.R. 643, designed by NHF, would prohibit the FDA from limiting dosages or ordering warning labels on any "food supplement" that is not "intrinsically injurious to health." Such a bill would cripple FDA activity against misleading sales claims for supplements.

To promote H.R. 643 (also known as the Hosmer Bill), NHF adopted the pose of public defender. "Fight for your right to good nutrition!" was the battle cry. Article after article is appearing in the NHF monthly *Bulletin*, *Prevention* magazine, national chiropractic journals, and health food catalogues. Readers are told how to urge their congressmen to cosponsor H.R. 643. Letter-writing kits have been distributed to NHF members, chiropractors, and health food stores. To arouse public concern, NHF is claiming that the new FDA rules will raise vitamin prices and make them harder to get. These claims are false, yet the NHF campaign stimulated hundreds of thousands of letters to Congress—which, in turn, lined up more than 200 congressmen as cosponsors of the Hosmer Bill. The same tactics facilitated chiropractic inclusion in Medicare.

The "Organic" Food Fad.   Promoters of so-called "organically grown" foods claim that they are grown "naturally," without the use of pesticides or "artificial" fertilizers. Sometimes they claim nutritional superiority. These claims, as well as the definitions upon which they are based, are misleading. All foods are "organic." Plants cannot tell whether chemicals are prepared in factories or come from natural sources. Pesticides, when used properly, do not threaten human health. Foods grown "organically" are not more nutritious than those grown conventionally. Public confusion, however, has enabled the "organic" label to command a higher price.

Rodale Press is the primary promoter of the "organic" fad. It has established a certification plan which it has been trying to persuade state agriculture departments to adopt. The Pennsylvania Department of Agriculture seems quite interested in this possibility. Together with Rodale Press, it has conducted surveys of "organic" farmers, retailers, customers of supermarkets with "health food" departments, and readers of *Organic Gardening* magazine. During the past year and a half, I have spoken to Pennsylvania Agriculture Secretary James A. McHale and members of his research and public information staffs. All seem oblivious to the concept that "certification" of "organic" foods would be an endorsement of consumer deception. One staff member, however, indicated that McHale "wants to do something to help the small farmer." A few other states are considering the certification question and Oregon will begin a certification program in October 1974.

Fluoridation is an extremely efficient public health measure. It reduces the incidence of tooth decay by two-thirds (Ast 1962). Although the question of its safety is nonexistent from the viewpoint of medical science, it has been the focus of sharp political controversy. "Scare" propoganda can lead people who do not understand biochemistry into fearing that fluoridation is dangerous. Rodale Press, the National Health Federation, chiropractic, and virtually all nutritional hucksters oppose fluoridation—a curious inconsistency when compared to their clamor for "prevention" through nutrition. Politically, fluoridation has special significance because it can be used as an issue to mobilize people for grass roots political action favorable to pseudoscientific causes. Anti-fluoridation groups have been easy to mobilize for the anti-FDA vitamin bill.

Public Confusion.   Despite the fact that scientists know more about nutrition than ever before, the majority of Americans hold many confused ideas about it. Many theories have been offered to explain why this is so:

1. Nutrition education has alerted people to the fact that they need an adequate supply of specific nutrients, but it has not stressed how easy it is to get what they need from food (Deutsch 1967).
2. Pseudoscientists have certain advantages in promoting their ideas. Motivated by missionary zeal or profit, they work harder. They tend to appear very confident and interested in the welfare of their followers.
3. People tend to be attracted to easy methods of achieving success. The possibility that food supplements will bring superior health has great appeal—especially when the use of such supplements is seldom harmful.
4. People are easily frightened by what they do not understand. Pseudoscientists warn that our food supply is poisoned. The rise of legitimate public concern about pollution has made their warnings seem more realistic. At the same time, science and organized medicine have fallen somewhat in the public favor.
5. Strengthening of consumer protection laws has led many people to think that claims about products could somehow not be "allowed" if they were false.
6. Modern communication enables ideas to spread very quickly and far. Because the mass media's primary concern is of an immediate nature, the sensational claims of health fads are more likely to be covered than the more sober facts behind them.

Public Apathy. Public protection can be increased by better education and stronger laws. Unfortunately, most people do not see the issues discussed in this paper as problems which touch them personally. Consumers of pseudoscientific ideas and methods are generally satisfied with their use. Many who take one multivitamin pill daily regard it as cheap "insurance" against deficiency. If they spend less than one cent per day, the fact that their purchase is not necessary is not likely to interest them. People who go to extremes, commonly known as "health food nuts," may waste hundreds of dollars per year. They may also delay proper medical care if they rely too heavily upon nutritional gimmicks to protect them from disease. Those who reach this degree of involvement can seldom be re-educated to give up their delusions about nutrition. In fact, they can often be mobilized to crusade against those who want to protect them from being exploited.

Non-users of nutritional supplements, "organic" foods, and chiropractic seldom get indignant about the money wasted by users—particularly when the individual amounts are small. People who do not go to chiropractors tend not to care about the danger posed by the inadequacy of chiropractic training. Rather than feel sorry for the victims of quackery, many people agree with the viewpoint expressed in 1924 by H.L. Mencken: " . . . nothing operates more cheaply and effectively [to rid the world of half-wits] than the prosperity of quacks." Thus, large segments of the public do not hold these issues high on their lists of educational or political priorities.

Combatting Health Nonsense. Scientific efforts to combat health nonsense must take two directions—educational and political. In the long run, the most effective way to combat health confusion is to prevent its development by increased emphasis on consumer protection in the school system. Education of adults who no longer attend school is more difficult for two reasons. First, adults have already established most of their health habits. Second, large-scale efforts at public education are likely to encounter political interference from promoters of pseudoscience.

In the battle between health science and pseudoscience, too many people perceive pseudoscientists as underdogs. Health scientists must arouse public indignation against those who divert health dollars to ineffective or dangerous practices. Health scientists must work toward a political network equal and opposite to that of the pseudoscientists. We must care more, speak out more, write more, spend more, and organize more. We may not be able to match the quacks word-for-word, letter-for-letter, or dollar-for-dollar—but with truth and ethics on our side, that should not be necessary.

REFERENCES

Anon. 1973a. *Data sheet on NHF*. American Medical Association, Chicago.

Anon. 1973b. *The Prevention market for mail order vitamins, supplements and health foods*. Rodale Press, Emmaus, Pa.

Ast, D.B., and Fitzgerald, B. 1962. Effectiveness of water fluoridation. *Journal of the American Dental Association* 65:382.

Beloin, A. 1973. Nutrition labels: a great leap forward. *FDA Consumer* 7(7):15.

Cohen, W.J. 1968. *Independent practitioners under Medicare—a report to Congress*. U.S. Dept. of Health Education and Welfare, Washington, D.C.

Davis, A. 1972. *Let's get well*. Harcourt Brace Jovanovich, Inc., New York.

Deutsch, R. 1967. *The nuts among the berries*. P. 305–16. Ballantine Books, Inc., New York.

Mencken, H.L. 1924. Chiropractic. *The Baltimore Sun*.

Rodale, J.I. 1954. *This Pace is Not Killing Us*. P. 3. Rodale Press, Emmaus, Pa.

Rynearson, E. 1973. Adelle Davis' books on nutrition. *Medical Insight* 15:32.

How Safe Is Our Food Supply?

by Thomas H. Jukes, PhD

To judge from the fuss being made by "consumerists" in books, magazines, newspapers, and on the radio and television, we are in tremendous danger from our food supply. We are told that some of the substances added to foods or present as contaminants may give us cancer. Prominent in the list are nitrosamines, saccharin, food colorings, and diethylstilbestrol (DES). If we escape these dreadful intruders, we are warned that saturated fatty acids in our foods can cause cancer of the large bowel, and we are advised to devour large amounts of wheat bran to stave off this fate.

However, after eating three meals a day for a good many years, my own opinion is that food is one of the safest things that I encounter in my everyday life. Our food supply in the United States is in its golden age of safety, adequacy, variety, and abundance. It has reached this stage first as a result of a free and open marketplace in which producers and processors compete for the attention of consumers and second, because of the flowering of science and technology during the past century. These facts are evident to anyone who compares the contents of a modern supermarket with the flyblown grocery shop of past years with its cracker-barrel, salt pork, rancid lard, and wormy apples, or with the meager, contaminated, and nutritionally inadequate diet that has to suffice for the majority of the world's population. The only really important problem with the diet of the United States is that people eat too much.

The history of our species shows that we have had always to walk a tightrope, as it were, between toxicity and adequacy of our daily diet until recent years, when the tightrope has become a fairly broad pathway. Among the many scientific advances are the discoveries of the essential vitamins, minerals, and essential amino acids. These discoveries have led to great reductions in many nutritional-deficiency diseases, such as rickets and beriberi, in underdeveloped countries.

From the *Archives of Internal Medicine,* May 1978, Vol. 138. Copyright 1978, American Medical Association. Reprinted by permission.

SOURCES OF FOOD HAZARDS

The U.S. Food and Drug Administration (FDA) is the "clearing house" for matters arising from the lack of safety of foods. Within the past few years, the FDA has listed and ranked the sources of food hazards. Microbiological contamination is put in first place. It results in food-borne disease that attacks about 10 million people annually. *Salmonella* and staphylococci are leading causes; they can grow in foods and produce severe symptoms of food poisoning that are sometimes erroneously called "intestinal flu." In the second spot are nutritional hazards resulting from overeating, improper choice of foods, and deficiencies of essential nutrients. Such departures from "good nutrition" may result from ignorance, indifference, or poverty. Overeating is the biggest of these hazards and it must be blamed on the consumer rather than the food supply. Overeating leads to obesity, which can be a prelude to cardiovascular disease and diabetes. In third place, and probably only one thousandth as important as the preceding two, are environmental contaminants of food. An example is the case of polybrominated biphenyls (PBB) that entered the food supply when they were used inadvertently in cattle feed in Michigan. Mercury as a contaminant of estuaries and lakes is in this category. Rare cases of human sickness and death have arisen from such causes.

Toxicants that occur naturally in foods are listed as number 4. A recent example is amygdalin or laetrile, which is present in apricot seeds. These also contain an enzyme that sets hydrocyanic acid free from amygdalin, and there have been several cases of cyanide poisoning in people who ate "apricot seed milk shakes" prepared according to a recipe from the "health food" literature.(1) Amygdalin and related cyanogenic glycosides occur in many crop plants, including almonds and lima beans.(2) Strains of these have been selected by plant breeders so as to be low in these compounds. Aflatoxins are carcinogenic substances produced by common molds that grow on farm crops such as corn, soybeans, and peanuts. The FDA has set a tolerance of parts per billion 20 (ppb) for aflatoxin in food for human beings. This level will produce cancer in laboratory animals. Aflatoxin poisoning, including fatalities, is often reported from tropical countries where molds grow rapidly on foods.(3)

Natural foods contain thousands of different chemicals, practically none of which have been tested for safety by the standard procedures used for food additives. Many of these substances are well known to be toxic at levels only moderately higher than those reaching the consumer. Some examples are solanine (present in potatoes), antithyroid substances that are present in members of the cabbage and mustard family (such as broccoli and radishes), tannin in tea and coffee, and arsenic in shrimp. Time-honored cooking procedures also contribute to this list, such as polycyclic hydrocarbon carcinogens in smoked or barbecued meat.

The FDA placed at the bottom of the list the hazards from pesticide residues in foods and from food additives. The rarity of harm from these is because they are the subject of intensive scientific and regulatory efforts. These efforts are increasing. Despite the fact that billions of pounds of pesticides have been used on food crops, there is no single known case of human injury or death from a pesticide residue in food. Modern food additives are subjected to such close scrutiny and rigorous testing that their safety is greater than that of most natural ingredients in foods. Since 1958 the laws and regulations for new food additives have included extensive toxicity tests with animals.(4) The FDA "rule of thumb" calls for a 100-fold margin of safety between the level recommended for use in foods and the toxic level in animals.

CHEMICALS IN FOODS

The editor has asked me to respond to widespread concern about "chemicals in foods." Scientifically speaking, we are in the midst of a big overhauling of "chemicals" that are used in foods and, indeed, many of the foods themselves are getting a close new look. I see no reason for a panic as long as we remember that one of the most basic of all medical principles is that "the dose determines the poison." In other words, there is a safe level and a toxic level for every substance. We survive and thrive by keeping our intakes below the toxic levels. The fact that overconsumption of salt may cause or aggravate hypertension shows that moderation is important, but if a rat dies because it has eaten a diet containing 10% of table salt, this does not mean that we should immediately exclude salt from our diet.

The term "food preservatives" has "bad vibes" probably because in days gone by, substances such as formaldehyde and boric acids were used to preserve foods and their use was discontinued as being undesirable. The term "embalmed beef" dates from this era. In contrast, certain modern food preservatives have a beneficial role. Some examples are propionates, sorbates, and certain synthetic antioxidants. The first two of these are metabolized to carbon dioxide and water in the body. They are valuable for inhibiting bacterial and mold growth. Most people throw moldy food away, and recent research has shown that molds can produce carcinogenic substances such as aflatoxin, which is mentioned above. Antioxidants prevent or delay rancidity, which can be accompanied by destruction of vitamins A and E and can make the food unappetizing and injurious. Vitamin E itself is an antioxidant and so is ascorbic acid. These two substances have been proposed for use in cured meats, including bacon, because antioxidants inhibit the formation of nitrosamines.

Antioxidants have repulsive names such as "butylated hydroxytoluene." Such names on the label of processed foods do very little to stimulate the appetite. However, if the natural ingredients of foods were named on the label, they would sound just as bad or worse. For example, coffee contains chlorogenic acid and radishes contain 3-indolylmethyl glucosinolate, which is a goitrogen.

Several food colorings have recently been banned (delisted). Indeed, the number of permitted food colorings has been dwindling for many years, especially the synthetic dyes that were introduced in foods many years ago before the advent of adequate toxicity tests. The levels of dyes fed to animals in such tests are so enormous that some people wonder whether the tests are meaningful. Similar objections have been raised to animal-feeding tests with saccharin and cyclamates. More of this will be discussed later. However, it is probably best to be on the safe side with colors, and we may expect to see increased use of pigments obtained from vegetable sources, such as beet juice, carrot oil, grape skin extract, and paprika. These are color additives "permanently listed for food use."(5)

DIETHYLSTILBESTROL

Do DES residues make meat unsafe? This question has alarmed many people because of the finding that some cases of vaginal adenocarcinoma appeared in women who had been exposed 15 or 20 years ago to DES while they were in the uterus. The risk rate of this "time bomb" effect was recently estimated as between 0.14 to 1.4/1,000 exposures. In one series, 12.3 g of DES were administered per patient per pregnancy and no cases of cancer were reported in the 110 women exposed; however, vaginal adenosis was observed in a number of the women, and this may be a precancerous lesion. Such findings drew attention to the use of DES in beef production. Diethylstilbestrol administered to cattle can sometimes be detected in traces in livers of animals but not in muscle meat. In experiments with cattle fed large doses of DES, the amount of DES in beef muscle of treated animals was not more than one tenth the amount that is found in the liver. It is not possible to be more precise than this because DES is not detectable in the muscle meat of cattle that have been treated with DES by approved methods. In a survey conducted by the U.S. Department of Agriculture (USDA) (1973 to 1975), no DES was detectable, i.e., there was less than 0.5 ppb in 8,241 of 8,293 liver samples examined. In one investigation, DES was made artificially radioactive, and a level of radioactivity corresponding to 0.12 ppb of DES was found in livers of beef cattle that had been implanted in the ear with pellets of the radioactive DES. The level detected in this experiment is such that 100,000 tons of the beef liver would contain 12.3 g of DES. This was the dose received by each pregnant woman in the study mentioned above. Natural estrogens and DES both increase the number of breast tumors in special strains of laboratory mice.

The amounts of orally active estrogenic substances entering the diet from vegetable sources are greater in terms of biologic potency than the amount of DES that could possibly be derived from beef. Furthermore, the circumstance that estrogens are produced daily in the body indicates that the physiological effect of DES in beef would be completely lost in the much larger background of estrogens from other sources. The use of DES by cattle raisers leads to the production of beef with a lower fat content,(6) and this is desirable from the standpoint of public health.

NITROSAMINES, NITRITES, NITRATES

Nitrosamines produced in bacon during frying have been much in the news. Nitrosamines are carcinogenic to various species of laboratory animals at low rates of dose. Nitrosamines can be formed by a reaction between nitrites and secondary amines. This reaction can take place in the stomach. Most of the nitrites reaching the stomach originate in saliva. Their presence in saliva results from reduction of nitrates in foods by bacteria in the digestive tract, including both oral and intestinal bacteria. Many common vegetables are high in nitrates, especially celery, spinach, lettuce, and beets. In one investigation, high levels were found in "organic" carrots grown on muck soil. It is not quite clear how we can escape contact with nitrosamines, but the USDA stated on Aug 31, 1977, that "The immediate objective of both USDA and FDA is to identify and propose to eliminate all uses of nitrites and nitrates in products in which cancer-causing nitrosamines are formed . . ."(7) Nitrites inhibit the growth of botulism organisms in cured meats. The statement by the USDA is particularly interesting because raw tobacco contains far higher levels of nitrosamines than are found in meat or any other food. So light up a cigarette, but beware of bacon.

ARTIFICIAL SWEETENERS

Bans of cyclamates and saccharin aroused wide public interest and reaction. Many consumers resented the ban on cyclamates, but when saccharin "got the axe," it was the last straw. Cyclamates were banned in 1969 because bladder tumors were found in four out of ten rats that had received a 10:1 mixture of cyclamate and saccharin, respectively, in a feeding study that lasted two years. Efforts to demonstrate conclusively that cyclamates are indeed tumorigenic have given negative or indefinite results. In 1976, the FDA announced that because of "unresolved safety questions" it would not lift the ban. A decision to prohibit the use of saccharin in foods was announced on March 9, 1977, following a report that bladder cancer developed in laboratory rats that had received a diet containing 5% of saccharin. A strong public reaction against the ban was immediately voiced. Saccharin was the only artificial sweetener available for most purposes, especially for "diet drinks," after cyclamates had been banned. Many critics seized on the fact that rats in the test received an intake of saccharin corresponding to 800 twelve-ounce cans of diet soft drinks for a person daily. However, it is necessary to use high dose levels in such tests to keep the number of rats within bounds.

SUGAR

Sugar, which is a food, is used extensively as an additive. Sugar usage in food products, including soft drinks, increased from 28 lb per capita, from 1925 to 1929 to 70 lb in 1971. Simultaneously, the household usage decreased from 65 lb to 28 lb, so that the total consumption remained about the same. There is no evidence that sugar itself leads to increases in cardiovascular disease or adult diabetes, but overconsumption of calories, especially fatty foods, is undoubtedly prejudicial to health. Sticky candies can cause tooth decay in children.

PESTICIDE RESIDUES IN FOODS

Not a single case of illness or death is on record as a result of pesticide residues in foods. This remarkable record probably reflects the careful control by the regulations under which pesticides are used on crops, and by monitoring the content of pesticides in "grocery store" foods.

Dr. Ernst Wynder[8] warned against drawing conclusions from animal experimentation "in which such components were administered in unrealistically high concentration." Nevertheless, dichlorodiphenyltrichloroethane (DDT) always seems good for a headline, and the question of DDT in breast milk has been used at regular intervals for several years as a "scare topic." Levels of DDT in human milk tend to be higher than in cows' milk because women excrete DDT readily in their milk, about 80-fold more readily than cows do.[9] It has been reported that DDT produces liver tumors in certain highly susceptible strains of laboratory mice. No tumors have been produced by DDT in nonrodent species and there is no link between DDT and cancer in human beings, even in people who have received DDT for many years at levels hundreds of times higher than those to which the general population has been exposed.

The average concentration of DDT in human milk was found to be 0.13 ppm in 1950 and 0.07 ppm in 1961, which indicates a downward trend that presumably has continued because of the general lowering of DDT intake and of the DDT content of human tissues that has taken place since 1961. The 1961 level of DDT in breast milk corresponds to a daily intake of about .004

mg of DDT for an infant, or about 0.0012 mg/kilo of body weight. A level about 8,000 times as high as this was fed to beagle dogs through three generations in studies by Ottoboni and co-workers.(10) The study was carried out because of apprehension concerning the effect of DDT in human breast milk. There was no effect of DDT on survival, growth, morbidity, mortality, or histological findings in the dogs. A total of 650 pups were produced in the experiment. In view of these findings and considerations, it seems unnecessary to alarm nursing mothers with headlines about DDT in their milk.

Providing a huge urban population with food is an unprecedented feat of the 1970s that is made possible only by using chemical technology in agriculture and food processing. Without chemical fertilizers, pesticides, and food additives, it would not be possible to feed the nation without a tremendous increase in intensively cultivated land. Many city dwellers would be forced into subsistence farming. Fortunately, technology has so far met the challenge of providing safe food in abundance. (Further discussions of food additives are in references 4 and 5. Good general discussions of nutrition and the food supply are in references 11 and 12.)

REFERENCES

1. Cyanide poisoning from apricot kernels, in *California Morbidity*. Sacramento, Calif, State Department of Public Health, Sept 1, 1972; Nov 14, 1975; Dec 26, 1975.
2. Conn EC: Cyanogenetic glycosides, in *Toxicants Occurring Naturally in Foods*, ed 2. Washington, DC, National Academy of Sciences, 1973, pp 299–308.
3. Krishnamachari AVR, Nagarajan V, Bhat RV, et al: Hepatitis due to aflatoxicosis: An outbreak in Western India. *Lancet* 1:1061–1063, 1975.
4. Food Protection Committee: *Evaluating the Safety of Food Chemicals*. Washington, DC, National Academy of Sciences, 1970.
5. Furia TD (ed): *Handbook of Food Additives*, ed 2. Cleveland, CRC Press, 1972, p 599.
6. Preston RL: Biological responses to estrogen additives in meat producing cattle and lambs. *J Anim Sci* 41:1414–1430, 1975.
7. USDA follows FDA in requiring research on nitrosamines in cured meat. *Food Chem News* 19:47, 1977.
8. Wynder EL: Nutrition and cancer. *Fed Proc* 35:1309–1315, 1976.
9. Quinby GE, Armstrong JF, Durham WF: DDT in human milk. *Nature* 207:726, 1965.
10. Ottoboni A, Bissell GD, Hexter AC: Effects of DDT on reproduction in multiple generations of beagle dogs. *Arch Environ Contam Toxicol* 6:83–101, 1977.
11. White PL, Selvey N (eds): *Lets Talk About Food: Answers to Your Questions About Food and Nutrition*. Acton, Mass, Publishing Sciences Group, 1974.
12. Clydesdale FM, Francis FJ: *Food, Nutrition and You*. Englewood Cliffs, NJ, Prentice-Hall Inc, 1977.

Regulating Carcinogens—
the Bitter and the Sweet

by Robert H. Baldwin

Two years ago the FDA banned the use of saccharin because it felt that such a ban was required by law in view of animal tests reported by Canadian investigators. Then Congress, reacting to public outcry, deferred FDA's ban until May of 1979. We can thus now expect considerable debate over what the next step should be including modification of the law, the Delaney Amendment, under which the ban was imposed. But it's not just saccharin or the Delaney Amendment that's at issue. In the last two years concern over chemical carcinogens, and appropriateness of their regulation has broadened dramatically. We now have regulation under the Toxic Substances Control Act (TSCA), the Occupational Health and Safety Administration (OSHA), Environmental Protection Agency (EPA), Consumer Products Safety Commission (CPSC), and other agencies. Reactions to their activities from many quarters not only oppose the banning of saccharin, and the Delaney Amendment *per se*, but more broadly question the use being made of animal feeding tests which employ massive doses of suspect chemicals, and the regulatory actions that derive from these tests.

Thus while saccharin may be the center of the debate, there is a growing realization that much more is at stake than this venerable synthetic sweetener. The larger question involves the whole area of the safe manufacture, handling, use, and disposal of a variety of chemicals. Also at issue is regulation of plant operations and new products.

The debate really encompasses two major issues—one scientific; the other political. The scientific question deals with how chemicals are involved in causing cancer, and the kinds of tests and investigations needed to supply appropriate answers to this question. The political question centers on the Delaney Amendment because it implicitly seeks the unattainable goal of "zero risk"; it allows no consideration of a "threshold," or "no-effect," dose level of a suspect carcinogen.

A spirited debate is going on in both political and technical circles on these matters, but the complexity of the physiological, genetic and pharmacological factors is such as to suggest that it may be years before we have adequate scientific knowledge to form the basis for proper value judgments.

Reprinted with permission from *Chemtech*, volume 9, number 3, March 1979, pp. 156–162. Copyright 1979 American Chemical Society.

Yet judgments must be made and made now, and such judgments, of necessity, fall in the realm of politics.

Let us here, however, first deal with the scientific problem. It comes into focus most sharply when we look at the two countervailing schools of thought on chemical carcinogenesis—the "one-molecule" hypothesis and the "threshold-level" hypothesis.

THE "ONE-MOLECULE" HYPOTHESIS

One major school of thought is characterized as the "one-molecule hypothesis." Let me try to delineate this school of thought by deducing its "tenets." I'm sure that in most instances the concepts we'll discuss must have been set forth in many places, so that my citations are a matter of personal convenience. I've made no attempt to cite the prime source. In most instances I have attempted to state each tenet by slightly rephrasing some original statement, while retaining sense of each precept. Here is my interpretation of the thinking that underlies the "one-molecule hypothesis":

1. Cancer is induced by the reaction of a single molecule with a single, critical cell site—e.g., a DNA molecule in a single cell.(1)
2. This reaction between the carcinogenic molecule and the DNA is irreversible and probably results in a malignant neoplasm.(1)
3. A two-step, or two-stage, process may be involved in which reaction is required by two different chemical agents—one as "initiator" and the second as "promoter," or "co-carcinogen." These two steps may occur months or even years apart.(2)
4. Carcinogenic activity of a chemical in *any animal*, by *any test* is evidence that this chemical could cause cancer in man.(3)
5. The effects of chemical carcinogens are cumulative, hence there must be concern for a single exposure to any carcinogen or more than one.(3, 5)
6. Two chemical carcinogens can be synergistic to give an effect greater than the sum of the two.(3)

The overall one-molecule position is often summarized by the statement, "It is impossible to set a safe level of intake for any substance that might cause cancer in animal or man."(2, 3)

THE "THRESHOLD-LEVEL" HYPOTHESIS

In opposition to the "one-molecule" view of carcinogenesis are the proponents of the "threshold" hypothesis. They have been helpful in discerning and stating the opposing "one-molecule" precepts. Here are the basic tenets of this school of thought.

1. Animal defense systems include detoxifying mechanisms that dispose of a variety of "strange" chemical compositions—i.e., chemicals uncommon to the normal digestive and respiratory processes.(4–6)
2. These detoxifying processes have capacity limitations, so that they cope adequately with modest levels of "strange chemicals," but massive doses overload them. When overload occurs, secondary coping mechanisms may come into play to continue detoxification and disposal. There may also be an increase of the retention level of the "stranger," or its metabolites in the body as the intake level increases. Eventually higher dosage levels can overwhelm all systems and toxic effect, including carcinogenesis, may occur.(4–6)
3. Animal systems have "repair mechanisms" that reverse the initiation reaction of the intruding chemical "stranger" or its metabolite. These repair mechanisms can also be overloaded. If the extent of damage (initiating reactions) is great, the repair time may be longer. In extreme cases the repair system can be overwhelmed, the damage becomes irreversible, and malignant lesions may appear.(6)
4. Differences in metabolism among different animal families, genera and species are frequently encountered. As yet there is no certain way to predict that any given chemical "stranger" will be metabolized and/or secreted in the same way by rodents, carnivora, and primates. The differences among animal species, genera and families with respect to electrolyte balances, retention and elimination of metabolites are likewise considerable and may produce substantial differences in reactions to chemical "strangers," particularly in massive doses.(1, 6)
5. Animal tests at moderate and low dosage levels are thus essential to assess the thresholds of effectiveness of detoxifying mechanisms and repair systems.(1, 4, 6, 8)
6. Animal tests in families and genera closely related to man—i.e., primates—are most likely to indicate how humans will react.
7. Human epidemiological information should always have precedence over animal tests (assuming, of course, that the epidemiology is based on valid methods of obtaining and handling the data).(8)
8. It is almost always possible to establish a finite, "no effect" level of intake for a chemical suspected as a carcinogen (possible exception may be certain direct alkylating agents).(4, 6, 8)

DIFFICULTIES WITH THE "ONE-MOLECULE" HYPOTHESIS

I have five problems in trying to adopt the "one-molecule" view of carcinogenesis:

- the confusion between correlation and causation that seems to prevail in much of the animal test work;
- the smallness of the quantity of a single molecule—so awfully close to zero—boggles my mind as I try to grasp it as a real causative agent;
- the problems in extrapolation of data, as I perceive them, strain my credibility;
- my attempts to apply this "one-molecule" concept to a real case—the long-time, steady user of saccharin;
- my attempts to visualize how I can assure even myself (to say nothing of a skeptic) that I can devise any kind of experiment that is free from extraneous contamination by other "uncontrolled" molecules. Let's look at each of these briefly.

It is a well-known fallacy of logic to attribute causation to a situation in which only correlation is entailed. To my mind much of the animal test work is at, or close to, this pitfall(9). A common cure for this fallacy is to postulate a mechanism that seeks to explain the phenomenon under consideration and to devise experiments to test the model; i.e., to try to establish a causative mechanism relating to the observed results and to "prove" that the relationship is causative. Beyond this I have difficulty swallowing statements such as have been made repeatedly by the Food and Drug Administration (FDA), and are now required in saccharin labeling, to the effect that, "Saccharin has been shown to cause cancer in animals." Now this requirement begs the question, "What do you accept as proof?" The FDA reference in its proposed ban on saccharin referred to the Canadian Health Protection Branch tests as the basis for the "has been shown" statement. But these tests have been challenged on several grounds (lack of dose-response data, upsets in electrolyte balance in the renal system of the rats, questions of transplacental transfer and in utero dosage levels, etc.) In fact, the tests were not designed to elicit data on saccharin per se, but rather on o-toluene sulfonamide. With so many unresolved questions the skeptical observer must reserve judgment. It is thus only the true believer in the "one-molecule" hypothesis who can say, "It has been shown . . . ."

When I contemplate the concentration of reactant that a lone molecule represents, I find almost nothing—zero. To sharpen this point let's look at how many molecules are involved in the smallest amounts of a chemical we can detect with our newest and most sophisticated instrument—the GC-mass spectrograph systems. Some of the more readily identified organic molecules are detected in amounts as small as one picogram, i.e., 10^{-12} grams. Though saccharin may not be detectable at this level, let's assume for the moment that it is. Its sodium salt, dihydrate, has a molecular weight of 241, so that we would find in our picogram more than two billion molecules. Thus I have no quarrel with the idea that in any reaction some one molecule will always be first. But, that lone molecule represents such a minute concentration that I am unable to imagine that it will ever, in any time short of infinity, find *the* reactive site. Or, to put it another way, the statistical probability of a single, lone molecule finding and reacting at some single critical cell site is so infinitesimally low as to be negligible to my imagination—like making a hole-in-one on the planet Mercury from a tee shot on Earth.

In trying to grasp the extrapolation problem, I may be a prisoner of my engineering background. If so, forgive me. In Figure 1 I visualize two tests: the circles represent three points on a curve AB, the squares three points on a curve CD. In both cases I assume a simple linear relationship which I extrapolate to the axes. In the case A'AB my intercept at zero ordinate is a positive value on the abscissa. This I interpret as a "no effect" dosage level of A'. In the case of the squares, I extend CD to zero abscissa at C' where I also plot the control group's spontaneous tumor incidence as C'. Now if C' happens to be the control group for the series AB, do I have a "blank" value which I should subtract from AB to get an adjusted curve A''B''? So doing implies a new, and higher, no-effect dosage level, A''. Of course, to avoid these dilemmas I can just assume that the origin is on each curve; but may I?

I perceive another kind of problem (Figure 2). Here my test points are triangles at three dosage levels, but only the highest level, A, shows a tumor incidence significantly different from the control, D. Now how do I extrapolate? My engineering background says subtract the blank (D) and get a new curve A'B'. But even here I have trouble—I need a point between A and B since B becomes the corrected B' a zero. But what I seem to be hearing in the conclusions drawn from Figure 2 is an extrapolation OA. This says in effect only the point A is significant and the other points are of no consequence. I find the logic of "extrapolating a point" somewhat dubious. But this is what I think I hear and it is part of my problem with the "one-molecule" hypothesis.

Now none of this is a problem if you subscribe to the "one-molecule" idea already—then it is perfectly logical to use *the* point that shows a positive effect and to extend it to the origin. But it seems to me that you have to adopt the hypothesis as an article of faith. I don't impugn this faith for a moment, as I have friends who hold this faith; but they are candid enough to admit that their brief is a matter of faith, not of scientific proof.

Now Dr. Gehring(1) says that the proper method for plotting dose-response data is to plot the log of the dosage rate vs. the percentage tumor incidence. Doing so will, of course, eliminate the zero on the abscissa and

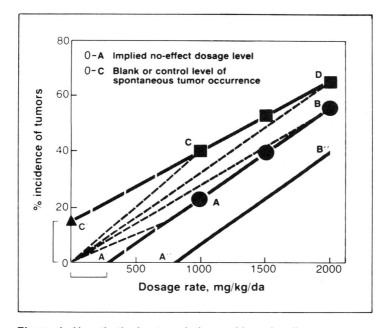

Figure 1. Hypothetical extrapolation problem visualizes two sets of data, one represented by the circles and by the line AB; the other represented by the squares and the line CD.

Also plotted on the ordinate (zero abscissa) is the point C′ which could represent the "blank" or "tare" value of "spontaneous" tumor occurrence in the "control" group. Line AB is extrapolated to zero ordinate to give an indicated "no-effect" dosage level of 300 mg/kg/da. Line CD extrapolates conveniently to C′ the "control" group response. The line A″B″ results from subtracting the "control level" or "blank" from AB to show a "no-effect" level of 800. There seems to be an aversion to such extrapolation in some quarters where zerophiles insist on making everything extrapolate to zero as in OCD or OD and OAB or just OB.

permit only successively lower and lower dosages, but never zero. Let me go one step further and propose that we use log-probability paper, plotting tumor incidence on the probability scale. After all, we are talking about a probabilistic phenomenon. Now we have eliminated the zeros from both scales. Dosages can get smaller by decades and incidences can get over smaller, but never zero. Whatever the problems of extending lines (which may not always be straight), I see a distinct psychological advantage in having no zeros anywhere. (Figure 3 is such a plot of the points in Figure 1.) There is never a zero-risk point and never a zero-dosage point. I particularly like this device for removing the idea of "zero-risk" from our thinking because I don't believe that it does exist in this vale of tears.

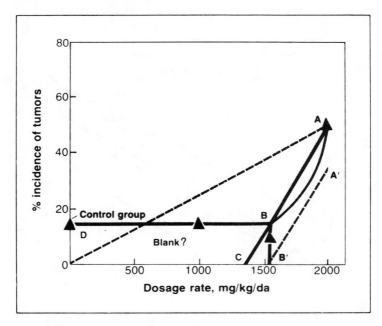

Figure 2. A second hypothetical extrapolation problem wherein the triangles represent the data at three dosage levels and the zero control (D).

An engineer would draw the line DBA through the points. Or he would subtract the "blank" or Control Group response and extrapolate A'B'. Again there appears to be strong affinity in some quarters for zero with the point A extrapolated to the origin as in OA.

My fourth problem with the "one-molecule" hypothesis comes about from trying to put it to test on the considerable group of people who have used saccharin on a regular daily basis over a long period of years. The recent National Academy of Science study estimated that 4 to 5 million people may have been using saccharin on a regular daily basis during 15–20 years. In the 20 years prior to 1962, and the advent of diet soft drinks, total saccharin consumption was of the order of 20 million pounds. Since industrial uses and non-ingestive uses (toothpaste, mouthwash, etc.) were substantial markets, the use as a table sweetener was probably only half the total or a half-million pounds per year. This amount would provide the steady saccharin user about 0.1 lb/y or about 8 one-quarter grain tablets per day. This amount is well below the "Allowable Daily Intake" of 1000 mg/day. When I convert this modest poundage into a daily intake of saccharin the figure astounds me. It comes out to 3×10^{20} molecules per day. So we have a sizeable group of people who have had a steady, day-in-day-out, year-in-year-out, measured

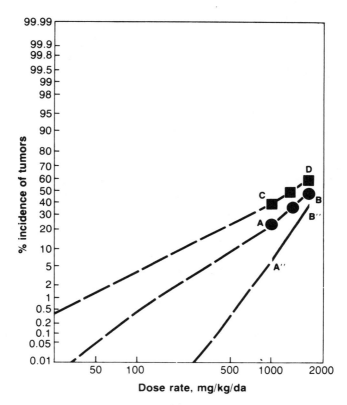

Figure 3. A third extrapolation using the same points as in Figure 1 but on a different graph paper.

Gehring prefers to plot dosage levels on a logarithmic scale. Since this eliminates one zero, I like it. Going one step further I propose plotting the tumor incidence as a probabilistic function on a probability scale—thus get rid of the other zero. A *no-zero* situation should have desirable psychological effects to say the least: There is no level of "zero risk" and there is no condition of absolutely zero exposure or intake. •

intake of a suspected carcinogen. In most cases of chemical exposure we have an unknown, and sporadic dosage from inadvertent and accidental contact via air, food, skin absorption, etc. But with saccharin users the dosage is reasonably well measured, very steady, and long term. Now with this situation I try to take on the "one-molecule" outlook. And this time my imagination tells me that if saccharin is a carcinogen (even a weak one, or a promoter), I have got to believe that every one of those 5 million long-time users must have bladder cancer. In cancer data terms that's 2500 per 100,000 or about 8 times the *total* incidence of all types of cancer in the U.S. and about 200 times the incidence of bladder cancer. This leaves me concluding that the "one-molecule" hypothesis is invalid, or that saccharin is not a carcinogen, or both.

My final problem with the one-moleculists comes as I try to visualize how any experiment can escape contamination from one molecule to say nothing of a few thousand or a few million molecules of whatever happens to be around. How can I assure myself that all extraneous molecules are excluded from the air, the water, the food, the hands, the tools, and the laboratory for the *two years* of an animal feeding test. Since the smallest amount of chemical detectable by our best techniques contains billions of molecules, how can I assure myself, or anyone else, that my test is not inadvertently contaminated on some given day? And, since we have only begun to identify those molecules we suspect may cause cancer, how can I possibly assure myself that a few thousand or million of these "bad" molecules have not somehow accidentally crept into my test group? I can only conclude that, for the present, it is impossible (for me, at least) to conceive a way to assure that any feeding test is not contaminated by at least one molecule that could do the damage—and I mean a molecule different from the one I seek to test. Thus I find the one-molecule hypothesis essentially unverifiable, at least until we can detect the presence of a single molecule.

So these are my problems with the "one-molecule" concept. They leave me in the camp of the "threshold-level" hypothesis. OK. What should we expect here?

· THRESHOLD

Does "threshold" answer all our questions now? Certainly not; but this hypothesis does hold promise. What do I expect from this school of thought? I see prospects for developing a broad, unified concept involving mechanisms of tissue generation, repair and degradation, including mechanisms for detoxification of "stranger" chemicals and DNA repair. I further see these processes coupled with pharmacokinetic understanding that will reconcile the disparate aspects of our current knowledge and give us a good appreciation of how animal organisms function from conception to demise. Finally, I hold the hope that we will be able to predict reactions to chemicals in many instances and to quantify risks.

I hope to see a body of knowledge that will show the relationship between mutagenesis and carcinogenesis, knowledge that will show how and why most cancer is associated with aging. I hope we'll soon understand how and why some individuals, families, and populations survive adverse environments to achieve great longevity without any incidence of cancer, and yet how and why certain types of cancer devastate some children.

Today we seem trapped in a time when all our ills, misfortunes and misbehaviors are blamed on the environment. We would hope to see the day when we can face the prospects of hereditary differences without apology. And it would be nice if we could also come to acknowledge that some (if not most) of our difficulties stem from our own follies.

Anomalies I would hope to see understood include latency, inhibition, dormancy, potentiation, and cumulative effects (if there are any such). I want to know why small amounts of certain chemicals or elements—e.g., tryptophan or selenium—are "essential," while they exhibit carcinogenic effects in only slightly larger amounts. And I look forward to our understanding the paradoxes in reactions among mice and men—e.g., 2-naphthylamine, a carcinogen to men, not to rats; thalidomide, a teratogen to men but not to mice; aspirin, a teratogen to mice but not to men, etc. There must be logical and rational explanations to these contradictions which we'll begin to understand.

NOW

However, it may be 5 or 10 or perhaps 25 years before we have such knowledge. Meanwhile, how do we operate? We have to keep about our business and certainly we will. But I am concerned over problems in intervening years.

First, it appears that animal tests which have been so prominent in the Delaney Amendment aspects of Food and Drug Administration's regulation are spreading rapidly into areas under the purview of Toxic Substances Control Act, National Institute of Occupational Safety and Health, Occupational Safety and Health Administration and Environmental Protection Agency. I perceive a momentum carrying us into echelons of tests on long lists of chemicals suspected of carcinogenic potential. I fear much of this effort will be discarded in the long run and may cause considerable confusion meanwhile. Some of this may be necessary and some is tolerable, but the regrets come from the diversion of so much time, money and talent into a go-no-go kind of testing that adds so little to knowledge and understanding. Furthermore, I'm concerned that a burgeoning of animal testing will encourage further regulation of industry on the basis that we know enough about cancer causation and enough about appropriate exposure levels and risk assessment—when I doubt that we do.

THE POLITICAL QUESTION

I thus have a second concern. It is that increasing animal testing and immediate use of results as the basis for regulation will ultimately discredit science in the public's view. Already we have cried "wolf" so often that there is concern that the appearance of a really serious problem in chemical carcinogenesis might be greeted by yawns. But more fundamentally my concern is that much of what is going on is poor science, and is bound to hurt the whole field in time.

The problem entails the interface between science and the political world, and the question is: "How do we use science to help us decide what and where and when and how to regulate our lives?" In tackling this problem I'd like to use three words in quite specific ways: They are Information, Knowledge, and Wisdom.

By *Information* I mean a fact or event—a verifiable result of some test.

By *Knowledge* I mean the understanding that science seeks from a study of many facts, and their relationships with each other. This knowledge is often stated in the form of a law or a principle—e.g., Newton's Law. And, the statement usually is predictive in form—that is, we say, "Whenever you do this, you will always get that;" or, "When you find so-and-so, you invariably also find thus-and-so."

By *Wisdom* I mean the use of knowledge to fashion means whereby we can live better as a society.

Now between each of these words there is a big jump in perception and comprehension of the world. It is a quantum leap from *information* to *knowledge*. And it is several such leaps from *knowledge* to *wisdom*.

The business of science is, basically, gaining *knowledge*—understanding how the world works. The many animal tests aim at a limited objective, at adding *information*, by showing what happens over a rat's lifetime at several levels of feeding of a suspected carcinogen. This information may be published and read by scientists around the world. Ultimately some brilliant fellow looks at all this information and says, "Hey, look at this! Every time you do this see what happens? You always get this—except when you also do so and so!" And we get a new law. All of this information has been raised to the level of understanding and we have knowledge. *And, right here the job of science, qua science, is done.*

Note that information is quite ephemeral stuff. Though each new paper gets a going over by other scientists, any given paper may be ignored, or become a landmark in the aggregation of information that sparks the genius who gives us the understanding.

Understanding develops slowly out of debate. The first attempts to state the new understanding are often modified quite a bit in the argument among scientists before a new "law" gets out into the secular world.

THE USE OF KNOWLEDGE TO ORDER SOCIETY IS THE BUSINESS OF POLITICS

Now after science has given knowledge of how things work, it is the job of all people in a representative democracy to decide how to use this new understanding. It is the body politic, through its elected representatives, that decides what kind of a society we want and how we might want to change it using the knowledge science gives us. It is *wisdom* we need in this business of deciding how to fashion a better world to live in—how to balance the *ends* we seek and the *means* for achieving them. And these two things—*ends* and *means*—are bound together in such a way that one always affects the other.

We may all agree to seek as *ends* a safe, clean, healthy, environment in which we are all free to make a wide diversity of choices. But if we propose to achieve these *ends* by regulation we have already given up some of the freedom that was part of the *ends* we sought. If we use regulation to excess, to protect us from all kinds of hazards, we find our freedom badly eroded. If we leave too much to individual choice we may find we live in anarchy, in a pretty messy world.

In this business of wisdom, the scientist is just another citizen. When he has given us new knowledge he must put aside his credentials and join the rest of society in seeking wisdom. He has nothing on the rest of us—and no special privilege to tell us how to do it politically. In this area the philosophers, historians, theologians, poets or novelists may be more helpful in seeing things in an overall balanced view. And, it is right here that I have a great concern that science has been getting out of bounds. We find scientists eager to influence the debate. Urged on by various activist groups, they bring into the public debate mere information—their latest test results—even before they have been subjected to peer review and publication. They urge regulation on the very flimsy basis of information, and remember, *information* at this stage in science is very fragile—subject to change or even discard before knowledge is achieved. The public is greatly confused by such antics. Information belongs in the halls of science until it emerges as knowledge. Much of the current debate is confounded by too much information and too little knowledge. In the area of food toxicology, we have much information, but we have far to go in really understanding how complex animal systems cope with all kinds of chemical components in our environment. What we do seem to understand— in the case of saccharin—is that a lot of people have eaten a lot of it over a long period without any demonstrable effect on cancer incidence.

It would be salubrious if the scientific community could recognize both the ultimate limitation on what scientific knowledge can and should do—and further to accept responsibility for the damage to the public image of a science that is being done by overweening efforts to influence public policy and regulation with premature and irresponsible dissemination of every new test result (mere information) with or without peer-review.

I'm not the first scientist to recognize the problem and speak to it.

Philip Handler, President, National Academy of Sciences said, speaking before the annual meeting of the Food and Nutrition Board early in December 1977,

> "There is no known epidemiological evidence that food additives are hazardous to health. Man-made chemicals are a trivial aspect of the burden of disease, and the issue is very emotional. The 80–90% of cancers attributed to environmental causes does not refer to man-made chemicals. The U.S. is going to have to live through a long period of risk aversion, in which a lot of chemicals may be found to be mutagens or carcinogens."(10)

Handler noted the current limitations of assessing carcinogenic potentiality, pointing out that in no case is it known how far the dose-response curve goes and how small an amount of a substance is likely to be carcinogenic, or whether it is dealt with by DNA-repair mechanisms. "In the end, some value system is going to dictate how we will behave (toward chemical additives), rather than science,"

Handler further stated, predicting one saccharin episode after the other, "without ever knowing what we're denying ourselves and whether the initial approach was right."

And early last year Morris Cranmer(11), Director of the National Center for Toxiciological Research, linked the Delaney clause to "strategies" that "encourage bad experimentation." He explained that, "More testing in more animals increases the likelihood of positive results," adding that, "This does not encourage a Petitioner to attempt to obtain more data on a compound."

It also is gratifying to find the secular press in some of its more prestigious journals taking science and the regulators to task quite severely.

A *Wall Street Journal's* editorial, addressing itself to the laetrile controversy, digressed to speak of saccharin and cancer causers generally said: "Regulatory agencies, in this case the Food and Drug Administration, offer us the worst face of science. By filtering scientific tenets through inflexible bureaucratic logic, they squeeze out all room for human judgment. The mission becomes one of protecting the public from itself. Thou shalt not make your own judgment about the risk of consuming saccharin or cyclamates. The public has repeatedly proved itself ornery about these matters; witness the consumption of cigarettes. Condescension, no matter on what scientific evidence, risks a backlash.

"Eventually science will unlock the secrets of cancer and laetrile will fade away. But there will always be things beyond the competence of science, and its friends will only do it damage by pressing its claims too hard where it has no answer."(12)

As a final comment, hear what Marvin Stone, editor of U.S. News and World Report had to say:

"How capricious does our Government intend to be—and how far can it be allowed to go—in limiting freedom of choice by individual citizens? That question is at the heart of the controversy over saccharin, which the Food and Drug Administration proposes to ban because of evidence that it is a cancer-causing agent in force-fed Canadian rats. From the start, the whole saccharin mess has been surrounded by a hypocrisy on the part of the Government. What is wrong with allowing Americans to make themselves aware of the arguments for and against the use of saccharin and then leaving them alone to make a free choice—much as they now are free to make a choice whether to smoke tobacco or, for that matter, whether to take the risk of driving on highways that claim 45,000 lives a year? Surely people in Washington have learned by now that, when common sense has fled from Congress and the bureaucracy, public outrage soon surfaces, and sometimes prevails. Prohibition of whisky, well intentioned as it may have seemed, failed as unenforceable. More recently, seat belts with ignition interlocks provoked a citizen revolt strong enough to force repeal. The Delaney Clause, while meritorious on the whole, needs to be changed to provide more flexibility. It offers no alternative to an outright ban on saccharin and as such prohibits voluntary decision making. Americans need not be treated like a mindless mass, with the most personal decisions stuffed down people's throats through restrictive legislation. The proper approach with saccharin is to tell people in plain English what may be the risk of using it, and let the people decide for themselves whether the risk is worth taking. As matters stand, the "state" is interfering in decisions that individuals should be making. At best this is capricious and condescending. At worst it is a growing danger and has gone far enough."(13)

SCIENTIFIC INADEQUACY AND ODIOUS REGULATION

These observers and commentators of the chemical carcinogenesis scene today emphasize two things:

(1) The scientific inadequacy of the Delaney-inspired, massive-dose animal test condemnation of chemicals on a zero-risk basis; and

(2) The odious and uncompromising affection of bureaucrats for regulation via bans and prohibitions when no clear danger is perceived.

There is also much talk of balancing "risks" and "benefits." But if the same bureaucratic thinking that deals as it does with risk is applied to assessing benefits, will we have made any significant progress? Perhaps if both risks and benefits can be viewed in subjective terms, as Handler says, in "some value system rather than science," we may be getting nearer to a liveable system for protecting ourselves from the hazards of all sorts. Why can't we use Lowrance's concept that, "A thing is safe if its risks are judged to be acceptable"(14). This really describes how the prudent person behaves in real life, does it not? Now, why not conceive "benefits" in this same frame: "A thing is beneficial if the values it affords are judged to be helpful or enjoyable?"

In either case there remains the question, "Judged by whom? And by what criteria?" This may not be an idle question. Food and Drug Administration Commissioner, Donald Kennedy, recently warned us (and the Congress) that a risk-benefit law would insert into Food and Drug Administration's powers the "new element" of "value judgment," observing that the two factors are "indivisible." He further warned that agency value judgments would not be subject to "statutory restraint" or to the traditional judicial review(15).

Congress should take care to provide the checks and balances we deem so valuable and should avoid setting up any agency that is prosecutor, judge and jury.

There are obviously two schools of thought here—the elitists and the populists—those who believe that only a small select group can make appropriate judgments of either risk or benefit—and those who hold that the average person supplied with reasonable knowledge of the situation can make reasonable judgment.

Trouble is we often don't have the knowledge adequate to the situation at the time of decision. So we need some middle way—an interim kind of *modus operandi*—pending development of the "knowledge" we need to make a final judgment. In this regard, John T. Dunlop has some worthwhile thoughts. He cites the "main reason for the attraction of regulation has been the belief that it is a speedy, simple and cheap procedure." He continues, "It should be apparent that the administrative procedure is by no means fast or inexpensive . . . ."(16).

He concludes: "It has well been said that the recreation and development of trust is the central problem of government in our times. The development of new attitudes on the part of public employees and new relationships and procedures with those who are required to live under regulations is a central challenge of democratic society. Trust cannot grow in an atmosphere dominated by bureaucratic fiat and litigious controversy; it emerges through persuasion, mutual accommodation and problem-solving."

Thanks go to John Weaver for catalyzing the relationship with Mr. Baldwin which led to this editorial.

REFERENCES

1. Gehring, P.J., *New Sci.*, August 18, 1977.
2. McGaughy, C., *Science*, **202**, 4372, December 8, 1978, pp. 1105–6.
3. Lijinsky, W., *Chem. Eng. News*, June 27, 1977, pp. 25–33.
4. Gehring, P.J., SOCMA Meeting, March 9, 1976, Atlanta, Ga.
5. Brown, Fears, Gail, Schneiderman, and Larone, *Science*, **202**, 4372, December 8, 1978, p. 1105.
6. Cohn, W.E., *Chem. Eng. News*, August 29, 1975, p. 5.
7. Gehring, P.J., *Chem. Week*, **121**(15), April 13, 1975, p. 32.
8. Coulston, F., *Chem. Eng. News*, June 27, 1977, pp. 34–37.
9. Hickey, R.J., *Chem. Eng. News*, January 1, 1979, p. 37.
10. Handler, P., *Food Chem. News*, December 12, 1978, p. 70–71.
11. Cranmer, M., *Food Chem. News*, February 13, 1978.
12. *Wall Street Journal*, July 7, 1977, p. 10.
13. Stone, M., *U.S. News & World Rep.*, April 4, 1977, p. 84.
14. Lowrance, W.W., *Of Acceptable Risk—Science and the Determination of Safety*, W. Kaufman, 1976.
15. Kennedy, D., *Food Chem. News*, December 11, 1978.
16. Dunlop, J.T., The Conference Board RECORD, March 1976, pp. 23–27.

4

Microbiological Hazards

Whenever any scientific regulatory body is asked to list the greatest hazards to health from food, the first hazard is always microbiological.

It has been estimated that over 2 million individuals each year in the United States suffer from some form of microbiologically related food borne illness.

It always amazes us that, with these facts, the public is not educated to a greater extent about sanitation and the handling of food.

One might suppose that since the consumer cannot see microorganisms they are not interested. We believe that this assumption is wrong and that early education should begin on this topic. Since such education does not exist to any extent we felt that a few papers on this subject could be included.

It seems there is little we have control over in our society but this is one area where we can exercise a great deal of personal control.

It is hoped that the text and pictures provided in this section might prevent one of you, who are reading this book, from suffering the pain of food borne illnesses.

Food, Hands and Bacteria

by G.A. Schuler, J.A. Christian and W.C. Hurst

Bacteria have their own population explosion going. They can reproduce every 20 minutes. There are so many of them that you now have on your body more bacteria than there are people in the United States.

Like people, bacteria may be good or bad, depending on what they do *to* you or *for* you. And like people, bacteria are here to stay. We can't get rid of them. So we must learn to live with them.

Some bacteria spend their lives in the small folds of the skin, on hair or under fingernails. Others cause body odor. Still others, called *pathogens,* cause disease.

The bacteria normally found on your skin we'll call *resident bacteria.* They exist on the skin of normal, healthy people, and are usually not harmful. They're always there, and can't be removed completely.

Other bacteria are transferred to your skin in one way or another. Let's call these *transient bacteria.* Think for a moment how many ways your hands have picked up bacteria today.

Your hands do all sorts of things for you. They write, pick up the telephone, handle money, fix meals, dress wounds. Your hands gather bacteria with each job they do. You can remove many of these bacteria by washing your hands and scrubbing your fingernails.

We can't see individual bacteria without using a microscope. But if they are allowed to grow and multiply on *agar,* we can see them. *Nutrient agar* is a special food used to grow bacteria in the laboratory. It contains everything bacteria need to grow and reproduce.

If we transfer bacteria to an agar plate and keep it warm *(incubate it),* the bacteria will reproduce rapidly. There will be so many that we can see them with the naked eye. These millions of bacteria, side by side, are called a *colony.*

HANDS

We transferred bacteria to agar plates by touching them with our fingers. First, we touched a plate with dirty fingers. Then we rinsed the fingers in cold water for 20 seconds. Next, we washed them with soap and water for 20

From *Cooperative Extension Service* bulletin 693, reprinted May 1979, University of Georgia, College of Agriculture. Reprinted by permission.

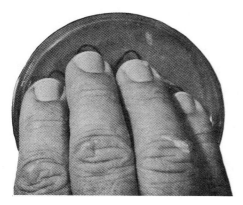

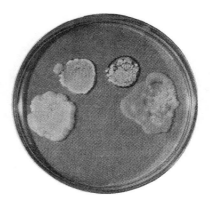

Dirty fingers touch agar.   **After 24 hours**

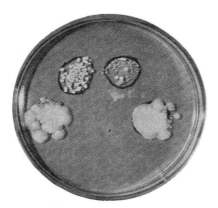

After cold water rinse

seconds. The fingers were then washed for an additional 20 seconds. Finally, we dipped the fingers into a sanitizing solution containing *chlorine*. We could have obtained similar results with a *bromine* or *iodine* solution. The fingers touched an agar plate after each cleansing. The plates were incubated at 98°F. for 24 hours. The photos show what happened.

The dirty fingers contained so many bacteria that the areas they touched on the agar plate were a mass of colonies.

The 20-second cold water rinse removed large particles of dirt and some bacteria. But there were still millions of colonies left. As you can see, rinsing your hands with cold water is not a good way to clean them.

Washing the hands with soap and water for 20 seconds reduced the number of bacteria. However, 20 seconds was not long enough. After the

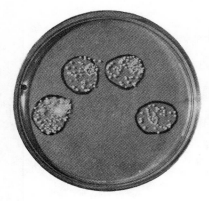

After 20-second wash with soap and water

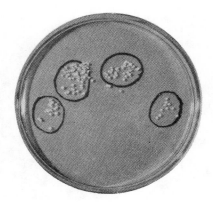

After additional 20-second wash with soap and water

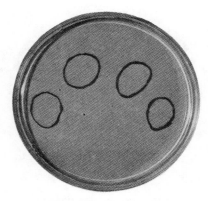

After using sanitizing solution

hands were washed again with soap and water for 20 seconds, the number of bacteria was reduced even more.

So hands should be washed at least 40 seconds with soap and water. It's even better to wash them a full minute.

The photos show that soap and water will reduce the number of bacteria on your hands. It's impossible to remove all bacteria with soap and water. The important thing is to reduce the number of *transient* bacteria on your hands. Just be sure to wash your hands thoroughly for at least 40 seconds before you handle food.

No bacteria grew on the agar plate after the fingers were dipped in a sanitizing solution. The bacteria may or may not have been killed, but the sanitizer stopped their growth. Of course, some people may not be able to use a sanitizing solution because it may irritate their skin.

**Effect of sanitizing solution
on sneeze**

This photo dramatizes the effect of sanitizing agents on bacteria. An agar plate was sneezed on, then a drop of sanitizing solution put in the center of the plate. Bacteria grew in the areas not touched by the sanitizer.

The demonstration shows the importance of covering your mouth and nose when you sneeze. Your mouth, nose and throat contain millions of bacteria all the time. Unless you cover your mouth and nose when you sneeze, you spray bacteria around like a spray can.

GLOVES

Like your hands, gloves also become dirty and covered with bacteria. In the next demonstration, a person wearing a dirty glove touched an agar plate. He then rinsed the glove in cold water for 20 seconds; washed it with soap and water for 20 seconds; then washed it again with soap and water for 20 seconds; and finally dipped it into a sanitizing solution. After each cleansing, he touched an agar plate. The photographs show how the plates looked after 24 hours.

The dirty glove contained many bacteria, as shown by the large number of colonies on the agar. The number of colonies was reduced after the glove was rinsed in water. As you can see, we can reduce the number of bacteria on gloves by just rinsing them in water.

The two 20-second washes with soap and water reduced the number of bacteria to a very low level.

So soap and water are better than a plain water rinse for removing bacteria from gloves.

The sanitizing solution stopped all bacteria from growing.

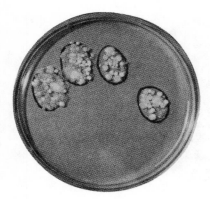

Effect of dirty gloves
after 24 hours

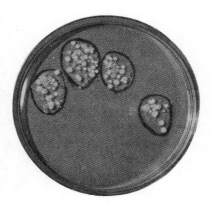

After 20-second cold water rinse

After 20-second wash with
soap and water

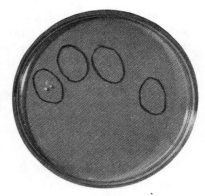

After additional 20-second wash
with soap and water

After using sanitizing solution

It was easier to remove bacteria from gloves than it was from the hands. Gloves have no *resident* bacteria; only *transient* bacteria. Gloves have no ridges or crevices in which bacteria can hide. It's possible to remove all bacteria from gloves, although we can't remove all them from our hands.

OTHER SOURCES

Well kept hair is attractive, but let's keep it out of our food. Nobody likes to see hair in what they are about to eat. It's a good sign that someone didn't follow sanitation rules when the food was processed or prepared. So always wear a hair net or a hat when you work with food.

To demonstrate the importance of this, we placed some human hair on an agar plate and incubated it for 24 hours. Look at the number of bacteria that grew around the hair.

Like hands, it's impossible to completely remove bacteria from your hair. Although you may have just washed it, it still contains many bacteria.

We can also transfer bacteria from dirty aprons to food. We touched a dirty apron to an agar plate and incubated it for 24 hours. The photo shows that the apron contained many bacteria. These bacteria could easily have been transferred to food. This points out the need for wearing clean clothes and clean aprons every day. If your clothes or apron get dirty during the day, change them.

Cutting boards are another source of bacteria, and should be washed thoroughly after each use. Do not use *wooden* cutting boards. Bacteria can hide in the wood fiber, making it impossible to remove all of them. If you use cutting boards or utensils on raw food, don't use them to hold, serve, prepare or carve *cooked* food before they are thoroughly cleansed and sanitized.

Flies, roaches and rats leave bacteria on everything they touch. To illustrate this, we let a cockroach walk on an agar plate. The photo, made after 24 hours, shows the number of bacteria the cockroach left on the plate.

Rats, flies, roaches and other insects leave bacteria as they crawl on food, garbage and people. So we must all work to keep these pests out of our homes, restaurants and food processing plants. The time you spend cleaning and sanitizing your food handling equipment is wasted if you allow insects and rats to walk on them after they're cleaned.

Even the best homes, restaurants and food processing plants have flies, roaches and other insects from time to time. But these pests should not be allowed to live in these places for long.

Ashes from tobacco contain very few bacteria. But, foreign material of any kind should not be tolerated in food. So do not smoke and do not allow others to smoke where food is being processed, stored, prepared or served.

Human hair after 24 hours

Effect of dirty apron after 24 hours

Cockroach after 24 hours

Cuts, bruises and sores on our hands also carry millions of bacteria. If the skin on your hands is broken anywhere, cover the wound completely before handling food.

Bacteria carried on hands may cause food to spoil. They may also cause food poisoning and food infection. As bacteria increase, the food develops an odd smell or taste when it is cooked. It just doesn't taste as good as it should. If the bacteria continue to multiply, the uncooked food develops a peculiar smell. As the bacteria develop further, the food becomes slimy. It will be slippery to the touch, like a bar of wet soap.

So if you handle or start to eat food with an objectionable smell, taste or feel, throw it away. Never taste food to see if it's spoiled—it may be.

Bacteria are everywhere and on everything. So we must learn to live with them. But we must try to keep the number of bacteria in our food as low as possible. We can do this by following the simple rules below.

- Keep food handling areas spotlessly clean.
- Wash your hands often with soap and water. Be sure you wash them thoroughly after using the restroom, dressing a wound and before handling any food. This will help get rid of transient bacteria which can cause disease.
- Don't handle food with hands that have cuts, bruises or sores on them.
- Don't sneeze or cough on food or in areas where food is being prepared.
- Keep your body and clothes clean.
- Wear a hair net or a hat when handling food.
- Keep rats, cockroaches, flies and other insects out of areas where food is processed, stored, prepared or served.
- Don't use wooden cutting boards—they can't be cleaned properly.
- Be sure cutting tools used on raw food are sanitized before you use them on cooked food.
- Don't smoke and don't allow anyone else to smoke in areas where food is processed, stored, prepared or served.

Food-Borne Disease I

by Edmund A. Zottola, Ph.D.

Do you enjoy eating raw hamburger? Do you occasionally taste uncooked, ground meat while preparing a meal? Has this unconcscious habit of yours ever resulted in an unexpected illness? If not, you are luckier than several homemakers in the Western United States who, as they prepared their family dinner of ground meat, sampled a bite of the raw, ground meat. A few days later they became ill with severe diarrhea. Some required hospitalization. They had contracted Salmonellosis, a type of food-borne disease common in the United States today. Their families ate only the cooked meat and did not become sick as the heat involved in the cooking killed the bacteria that caused the symptoms.(1)

How would you like to be on a transcontinental flight for many hours and suddenly have severe stomach cramps, nausea, vomiting and explosive diarrhea with 100 or so fellow passengers? It would not be a very pleasant experience.(2) Well, it has happened on several occasions. The cause is *Staphylococcus aureus*. This bacteria probably causes more cases of food-borne disease in the United States than any other microorganism.

Many such instances of food-borne disease probably occur each day all over the United States but they may go unrecognized or undiagnosed or passed off as "stomach-flu", a "virus" or something that's going around. The Center for Disease Control (CDC) in Atlanta, Georgia, is the agency responsible for reporting outbreaks of food-borne disease. Their activities depend upon reporting agencies in the 50 states and numerous municipalities throughout the United States. The CDC estimates that only 10% of the outbreaks of food-borne disease that occur each year are reported. If that assumption is true, then over 2 million individuals each year suffer from some type of food-borne disease.

The two stories above, Salmonellosis from raw hamburger and the outbreak of staphylococcal food poisoning on the aircraft, are examples of two different types of food-borne disease. There are: *food-borne infection* when specific bacteria are present in the food. After you eat the food, the bacteria grow in your intestines and bring about illness. Only a few bacteria are necessary to establish the infection. The second is *food intoxication* when specific bacteria grow in the food and produce a toxin or poison. When you eat the food, this poison causes illness.

From *Contemporary Nutrition, 2,* (9) 1977. Reprinted by permission of General Mills, Inc.

FOOD-BORNE INFECTION

Salmonellosis is a food-infection. In this type of outbreak, the food serves as a carrier of the causitive bacteria, *Salmonellae* species. Growth of the microorganism in the food is not necessary for the illness to occur. But growth in the food increases the likelihood of infection resulting. The organism grows in the gastrointestinal tract releasing an endotoxin, which causes the symptoms. Onset of symptoms is related to the number of bacteria ingested with the food, the greater the number of cells (millions per gram of food), the faster the onset of symptoms. Generally, occuring anywhere from 8 to 72 hours after ingestion of the contaminated food, Salmonellosis is characterized by an abrupt onset of diarrhea, nausea, abdominal pain, prostration, chills, fever and vomiting. Symptom intensity varies from slight to severe discomfort and, in extreme cases, can result in death. The mortality rate is low (less than 1 percent) and is generally confined to infants, older people and those suffering from other diseases.

The microbe, which causes Salmonellosis, may be any one of over 1,600 different serotypes that have been identified. Cultivation, isolation and identification in a microbiological laboratory requires several days and eventually serotyping with known antisera to positively identify the specific serotype. It is not a difficult task but requires a working knowledge of microbiological techniques and loboratory experience.

The organism is an inhabitant of the intestinal tract of warm and cold-blooded animals. It is usually associated with fecal material but can also be isolated from non-fecal material as well. Bryan in his summary on "The Status of Food-borne Disease in the United States" suggests that current epidemiologic evidence indicates that domestic farm animals are major sources of *Salmonellae*.(3)

The Salmonella cycle consists of animals becoming infected from feed or from the farm environment, i.e., manure from previously infected animals. The contamination increases as the animals are transported to abbatoirs, kept in pens with other animals and eventually slaughtered. In this situation, one infected animal can contiminate many. After slaughter, the offal (G.I. tract, stomach, hoofs, bones, etc.) are used as protein sources for animal feed. These waste products are frequently contaminated with Salmonella and, subsequently the animal feed is contaminated and the cycle continues.

In order for the outbreak of Salmonellosis to occur, the food, when consumed, must be contaminated with Salmonella in any of the following ways: (a) food contaminated with fecal matter during processing, (b) contaminated raw foods, such as hamburger in the above example, consumed raw or used in prepared foods that receive no further heat treatment, or are given heat treatment insufficient to destroy the *Salmonellae*, (c) cooked, prepared foods contaminated from unclean equipment previously used to handle raw food and (d) workers, who previously handled raw food or who may be carriers, with poor personal hygiene practices.(3)

Once the food is contaminated, further mishandling, such as improper storage temperature, allows the *Salmonellae* organisms to grow to numbers sufficient to cause the illness. Growth is not always necessary as small numbers of several serotypes can cause the illness. Two factors lead to outbreaks of food-borne Salmonellosis; the first, contamination of the food with the microbe and second, mishandling of the food allowing growth to occur.

Obviously, the food must be ingested before the illness results. Growth of these bacteria in the food does not alter the flavor, aroma, appearance and taste of the food in any way. The only way to ascertain the presence of Salmonellae in foods is by proper microbiological analysis in a laboratory accustomed to working with food.(4)

Control of outbreaks of Salmonellosis is dependent upon interrupting the Salmonella cycle described previously. If this cycle of infection can be broken in several places, then a reduction in numbers of outbreaks of Salmonellosis will occur. Regulatory agencies are attempting to reduce the occurences of Salmonellosis by controlling several of the possible sources in the cycle. But to achieve this control will require the cooperation of all who are interested in a safe food supply.

CLOSTRIDIUM PERFRINGENS FOOD-BORNE ILLNESS

How would you like to purchase 13,500 get-well cards? Improper handling of beef used in a school program resulted in this many cases of *Clostridium perfringens* food-borne illness.(5) The beef had been cooked the day before serving, improperly cooled overnight and inadequately cooked before serving—two important factors which contribute to outbreaks of this type of food-borne disease.

This illness is not as easily classified as an infection or intoxication as the two previously mentioned. Both elements of infection and intoxication are involved. Extensive growth of this microbe in the food is necessary before illness will result. Once ingested, the organism continues to grow in the intestinal tract producing spores. When the spores are formed, a toxic substance is released, which causes the symptoms.

In comparison to other forms of food-borne illness, *C. perfringens* food-borne illness is a relatively mild one. The symptoms are intestinal gas, diarrhea, cramps, occasional nausea and rarely fever or vomiting. How many times have you been affected with similar ones and passed them off as a virus or something that's going around?

This particilar food-borne illness has been tagged as a problem of the food service industry. Reported outbreaks are generally associated with banquets, picnics and meals that are served at large gatherings of people. It is most generally caused by food that is prepared in advance and kept warm until served.(5)

The microorganism involved, *Clostridium perfringens*, is an anaerobic, spore-forming rod with rather fastidious nutritional requirements. It requires several performed amino acids and vitamins for growth. Few foods, other than meat, poultry, soups and gravies made from these foods, contain these necessary growth factors. Since this microbe also forms spores, it can survive cooking.

The conditions needed for an outbreak of *C. perfringens* food-borne illness to occur are: (1) the food must contain *C. perfringens*, (2) the food must be suitable for its growth, (3) temperature of the food must be suitable for its growth, (4) there must be sufficient time for growth to occur and (5) the contaminated food must be eaten.

Outbreaks of *C perfringens* food-borne illness can be prevented by following the guidelines given below.

1. Preparing food several hours or a day before serving is hazardous and should be avoided.
2. Leftover, cooked meat should not be merely warmed up but heated to at least 165°F., internal temperature, to destroy the vegetative cells of *C. perfringens*. Or, cut the meat into small pieces and boil it until the meat is completely heated to assure destruction of vegetative cells.
3. Once reheated, leftover foods should be eaten while hot or kept hot until consumed.
4. Food to be served hot should be kept above 140°F. until served.
5. All foods not eaten while hot or that cannot be held at 140°F. must be chilled rapidly and refrigerated at 45°F. or below.
6. Never allow hot foods to cool slowly to room temperatures before refrigerating. The slow cooling period provides an ideal growth temperature for the bacteria.
7. Room temperature should not be used to cool foods. Mechanical regrigeration, particularly large walk-in type rooms with circulating air, are more efficient for rapidly cooling food.
8. Foods should be refrigerated immediately after removal from a steam table or warming oven.
9. Food in shallow pans cools much faster than food in deep pans. Ice baths or cold running water also can be used to rapidly cool food for storage.

Observation of these precautions will not only help prevent outbreaks of *Clostridium perfringens* food-borne illness but also others such as salmonellosis and staphylococcus food poisoning. In addition, food spoilage caused by the growth of other types of bacteria will be minimized.

REFERENCES

1. U.S. D.H.E.W. *Morbidity and Mortality Weekly,* Vol. 24, No. 52, Center for Disease Control, Atlanta, GA., 1975.
2. U.S. D.H.E.W. *Morbidity and Mortality Weekly,* Vo . 24, No. 7, Center for Disease Control, Atlanta, GA., 1975.
3. Bryan, F.L. Status of Food-borne Disease in the United States, *J. of Environmental Health,* Vol. 38, No. 2, 1975.
4. Zottola, E.A., *Salmonellosis,* Extension Bulletin 339. Agricultural Extension Service, University of Minnesota, St. Paul, MN., 1967.
5. Zottola, E.A., *Clostridium perfringens Food Poisoning,* Extension Bulletin 365. Agricultural Extension Service, University of Minnesota, St. Paul, MN., 1971.

Food-Borne Disease II

by Edmund A. Zottola, Ph.D.

Wash your hands before handling food! Do not work with food if you have a skin infection! How many times have you heard these rules or seen them posted in the kitchen of a food service establishment? Many times, no doubt. But do these rules, if followed, really serve a useful purpose? The Center for Disease Control in Atlanta, Ga., maintains yearly records of reported outbreaks of food-borne disease. Dr. Frank Bryan has summarized these statistics over a several year period and has shown that approximately 20% of the yearly outbreaks are caused by not following the simple rules given above.(1) They must be important!

The most common types of food-borne disease affecting consumers in the United States are Staphylococcal food poisoning. Salmonellosis and **Clostridium perfringens** food-borne illness. The latter two were described in "Food-borne Disease I." This issue will deal with Staphylococcal food intoxication.

Staphylococcal food intoxication is a true food poisoning. This type of food-borne disease differs from a food infection in that the bacteria must grow in the food for an outbreak to occur. As the microbes grow, they produce an enterotoxin, which is the causative agent of the illness. An outbreak can occur without demonstrating the presence of viable microorganisms in the food. Only the toxin is needed.

In order for an outbreak of Staphylococcal food poisoning to occur, four conditions are necessary: (a) the food must contain enterotoxin producing strains of **Staphylococcus aureus,** (b) the food must be suitable for growth of the organism and toxin production, (c) the temperature of the food must be suitable for growth of the organism and there must be sufficient time for enterotoxin production, (d) the enterotoxin-containing food must be eaten.

Staphylococci enter foods from two sources, humans and animals. These microorganisms are most commonly associated with warm-blooded mammals. The body openings of a human, particularly the nasal passages, are loaded with staphylococci. Boils, pimples, acne and skin infections are important sources of these organisms. They are responsible for mastitis infection in dairy cows, skin lesions and other infections of meat animals. Many of the staphylococci that cause these infections are able to produce enterotoxin and, thus, may be a source of an outbreak of food poisoning.

From *Contemporary Nutrition, 3,* (1) 1978. Reprinted by permission of General Mills, Inc.

The poison produced by this organism is called an enterotoxin because it causes inflammation and irritation of the lining of the stomach and intestinal tract. The illness caused by ingestion of this poison is probably the most common type of food-borne disease occuring in the U.S. today. The actual number of outbreaks occurring each year is difficult to determine since the majority go unreported. The illness is characterized by a rapid onset of symptoms, usually within 2 to 4 hours after the food is consumed. They are explosive diarrhea, vomiting, prostration, and abdominal cramps. Recovery occurs as soon as the toxin is removed from the system, usually within 24 hours. This type of illness may be inappropriately called ptomaine poisoning, which is an old term that was first applied to food poisoning in 1887.

Ptomaines are toxic amines formed when proteins decompose. In order for food to have toxic amines or ptomaines present, decomposition would have to occur to the point where food would be by current standards unfit for consumption. Today, outbreaks of food-borne disease are usually associated with foods that appear sound and unspoiled. Even though it has been demonstrated many times that food-borne illness is caused by microorganisms, the term "ptomaine poisoning" is still incorrectly used to describe the illness.

The germ, **Staphylococcus aureus,** is a gram-positive cocci, which appears under the microscope as masses or clumps of cells much like bunches of grapes. The range of conditions under which staphylococci will grow and produce enterotoxin in foods varies. Some of the toxin-producing staphylococci are very salt-tolerant, growing in 15% NaCl solutions. They also tolerate nitrates-nitrites to such an extent that they can grow under favorable conditions in curing solutions and on cured meats. Growth temperatures vary but, in general, they will grow from about 50°F. to approximately 120°F. Optimum growth temperature is approximately 98°F. These organisms also produce no detectable changes in the food while growing. There are no obnoxious odors, no flavor changes, no alteration in appearance by the growth of **Staphylococcus.** It is impossible to sense the presence of **Staphylococcus** or enterotoxin by the appearance of the food.(2)

There are several serologically different types of enterotoxins paroduced by **Staphylococcus aureus.** All are capable of causing the symptoms listed earlier. This bacterial enterotoxin is different from many other toxins produced by microorganisms in that it is not affected by high temperatures. Consequently, it is possible to have an outbreak of staphylococcal intoxication occurring without being able to demonstrate the presence of microorganisms.

If raw food containing enterotoxin producing staphylococci is mishandled, growth of these organisms and subsequent toxic products may occur. When this raw food is heat-treated in some way—cooking, for example—the microbes will be destroyed but the activity of the toxin will not be affected. Such circumstances have occurred on several occasions.

A laboratory procedure specific for the detection of enterotoxin is available. This test was only developed within the last 10 years and not all laboratories have the capacity to test for enterotoxin. However, the method has provided an answer to many outbreaks of food-borne illness that used to be classified unknown.(3)

Prevention of staphylococcal food-borne infection is dependent upon two primary techniques. (1) Keep the microbe out of the food and (2) handle and store food properly to prevent the growth of these poison-producing microbes.

Since staphylococci are indigenous to humans and humans handle food, it becomes practically impossible to produce food for consumption that will not contain some staphylococci. But if food is handled in a sanitary manner during preparation, the number of contaminating staphylococci can be kept at a minimum. If the food is then stored cold, below 45°F., or hot, above 140°F., growth of these few contaminates will be prevented and food poisoning avoided.

The story about the outbreak of staphylococcal food-poisoning on an airplane mentioned in "Food-Borne Disease I" will illustrate how disregard for the principles mentioned above caused the outbreak. The food served on this aircraft had been prepared by an individual with an inflamed finger lesion. **S. aureus** was cultured from the finger. In addition, the ham, which was the contaminated food, was held at room temperature for several hours, plenty of time for **S. aureus** to grow and produce toxin. This outbreak would have been prevented if the simple techniques indicated above were followed.(4)

PREVENTION AND CONTROL

At first glance, prevention and control of food-borne disease appears relatively simple. Yet it is not. As long as people are involved with handling and preparation of food, occasional oversights or poor food handling practices are going to occur and outbreak of food-borne disease will result. Prevention and control must be aimed at keeping the occurrences to a minimum.

There are many facets involved with prevention and control: education, surveillance, identification of the foods involved and the causative agent of the illness followed by corrective preventive measures.

Education has to be directed to all concerned with handling, processing and final preparation of foods. Statistics from the Center for Disease Control(5) summarized by Bryan(1) indicate that the majority of outbreaks are caused by mishandling of the food at the point of final preparation—restaurants and homes. The chief causative factor is improper storage temperatures of the prepared food. It appears, then, that food handlers must constantly be reminded to store food at the proper temperature. Most health agencies agree food should be stored below 40°F. or above 140°F. Avoid long holding times at warm temperatures by serving the food as soon as possible after preparation.

One aspect of surveillance that needs to be increased is **reporting of outbreaks**. If only 10% of those that occur are reported, what about the other 90%? This 90% will only be decreased when physicians and other public health officials recognize and report food-borne illness. Consumers must also be aware of what might be food-borne illness and consult with a physician to assure the proper treatment. The physician should be encouraged to report the outbreak.

It may not be possible to eliminate the food-borne illnesses discussed in this paper but by handling food properly at all times and reporting and investigating suspected outbreaks, it should be possible to markedly reduce the incidence of this type of disease.

REFERENCES

1. Bryan, F.L. Status of Food-Borne Disease in the United States, *J. of Environmental Health,* Vol. 38, No. 2, 1975.
2. Zottola, E.A. *Staphylococcus Food Poisoning,* Extension Bulletin 354, Agricultural Extension, University of Minnesota, St. Paul, Minn., 1968.
3. Ayers, J.C., Elliot, R.P., Foster, E.M., Niven, C.F., Jr., Olson, J.C., Jr. and Slocum, G.G. Prevention of Microbial and Parasitic Hazards Associated with Processed Foods. *A Guide for the Food Processors,* National Academy of Sciences, Washington, D.C., 1975.
4. U.S. D.H.E.W. *Morbidity and Mortality Weekly,* Vol. 24, No. 7, Center for Disease Control, Atlanta, Ga., 1975.
5. U.S. D.H.E.W. *Food-Borne and Water-Borne Disease Outbreaks,* Annual Summary. Center for Disease Control, Atlanta, Ga., 1975.

5

The Sugar Controversy

There doesn't seem to be much need to explain the reason for this section. Anyone who reads or watches TV must be aware of the great controversy which surrounds the consumption of sugar.

We feel that this controversy is completely out of balance and hope that the papers presented might shed some truth on the matter.

The first two papers utilize much of the same evidence and come to the same conclusions. However, the style of writing is so different that one gets completely different perceptions from fundamentally the same evidence.

After you read these see if you don't agree. This is a good lesson for the non-scientist to learn and was covered to some extent in the first chapter. Be careful, not only of non-science but also the words used to describe science.

Science tells us that sugar is a compound which is involved with dental decay. It provides calories and when eaten in excess causes weight gain just like any other food eaten in excess. However, there is room in a varied diet for moderate consumption of sweeteners including sugar.

It is not a super-energy food, it is not a poison. Like any other food it should not be eaten in excess.

Because of its known relationship with dental caries the third paper in this section covers that topic.

It is hoped that this section might provide some rationality to a topic which has received much more space in the minds of the public than it deserves.

Too Much Sugar

Which contains a greater percentage of sugar: *Heinz Tomato Ketchup* or *Sealtest Chocolate Ice Cream? Wishbone Russian Dressing* or *Coca Cola? Coffee-mate Non-Dairy Creamer* or a bar of *Hershey's Milk Chocolate?*

Unless you have a food-analysis laboratory in your basement, the answers might come as quite a surprise. The *Heinz Tomato Ketchup* is 29 percent sugar, compared to 21 percent for the ice cream. If you put *Wishbone Russian Dressing* on a salad, you're pouring 30 percent sugar, a proportion more than three times that of *Coke.* The *Coffee-mate,* which is supposed to be a substitute for cream, contains 65 percent sugar, against 51 percent for a *Hershey* bar.

Those were some of the results when CU analyzed 24 common food products to determine what proportion of their weight consisted of sugar. (When we use the word "sugar," we're referring to all varieties of sugars, including those in corn syrup, honey, fruit, and vegetables, as well as ordinary table sugar, or sucrose.)

When it comes to sugar, much of the food industry apparently operates on the assumption that the consumer has three taste preferences: sweet, sweeter, and sweetest. If you prepare your chicken with *Shake 'N Bake Barbecue Style,* you're geeting a coating that's 51 percent sugar. A bowl of *Quaker 100% Natural Cereal* gives you 24 percent sugar. If you munch on a *Ritz Cracker,* you know you're not eating a cookie, but you might not know it's 12 percent sugar.

A look at product ingredients on supermarket shelves reveals the difficulty of finding almost any type of prepared food product without sugar in it. It's used not only in sweet baked goods, desserts, and soft drinks, but also in sauces, many baby foods, almost all fruit drinks, salad dressings, canned and dehydrated soups, pot pies, frozen TV dinners, bacon and other cured meats, some canned and frozen vegetables, most canned and frozen fruits, fruit yogurt, and breakfast cereals. If you eat a hot dog, there is likely to be sugar in the meat, in the ketchup or relish, and in the bun. There is even a bit of sugar in many brands of salt. And for Fido, there's sugar in *Gaines-burgers* dog food.

What is all this added sugar—an average of 128 pounds consumed by every man, woman, and child in the United States last year—doing to us? It depends on whom you listen to. The Sugar Association calls it "one of our cheapest sources of food energy" and "the catalyst that makes eating pleasurable." Kellogg Co., which makes various brands of presweetened cereal, says that sugar is "a solution to some world hunger problems."

But to critics, sugar represents "empty calories," accompanied by a host of medical ills. Sugar has been blamed not only for heart disease and diabetes, but also for a list of afflictions ranging from acne to varicose veins—not to mention obesity and tooth decay.

Where does the truth lie? In this article, we'll take a look at what sugar is, how it is used by the body, and what is known about its effects on health. We'll also answer some of the questions most frequently asked about sugar: How much is really necessary in a proper diet? Is brown sugar better for you than that white refined stuff? Is the natural sugar in fruit and honey somehow different?

FROM SUNLIGHT TO HOSTESS TWINKIES

Sugar is the most fundamental of all foods. In converting sunlight into food, green plants first make simple sugars. The starch in a potato comes from sugar formed in the leaves of the potato plant. Wood is built from sugar made in the tree's leaves. The oil in a peanut, the protein in wheat grains, and the perfume of a rose are all developed from sugar by the plant. Except for their mineral content, in fact, all components of a plant are derived from sugar.

Although the main sugars in fruits are usually fructose and glucose, many fruits and some vegetables also contain modest amounts of sucrose, which is chemically identical to the table sugar used in the home. Apples, apricots, beets, carrots, corn, peas, peaches, plums, and soybeans, for example, all contain from 3 to 7 percent sucrose. Virtually all the sucrose our early ancestors ate came from fruits and vegetables.

Sugar was cultivated as early as 325 B.C. in India, but it remained a scarce luxury until Columbus brought sugar cane to the Caribbean in 1493. Within the next hundred years, sugar became one of the valued products of the New World, often plundered by pirates along with silver and gold. Large-scale cultivation of sugar beets came much later, when the Napoleonic wars cut off shipments of Caribbean sugar to France. Napoleon then issued a decree in 1811 spurring a vast increase in French production of beet sugar.

In the chronicle of sugar, however, Columbus and Napoleon emerge as mere pikers alongside 20th-century food processors. Within the span of a few generations, the food industry has converted sugar from a household condiment to a ubiquitous component of the average person's diet.

Between 1900 and 1970, world production of sugar climbed from 8 million to 70 million tons. On average, Americans now get about 24 percent of their calories from sugar. Only 3 percent comes from the sugar in fruits and vegetables. Another 3 percent is from lactose, the milk sugar in dairy products. The vast bulk—18 percent of all the calories we consume—is from sugar that is added to our food. Whether in packaged salad dressing or in *Hostess Twinkies,* sugar is the leading food additive in the United States today.

WHY WE'RE HOOKED ON SUGAR

Long before babies are exposed to Saturday morning candy and cereal commercials, they show an innate preference for sweets. The sweeter the solution, the more vigorously a newborn infant will suck—and the more the infant will consume. Even a five-month human fetus will increase its swallowing rate when saccharin is injected into the amniotic fluid of the mother.

Why do we have a seemingly inborn desire for sweets? A commonly held theory is that in primitive times sweetness served as nature's guide to what foods were safe to eat. Generally, the fruits and vegetables that tasted sweet were nutritious and healthful, while foods that tasted bitter were frequently poisonous. The process of natural selection might have produced an instinct for sweet taste, since the animals that preferred sweet things would have obtained the nutrients necessary for survival. This theory is substantiated by the fact that cats are among the animals that don't have a pronounced sweet tooth. Their ancestors never needed to develop one, since they hunted meat exclusively.

Whatever natural desire we have for sugar is quickly reinforced. The word "sweet" in our language stands for something good, something desirable. And for many young children, the attraction of sweetness is underscored by thousands of TV commercials extolling sweet-tasting foods.

Meanwhile, we now have far less control over the amount of sugar we eat than did previous generations. In 1930, 64 percent of the sucrose used in this country was purchased directly by consumers for home use, while only 30 percent went to industry. By 1970, those percentages were more than reversed, with just 24 percent being bought by consumers directly and 65 percent going to industry. (The rest went to restaurants, hotels, and government.) This means that much of the sucrose we eat has already been added before the food is brought home.

Some of the sugar in processed foods serves functions other than adding sweetness. It retains and absorbs moisture, which keeps foods from drying out rapidly. It depresses the freezing point, making ice cream and other frozen desserts smoother. It can act as a preservative, and it can enhance the appearance of some foods.

But much of the sugar used by industry seems to be related to two other factors: At around 10 cents a pound, sugar is much cheaper than many other ingredients. And many people like a sweet taste. The Senate Select Committee on Nutrition reported last year that "increased use of sugar is traceable in large part to the desire of food manufacturers to create unique food products with a competitive edge. Just recently, for example, Nabisco introduced an Oreo cookie with double the amount of sugar filling."

Food manufacturers insist that the percentage of sugar they use in foods results directly from the preference of consumer tasting panels. Yet they won't come out and say exactly what the total percentage is. You can look at the list of ingredients on the label, of course. But even then you frequently won't know where sugar ranks, because manufacturers can use different types of sweeteners and list each one separately.

Post Raisin Bran, for instance, lists sugar (sucrose) as its number three ingredient, corn syrup number five, and honey number seven. Together, those sugars might be the primary ingredient, but the purchaser won't know. As one father said in a recent television report on sugar: "What I didn't realize was that there's no place on the box that says there is 50 percent sugar or 55 percent sugar. So for most parents who only see a list of the vitamins stretched out, there's no way that they know that what they're feeding their children is candy, essentially."

The proliferation of sugar in food products is such that sometimes even company officials can't keep up. We asked a spokeswoman for Nabisco Inc. why *Ritz Crackers* had sugar in it. "There's sugar in Ritz Crackers?" she responded. After looking at the list of ingredients, she said the sugar was there for flavor, and that the difference between a *Ritz* cracker and a cookie was that "a cookie would have more sugar in it."

HOW MUCH SUGAR ARE WE EATING?

Defenders of sugar are quick to assert that sugar consumption in the United States has remained basically unchanged in the last 50 years—slightly under 100 pounds per person per year. That's true, but there's a catch. The figure is for sucrose only.

Food processors have increased their use of a second type of sugar in recent years. Derived from corn starches, it is variously called corn syrup, corn sugar, or corn sweetener. The per-capita consumption of corn syrup has jumped from 13 pounds in 1960 to an estimated 32 pounds last year. So per-capita sugar consumption—sucrose, corn syrup, and minor sweeteners like honey—has actually grown 14 percent since 1960, from 112 to 128 pounds. That's more than one-third of a pound of sugar a day for each person.

What happens to all this sugar in the body? Basically, it is digested and used like any other carbohydrate. Nearly all carbohydrates are ultimately converted into glucose, the primary fuel of the body. Glucose, or "blood sugar," is delivered by the bloodstream to the liver, where it is converted and stored as glycogen until needed by the body. With the help of the hormone insulin, blood glucose then enters nearly all cells of the body and is used as an energy source. The glucose that isn't needed by the cells is metabolized in the liver into fatty substances called triglycerides, which are transported in the bloodstream to the fat depots of the body. The body can later draw upon those stores of fat if it needs energy during fasting or dieting.

Why, then, in view of the body's basic need for energy, is there anything wrong with eating sugar? The problem is that sugar, unlike most other sources of carbohydrate, contains no nutrients except calories. It's a classic constituent of "junk food"—generally, a processed food that's relatively high in calories, lacks any significant amounts of protein, vitamins, or minerals, and contains comparatively large quantities of fats or sugar. Essentially, there's absolutely no dietary requirement for sugar that can't be satisfied by other, more nutritious foods, such as fruits and vegetables.

There isn't even a need for sugar for so-called quick energy, to fuel a morning of tennis, skiing, or the like. Unless you fast for more than a day or two, your body has sizable reserves of liver glycogen to call upon. If you eat sugar before exercising, the sugar will quickly be metabolized and move into storage with your other fuel reserves.

If you get 20 percent of your calorie requirement from sugar, you have to rely on the other 80 percent of your diet to supply the other nutrients you need—no dietary feat for most people, but a neat trick for anyone trying to lose weight.

Moreover, while the amount of sugar we eat increases, the average per-capita consumption of flours and grains has dropped by more than half over the course of this century. Therefore we're getting more and more of our carbohydrates from sugar—the carbohydrate supplying the fewest nutrients.

In a recent report, the Senate Select Committee on Nutrition called for a 45 percent reduction in sugar consumption. We see little sense in picking an arbitrary percentage, but many people would do well to pay attention to the amount of sugar they're consuming. A lot of sugar certainly does you no good nutritionally, and it may contribute to certain health problems. Exactly which ones, however, has often been obscured by emotional debate.

SUGAR AND HEALTH

Here is what is known about sugar's relationship to some common health problems:

Tooth Decay.　The link between dental caries (cavities) and sugar is no longer a matter of controversy. There is now overwhelming evidence from animal experiments and human studies to implicate sugar in tooth decay.

Sugar serves as food for the bacteria normally present in the mouth. One of the byproducts of bacterial activity on sugar is glucan, a thick, gel-like substance that sticks tenaciously to the tooth surface and hastens the buildup of bacterial plaque. Another byproduct is a group of acids, including lactic, formic, and acetic acid. Held against the tooth surface by the plaque, the acids attack the tooth with a success that depends on the protective quality of the saliva and the tooth's vulnerability to decay.

There is not, however, a simple, direct relationship between the amount of sugar consumed and the number of cavities you'll get. In addition to your individual predisposition to cavities, a key factor is how much sugar gets stuck to your teeth, and for how long. Sticky candy, for instance, can do far more damage to teeth than a soft drink, because the sugar in liquids is more easily washed away. Note, though, that frequency of exposure also plays a role. Several soft drinks a day might do more damage than one piece of toffee a week. Moreover, the acid content of many soft drinks, such as cola beverages, can also contribute to erosions, a chemical wearing away of the teeth at the gumline.

Tests on humans have shown that sugar eaten as part of a meal causes less damage to teeth than the same amount of sugar consumed as a between-meals snack. This is probably because the other foods and liquids consumed during a meal help remove the sugar from tooth surfaces.

The bacteria in your mouth don't care whether the sugar has been put there by nature or by industry. You can damage a baby's teeth by putting fruit juices, or even milk, in a bottle at bedtime and allowing the baby to fall asleep while sucking. That lengthens the time the sugar in the drink is in contact with the baby's teeth.

Obesity.   America as a nation is growing fatter. About one-third of the adult population is overweight—more than 10 percent above the normal weight for height. The National Center for Health Statistics recently released results of a weight study of 13,600 people checked from 1971 to 1974. Women under age 45 weighed 4.7 pounds more on average than women of equivalent height checked in a 1960 to 1962 study. Men under age 45 were 3.8 pounds heavier than their counterparts of a decade earlier, and those older than 45 were 4.8 pounds heavier.

Obesity is usually bad for a person's health. It increases the possibility that such disorders as heart disease, high blood pressure, diabetes, gallstones, varicose veins, back problems, and arthritis might develop or become more severe.

It's not sugar itself that makes you fat, of course. It's the total amount of calories you consume in excess of what you need. Sugar, like all other carbohydrates, contains four calories per gram, or 113 per ounce. But sugar-sweetened foods also tend to be those in which calories are highly concentrated, such as in pies, cakes, candy, and the like. And there's also the palatability factor: The presence of sugar in a food may tempt you to eat more of it.

If you're trying to lose weight, moreover, reducing your calorie intake without cutting sugar consumption means you probably won't get all the nutrients your body needs.

Diabetes.   Since diabetics frequently have to reduce their sugar consumption dramatically, many people have come to think of diabetes as a disease caused by excess sugar. Actually, the causes are much more complex than that; and the role of sugar in the onset of diabetes still isn't clear—if, in fact, it plays any role at all.

Although diabetes has been known since antiquity, its cause or causes remain unknown. Genetic predisposition seems to play an important role. Medical studies have not been able to prove that sugar intake *per se* can cause diabetes. There might, however, be an indirect effect. Excessive consumption of sweets can contribute to obesity, and obese people have been shown to be more resistant than lean people to the action of their body's own insulin, the hormone that helps the body "burn" glucose. This factor may contribute to the development of the disease in overweight, middle-aged persons.

Heart Disease.   Most experts in the field see little support for the theory that sugar consumption contributes to heart disease. As one sums it up: "I would personally say the matter of sugar and heart disease is the least demonstrable problem with sugar."

There are some people, however, who have a tendency to develop high levels of serum triglycerides (a factor that may contribute to heart disease) from carbohydrate foods. And sugar, of course, is a carbohydrate. Since many of these people are obese, the total calories in their diet may be considered as important as their carbohydrate intake. Hence, weight reduction as well as carbohydrate restriction helps to reduce triglyceride levels in those patients.

Basically, if you are in good health and not overweight, the amount of sugar in your diet needn't worry you so far as heart disease is concerned. If you are overweight, it's advisable to lose weight by lowering your customary intake of both fats and sugars. In that way, you may reduce your risk of developing cardiovascular problems as well as other disorders associated with obesity.

Apart from sugar's role in tooth decay and its potential contribution to obesity, there is little evidence to convict sugar of the catalog of health crimes it is accused of. Allegations linking sugar to various disorders often change with the times. Acne was once thought to be caused by eating sweets—particularly chocolate. But medical studies failed to demonstrate any association. More recently, sugar has purportedly been linked to such ills as hyperactivity in children, hypoglycemia, and others. But again, the allegations are either unproven or anecdotal.

Nevertheless, sugar's contribution to tooth decay and obesity is reason enough to approach sweets as an occasional treat rather than as a steady diet. And to that end, it would be helpful if food manufacturers were required to tell consumers clearly just how much sugar is really in their products. You should know that spreading two tablespoons of ketchup on a hamburger means you're about to consume more than a teaspoon of sugar.

ARE ALL SUGARS THE SAME?

If you read labels carefully in a "health-food" store, you would no doubt conclude that white refined sugar is rated on a par with DDT and arsenic. But that doesn't mean you won't find sugar in "health-food" products. So-called health breads, for instance, are often chock full of honey, molasses, brown sugar, or "raw" sugar. It's just white refined sugar that's considered to be the villain.

Is there any truth to the notion that one sugar is somehow better for you than another? Some sugars aren't quite as bad for your teeth as sucrose. Otherwise, there's virtually no difference among them worth worrying about. To understand why, it's necessary to look at how the most common commercial types of sugar differ.

There are more than 100 sweet substances identified as sugars. These include fructose (fruit sugar), dextrose (one of the sugars made from corn starch and chemically identical to glucose), lactose (the sugar in milk), and maltose (malt sugar, formed from starch by the action of yeast). But the word "sugar" is commonly used to refer to sucrose, which comes from sugar cane or sugar beets. In a typical manufacturing operation, the sugar cane is shredded into small pieces, crushed, and the juice separated. Processing causes the sugar in the juice to crystallize, forming sugar crystals and syrup. These are separated by a mechanical device into the end products, raw sugar and molasses. Then comes a washing and filtering, and the raw sugar is eventually turned into refined white sugar.

Raw sugar is banned in the United States, for good reasons: It contains such contaminants as insect parts, soil, molds, bacteria, lint, and waxes. When it's partially refined to make it sanitary, it can be sold as "turbinado" sugar. Brown sugar consists of the sugar crystals coated with some molasses syrup. Most refiners make it by spraying syrup onto refined white sugar.

Brown and turbinado sugar might look more healthful because of their dark color and distinctive odor. But the few additional nutrients they contain are so minuscule in quantity that for all practical purposes they're worthless. The nutrients simply aren't there in the usable parts of the sugar cane or sugar beet plant to be refined out.

Honey is formed by an enzyme from nectar gathered by bees. Depending on where the nectar comes from, honey can differ in composition and flavor. But all honey is a blend of a number of different sugars, largely fructose and glucose. Like brown sugar, honey has a few nutrients—mainly potassium, calcium, and phosphorus. But, again, they're scant. You'd have to eat 91 tablespoons of honey each day to get your recommended daily requirement of potassium, 200 for calcium, and 267 for phosphorus. There's no evidence that honey is easier to digest than other sugars. When you eat table sugar, your body breaks the sucrose down into fructose and glucose, the two leading ingredients of honey.

What about substituting honey for sucrose in cooking or in your coffee to get more sweetening power per calorie? It is true that some batches of honey can be as much as 40 percent sweeter than sugar (although other batches can actually be less sweet). A cup of honey has only 23 percent more calories than a cup of sugar. So with a little luck, you do get more sweetening power per calorie. But substituting honey will change the character of the food you're preparing, meaning you might have to alter the cooking time or some other aspect of the recipe.

Remember, finally, that sucrose is a "natural" substance; it comes from a plant. In the same way, nature has put sugar in other fruits and vegetables. Just because a bottle of apple juice says "unsweetened" or "no sugar added," it doesn't mean that sugar wasn't there in the first place. The natural sugars in orange, apple, and many other fruit juices make them slightly higher in total sugar than a bottle of *Coca Cola*. But there are two important differences: The fruit juices give you other nutrients besides calories, and one of their principal sugars (fructose) is somewhat easier on tooth surfaces than sucrose.

Accordingly, if you're concerned about nutrition or your teeth, try to satisfy your craving for sweets with fresh fruits and fruit juices. Brown sugar, turbinado sugar, and the like offer no health advantage over the undisguised white stuff.

Meanwhile, even if you want to substitute nutritious foods for that one-third of a pound, or 600 calories, of sugar the average American eats daily, you may still find yourself thwarted by the lack of information on product labels. Manufacturers can use several different sugars to avoid putting the word "sugar" at the head of their ingredients list. Until a government agency acts to require a clear revelation of sugar percentage in processed foods, all you can do is to check the label to see which sugars have been added. As a key, look for any word ending in "ose," such as maltose or dextrose. "Corn syrup" or "corn sugar" is a commonly used sucrose substitute. Ultimately, they all mean the same thing: You're buying sugar.

SWEET TALK ABOUT SWEETENED CEREALS

Late last year, during an investigation of advertising aimed at children, the Federal Trade Commission took a particular interest in the promotion of highly sweetened cereals to youngsters. Kellogg Co. showed up to defend the nutritional quality of its products. At about the same time, Kellogg apparently decided to take its case to the public.

In mid-November, the two-page ad shown above appeared in newspapers in Boston, Chicago, Detroit, Los Angeles, New York, and Washington, D.C. The body of the ad presented a list of bold-faced "facts"—or, more accurately, assertions. The assertions merit some comment.

Kellogg says: "Ready-sweetened cereals are highly nutritious foods."

Some cereals are highly nutritious, and some aren't. But the presence of sugar or other sweeteners adds nothing except calories to a cereal's nutritive value. When CU last tested cereals (see *Consumer Reports,* February 1975), Kellogg's presweetened *Sugar Frosted Flakes, Sugar Smacks, Sugar Pops,* and *Cocoa Krispies* were among those "judged of sufficiently low nutritional value to be considered deficient."

Kellogg says: "Ready-to-eat cereals do not increase tooth decay in children."
Kellogg points out that three clinical studies found no relationship between the amount of cereals consumed, whether ready-sweetened or regular, and the incidence of tooth decay in children.

Kellogg does not point out, however, that the authors of one of those studies stated that "this conclusion must not be construed to dilute in any way the evidence associating dental caries with sucrose in general."

Essentially, it's not cereals that increase tooth decay, but the total aggregate of sugars in cereals, sweets, and numerous other processed foods. As Dr. W.H. Bowen of the National Caries Program at the National Institutes of Health commented: "There is now an overwhelming abundance of evidence from experiments carried out in animals (both rodents and primates), epidemiological studies in humans, and kindred other bodies of evidence that proves quite conclusively . . . that the development of caries and ingestion of sugar are closely associated."

Kellogg says: "Ready-to-eat cereal eaters skip breakfast less than non-ready-to-eat cereal eaters." The supporting text cites Kellogg's own analysis of an unpublished study. (The analysis involved only 250 children.)

It's probably churlish of us to point out that no comparison is made between eaters of ready-sweetened cereals and eaters of unsweetened cereals. The ad speaks only of "ready-to-eat" cereals and "nonready-to-eat" (or cooked) cereals. It's hard, therefore, to conclude that failure to *presweeten* a cereal will produce an epidemic of breakfast skipping.

Kellogg says: "There is no more sugar in a one-ounce serving of a ready-sweetened cereal than in an apple or banana or in a serving of orange juice."

Perhaps not. But Kellogg's presentation is comparing *one ounce* of cereal with servings of fruit that weigh at least four times as much. To detect that thumb on the scales, a consumer would have to know that there are about 28 grams in an ounce, and that a medium apple or banana each weighs about 115 grams. Moreover, the percentage of sugar in food may play a role in tooth decay. With that in mind, let's compare the data Kellogg presented with a factor the ad didn't mention—the sugar's concentration:

Food	**Mentioned** *Total Sugar Content Per Serving*	**Not Mentioned** *Sugar Concentration*
Kellogg's Sugar Frosted Flakes (1 oz.)	11 grams	39%
Kellogg's Apple Jacks (1 oz.)	16 grams	57%
Apple (1 med.)	17 grams	11%
Orange Juice (6 oz.)	17 grams	9%
Banana (1 med.)	29 grams	19%

Kellogg says: "The sugars in cereals and the sugars in fruit are chemically very similar." Supporting text notes that the principal sugars in cereals are sucrose and glucose, and that fruits contain those sugars plus fructose.

True, sucrose is sucrose and glucose glucose, whether in a cereal or in a fruit. But fruit sugars frequently include a relatively high percentage of fructose, which is somewhat less conducive to dental decay than sucrose.

Kellogg says: "Ready-to-eat cereals provide only 2 percent of the total consumption of cane and beet sugars in ths U.S."

But the use of sucrose in processed foods, including breakfast cereals, doubled between 1940 and the present. And among the uses of sugar Kellogg mentions (beverages, baked goods, confectionery, ice cream, and the like), breakfast cereals are perhaps the single category most directly promoted to young children.

Kellogg says: "On the average when children eat ready-sweetened cereals as part of a breakfast, the nutrient content of that breakfast is greater than when they eat a non-ready-to-eat cereal breakfast."

Read that statement carefully, for it does not compare the nutritive contents of presweetened and unsweetened dry cereals, nor does it compare dry cereals (with or without sugar) with cooked cereals. Rather, the ad refers to the relative nutrient content of the *breakfasts* eaten by some 250 children in an unpublished study. Even so, Kellogg's nutrient chart shows that the cooked-cereal breakfast surpassed the other in protein content, as well as in phosphorus, magnesium, and zinc. Moreover, as CU's 1975 cereal study demonstrated, an important factor is the biological availability of nutrients. The nutrients that occur naturally in foods are apt to be used by humans to a greater extent than nutrients added to a food.

Kellogg says: "Most ready-to-eat cereals are consumed with milk."

Probably true—although we wonder how many parents have observed their children nibbling on dry, ready-sweetened cereals as a snack. As consumer reporter Sidney Margolius once observed, "If milk is the main nutritional value in eating dry cereals, then obviously there are easier ways to drink it than with a spoon." In any event, the statement tells us nothing about any differences between ready-sweetened and unsweetened cereals, since the subject is "ready-to-eat" cereals, not "ready-sweetened" cereals.

Kellogg says: "On the average when children eat ready-sweetened cereals as part of breakfast, consumption of fat and cholesterol is less than when they eat a non-ready-to-eat cereal breakfast.

Again, the data source is an unpublished study. And again, the statement by Kellogg makes no comparison between ready-sweetened and unsweetened ready-to-eat cereals (the comparison is between *breakfasts* that include either a cooked or an uncooked cereal). Instead, it plays on dietary scare words such as "fat" and "cholesterol," which have nothing to do with the cereals themselves.

Kellogg says: "The per capita sugar consumption in the U.S. has remained practically unchanged for the last 50 years."

The graph that Kellogg presents with this statement shows, accurately enough, that per-capita consumption of cane and beet sugar (both sucrose) has held fairly steady at some 90 to 100 pounds per year since 1920.

But a closer look at the graph also shows that per-capita consumption of all sugars, including corn sugar, has increased nearly 30 percent since 1920. The graph doesn't show that much of the sugar we now eat is added to food before we buy it—and in amounts unknown to the buyer.

The ad is Kellogg's slippery way of responding to the chorus of complaints about television commercials peddling highly sugared foods to children. Last year, several public interest groups, including the Committee on Children's Television and the California Society of Dentistry for Children, sued another cereal-maker, General Foods Corp., over commercials for what they call "candy breakfasts" sold as part of the company's Post Cereals line.

The lawsuit charges that General Foods "exploits trusting children in order to sell sugar concoctions as nutritious breakfast cereals." It alleges that the company, through the expenditure of approximately $1-billion in television advertising and marketing, has "induced the formation of lasting poor nutrition habits and tooth decay in millions of children, particularly youngsters from low-income families."

The suit, which asks General Foods to change its labeling and advertising and pay more than $1-billion in penalties, isn't the only problem manufacturers of sugared foods for children are facing. Two activist organizations, Action for Children's Television and Center for Science in the Public Interest, have separately petitioned the FTC to ban television commercials to children for candy and other sugary snack food. The Center's petition was supported by more than 10,000 physicians, dentists, dietitians, nutritionists, and health students.

The FTC is currently considering a number of proposals to crack down on advertising aimed at children. The result could be an outright ban on commercials for highly sugared products on children's programs, or else strict guidelines for those commercials and perhaps a requirement that braodcasters set aside time for counter-commercials. Any such proposal, however, is expected to face years of hearings and court challenges from industry.

Sugar in the Diet of Man
A Summary

by Ronald M. Deutsch

SUGAR AND SAFETY

Sugar has lately been blamed for human ills from obesity to heart disease, from tooth decay to madness, from epilepsy to diabetes.

Such charges are disturbing, for we use sugar not as a sweet extra but as a basic of our food supply. In the United States last year, slightly over 100 lbs. of sugar disappeared from the market for each living American, about 15 to 20 per cent of our total calories. If sugar were removed from the market, all the calories needed to feed at least 36 million Americans would be lost.

Worldwide, many nations—such as Great Britain, the Netherlands, Denmark, Australia and Israel—use as much or more sugar per capita than the United States. And consumption is rising in other lands, especially in developing nations. The U.N. reports an increased use of sugar unmatched by any other food for humans, predicting that by 1980 the world will consume some 186 billion lbs. a year.

But one writer(1) says this food is "probably a major factor in the deaths of hundreds of millions of people." Another(2) writes: "If only a small fraction of what is already known about the effects of sugar were to be revealed in relation to any other material . . . that material would promptly be banned."

In 1973 a team of noted scientists all of whom were either physicians or dentists—aware both of such threats and of sugar's mounting importance as a food—began to study what was actually known about sugar's effects on health. Working independently, at medical centers and universities across the nation, they combed the archives of scientific research. This is a summary of the six recently published papers in which they report their findings (*World Review of Nutrition and Dietetics,* Vol. 22, pp. 237–326, 1975).

Reprinted by permission of the Sugar Association, Inc.

Ronald M. Deutsch is a well-known author and lecturer whose special interest is in the fields of medicine and public health. He has written six books and more than 200 articles for major magazines. A frequent speaker to groups of professional nutritionists, physicians, home economists and food technologists, Mr. Deutsch served on the President's White House Conference on Food, Nutrition and Health in 1969. He was commissioned to prepare this summary by the Food and Nutrition Advisory Council of The Sugar Association, Inc.

HOW WE USE SUGAR AS A FOOD(3)

Harvard's Dr. Fredrick Stare reports that of the roughly 100 lbs. of sugar consumed each year by an average American only some 80 lbs. are actually eaten. This amount has scarcely changed in half a century. So claims that sugar consumption is rising in the United States are untrue. Industrial sugar use has grown, but direct consumption of sugar by the consumer has declined proportionately.

About 15 to 20 per cent of a typical American's calories come from sugar—about 12 per cent for adults and 20 per cent or more for teenagers. That sugar is seen by scientists as a compact source of energy, our primary nutrition need.

Energy, Dr. Stare points out, can come from any of three food sources— proteins, fats or carbohydrates. Protein is expensive and scarce; it provides only about 15 per cent of our calories. Excess fats may offer health hazards. So the bulk of our energy has to come from carbohydrates.

(Many people are unaware that virtually all carbohydrates in our food are either sugars, or, as in the case of starches, are chains of sugars. *Sucrose,* the scientific name for table sugar, is one of the most common sugars found in plant foods.)

The energy we get from sugar is scientifically no different from that in any other food. But most other carbohydrate-containing foods, such as fruits and vegetables, have much bulk with few calories. So, Dr. Stare concludes that in the absence of a *compact* carbohydrate energy source, such as sugar, it could be hard to give youngsters enough calories without giving an unhealthful excess of fat.

This energy compactness, coupled with high agricultural yield, makes sugar a solution to some world hunger problems. No other major crop yields so many calories from so little soil—about 1 million calories from an eighth of an acre. To produce so much energy, potatoes take four times as much land, beef 125 times. And energy, fertilizer and refining costs for sugar are relatively low.

Are sugar calories "empty"? Though they carry with them no vitamins, minerals or protein, Dr. Stare notes that sugar is rarely eaten alone. And often it makes more palatable many foods such as cereals and fruits that supply other valuable nutrients.

Does the consumption of sugar risk illness and death? Dr. Stare cites a number of opinions to the contrary. In very specific terms, the question is answered by other papers.

SUGAR AND HEART DISEASE(4)

Doctors have long known that coronary heart disease (CHD) is linked to a degeneration of blood vessels called atherosclerosis and for decades they have suspected that *atherosclerosis* was speeded up by the saturated fats and cholesterol we eat.

Recently sugar has been charged with having the same effect. But Dr. Francisco Grande finds little or no evidence for the idea.

One argument is that CHD deaths are higher in countries where more sugar is eaten. This is often not true. Finland and Sweden use similar amounts of sugar, but the Finns have far more CHD. And a number of nations—such as Venezuela, Cuba, Colombia, Costa Rica and Honduras—consume much sugar but have a low incidence of CHD.

Another idea is that increases in heart deaths can be accounted for by rising sugar use. But Dr. Grande finds that the increase of CHD deaths in the United States during the last 50 years occurred while sugar use stayed constant.

Dr. John Yudkin (author of nearly all the medical papers linking sugar to CHD) says that 20 of his heart patients ate more sugar than the usual. But nine other studies controvert this finding. In two of them the heart patients ate *less*. In one, Canadian veterans with CHD averaged 47 grams of sugar a day; but a matched group of healthy veterans ate 65 grams!

A fourth claim is that sugar eating causes fatty materials in the blood, such as cholesterol, to rise, indicating a higher risk of CHD. When large amounts of carbohydrates replace large amounts of fat in the diet, there is a rise in some people of certain fats in the blood (triglycerides). But this rise is temporary. And people who regularly eat much carbohydrate prove to have *lower* levels of such fats in their blood.

Does sugar by itself cause cholesterol or blood fats to rise? Reviewing scores of studies—in some of which sugar was the source of 75 per cent or more of calories—Dr. Grande can document no such effect. The only indicators have been a few experimental studies of people who already had high levels of blood fats and who were fed huge amounts of sugar in a special dietary far different from any normal eating pattern. Such anomalies can hardly explain a disease so common that it is our worst killer.

"To conclude," says Dr. Grande, "the evidence available does not support the view that sugar, in the amounts present in diets such as those consumed in this country, is a causative factor in the development of CHD."

SUGAR AND OBESITY(5)

Does sugar make us fat? Three University of Pittsburgh teachers of medicine—Drs. Thaddeus Danowski, Sean Nolan and Thorsten Stephan—review the evidence and conclude it does not.

The stage seems to be set for obesity when some of us are either born with more of the storage cells that hold body fat or increase them by over-feeding in infancy. Even if one loses weight, these fat cells are not destroyed.

The fat cells can be filled or emptied depending on how many calories of energy we get in food and how many we burn with exercise. It does not matter which food the calories come from. Any excess is stored as fat.

Most such excesses seem small and steady. The experts conclude that often they result from learning to deal with emotional stress by eating more. Conversely, excesses may result from declines in activity, as with aging.

Two other possibilities are suggested to account for individual tendencies to fatten. One is that while some of us stir and bustle more others are more economical of energy. Also, some of us may use fuel more efficiently, like cars that get more miles from a gallon. In either case tiny excesses can add up. Even a 1-per-cent-more efficient use of fuel could mean a gain of 40 lbs. over 20 years!

Because only *total* calories matter, it does not help weight control to restrict only starches or sugars. Like protein, they provide some four calories to the gram. Some restriction of fats may be useful, however, for they have nine calories to a gram.

Unhappily, most people who want to reduce tend to limit their diets to a few foods and eliminate many others. This leads to boredom and failure and to poor nutrition.

For example, low-carbohydrate diets are pointless and may be hazardous. And when such diets emphasize meats they prove to be very high in fat. Although they seem to work for some people, they can cause nausea, loss of appetite, and the loss of body fluids (dehydration). The AMA has warned doctors of their medical dangers.

Even skipping meals is self-defeating. For the body tends to deposit more fat with only one or two meals a day then with several, although the caloric intake is the same.

"The most successful programs of caloric restriction," say the authors, "deviate least from ordinary eating. . . . Any excess of calories, be it from food, alcohol or inactivity, is inevitably stored as body fat. It is this excess of calories, and not the type or amount of sugars, starches, protein or fat in foods . . . that results in obesity."

SUGAR AND DIABETES(6)

In 1971 the American Diabetes Association surprised many with a statement that: "There no longer appears to be any need to restrict disproportionately the intake of carbohydrates in the diet of most diabetic patients."

Explaining this statement, Drs. Edwin Bierman (who chaired the committee that wrote it) and Ralph Nelson note that today patients rarely die of the direct effect of diabetes. They are lost to ills of the heart, blood vessels and kidneys, all of which may be related to high-fat diets. And a diet low in carbohydrates, such as the traditional diabetic diet, is high in fat. As the ADA statement observes: "A liberalized carbohydrate intake . . . will necessarily be associated with a decrease in dietary fat and cholesterol."

But aren't carbohydrates harmful to diabetics? Newer studies indicate that carbohydrates seem not only to stimulate the body to produce insulin, but also to trigger enzymes that put sugars in the blood to work. Experiments using diets up to 80 per cent sugar actually improved the glucose (blood sugar) tolerance of both normal people and diabetics.

Bierman and Nelson cite evidence that total calorie control is the main nutritional need of diabetics. If there is such control, diabetics can eat as much carbohydrate as the normal American—45 per cent or more of the calories they consume.

Will more carbohydrate and less fat help diabetics live longer? No one is yet sure. But in Japan, where diabetics eat more carbohydrates than their Western counterparts, they show less glucose intolerance and suffer less the complications of gangrene, while other functional disturbances are similar for both groups.

Regulating the diabetic's diet is still important. It must be adjusted to medication, activity and, above all, to calorie needs. And sudden surges of blood sugar (as can be caused by large amounts of sweets) must still be avoided. For the obese diabetic total calorie restriction (calories from all sources, not just sugar) is not relaxed.

This does not mean that sugar, as some claim, can cause diabetes. "There is no evidence," the researchers emphasize, "that excessive consumption of sugar causes diabetes."

SUGAR AND LOW BLOOD SUGAR(7)

"Low blood sugar" (hypoglycemia) is a new way to explain many discomforts, especially emotional ones. "We may find it easier," say the experts who studied the data, "to say, 'My blood sugar is low,' rather than, 'I can't cope.' "

But contrary to popular belief, not all of those people who show somewhat low blood sugar levels in tests are ill and need special care. Indeed, Pittsburgh's Drs. Danowski, Nolan and Stephan find that 20 to 30 per cent of normal people can show such readings in glucose tolerance tests.

These slightly low blood sugars are not, as some claim, the cause of psychological disorders. Nor are they the result, as some popular writers insist, of too much carbohydrate, especially sugar, in the diet.

Low blood sugar is simply a sign—one that should be checked to eliminate the possibility of serious underlying disease. This is especially true if the hypoglycemia is moderate or marked.

In most cases of mild hypoglycemia (blood sugars of 45 to 60 milligram per cent) there is nothing more than a variation of normal. But even such patients should be followed for a time.

In moderate hypoglycemia, however (30 to 45 mg. per cent), the low blood sugar may signify a prediabetic state. In a Public Health Service survey, within 10 years over 50 per cent of those with moderate hypoglycemia progressed to actual diabetes. All cases showing very low blood sugars (zero to 30 mg. per cent) are unusual. And blood sugar at this level may be the indicator of poorly controlled diabetes mellitus or of some rare and serious diseases, such as disorders of the nervous system, the liver, certain glands and the life.

Whatever the reason for low blood sugar, it is the result of either an individual quirk or a disease state, not of eating starches and sugars. A diagnosis of "low blood sugar," the authors' studies of research suggest, is not a diagnosis at all. In many cases it is meaningless. In some others it is a signal to look for what could be an underlying disease.

SUGAR AND DENTAL DECAY(8)

It is a widely accepted idea that table sugar is the cause of tooth decay. But the facts are not so simple.

For example, in a five-year study at a Swedish mental institution patients were divided into seven groups. The first group got no sugar but still developed some cavities. Two other groups received sweet drinks at meals but had no increase in decay.

Four other groups received between-meal sugars—as beverages, chocolate, caramels or toffee. The beverages and chocolate had no significant effect on decay, but the sticky candies did increase decay markedly when taken between meals.

From this and many related studies, Drs. Sidney Finn and Robert Glass conclude there is not a one-to-one relationship between total sugar consumption and decay. But there is strong association between cavities and between-meal eating. It seems to be long and frequent exposure to certain foods in certain forms that does the damage.

Which foods? Nearly all sugars tested cause about equal decay. "Natural" sugars, such as honey, are as decay-producing as table sugar. The common sugars of grains, fruits, vegetables and even milk may produce decay. And cooked starches can be as troublesome. For two years 979 children were given as much unsweetened or presweetened cereal as they wanted; regardless of the kinds or amounts of cereal consumed, the amount of decay was similar.

Why? Drs. Finn and Glass describe decay as an infectious disease. For mouth bacteria, which flourish on carbohydrates, produce an acid waste that eats into tooth enamel. Good hygiene helps to reduce tooth-adhering plaque and bacteria harbored by the plaque but never eliminates them entirely.

Many other factors enter into decay—heredity, the shape, alignment and hardness of teeth, the chemistry of the saliva and so on. But there are few of these factors we can control. We cannot keep our mouths bacteria-free or go without all the foods on which the bacteria can feed.

We can practice good dental hygiene, including regular visits to the family dentist. We can avoid sticky foods containing sugar, particularly between meals and at bedtime, and opt for sweets in liquid or quick-dissolving forms. But above all, we can add fluorides to school and community water supplies to harden young teeth early. It is estimated that for about 25 cents per person annually community water supplies can be fluoridated and some 60 per cent of dental decay (and hence dental bills) can be eliminated.

IS SUGAR SAFE TO EAT?

Many other human ills have been charged to sugar. But in these evidence is either non-existent or so slight that the scientific reviewers saw no reason for further study. In general they conclude that sugar, like any other widely used food, is harmless when eaten in reasonable amounts.

Considering all that science has learned of sugar and health, Dr. Stare sums up: "Sugar, a pure carbohydrate, is an important nutrient and food in the U.S. diet when used in moderation. . . . Studies of actual intake suggest that the percentage of calories taken as sugar are higher during the growing and adolescent years when energy demands are high, and lower during adult and later years. . . . There being no valid evidence to the contrary, this rate of intake (between 10 and 30 per cent of total calories, with the average at 15 to 20 per cent) may be considered moderate."

Discussing the conclusions of the investigating team, Dr. Stare concludes, simply "At these levels sugar contributes to good nutrition, to the enjoyment of our meals; and it is safe."

REFERENCES

1. Patrick, J.: Are You on the "Stuff?" Nat. Health Federation Bulletin, Vol. XXI, No. 2, pp. 9–13 (1975)
2. Yudkin, J.: *Sweet and Dangerous,* Peter H. Wyden, New York, (1972)
3. Stare, F.J.: Role of Sugar in Modern Nutrition. World Review of Nutrition and Dietetics, Vol. 22: 239–247 (1975)
4. Grande, F.: Sugar and Cardiovascular Disease. World Review of Nutrition and Dietetics, Vol. 22: 248–269 (1975)
5. Danowski, T.S., Nolan, S. and Stephan, T.: Obesity. World Review of Nutrition and Dietetics, Vol. 22: 270–279 (1975)
6. Bierman, E.L. and Nelson, R.: Carbohydrates, Diabetes and Blood Lipids. World Review of Nutrition and Dietetics, Vol. 22: 280–287 (1975)
7. Danowski, T.S., Nolan, S. and Stephan, T.: Hypoglycemia. World Review of Nutrition and Dietetics, Vol. 22: 288–303 (1975)
8. Finn, S.B. and Glass, R.L.: Sugar and Dental Decay. World Review of Nutrition and Dietetics, Vol. 22: 304–326 (1975)

INFORMATION ABOUT THE AUTHORS

Fredrick J. Stare, Ph.D., M.D., is Professor of Nutrition and Chairman, Department of Nutrition, Harvard School of Public Health.

Francisco Grande, M.D., is Professor of Physiological Hygiene, School of Public Health, University of Minnesota and Jay Phillips Research Laboratory, Mount Sinai Hospital, Minneapolis, Minnesota.

Thaddeus S. Danowski, M.D., is Professor of Medicine, Department of Medicine, University of Pittsburgh and Shadyside Hospital, Pittsburgh, Pennsylvania.

Sean Nolan, M.D., is Clinical Instructor in Medicine, Department of Medicine, University of Pittsburgh and Shadyside Hospital, Pittsburgh, Pennsylvania.

Thorsten Stephan, M.D., is Clinical instructor in Medicine, Department of Medicine, University of Pittsburgh and Shadyside Hospital, Pittsburgh, Pennsylvania.

Edwin L. Bierman, M.D., is Chief, Division of Metabolism and Gerontology, Veterans Administration Hospital; Professor of Medicine, University of Washington School of Medicine, Seattle, Washington.

Ralph Nelson, M.D., is Chief, Clinical Nutrition and Nutrition Therapy, Mayo Clinic, Rochester, Minnesota.

Sidney B. Finn, D.M.D., is Professor of Dentistry, University of Alabama, Birmingham, Alabama.

Robert L. Glass, D.M.D., Dr. P.H., is Associate Clinical Professor of Ecological Dentistry, Harvard University and Associate, Forsyth Dental Center, Boston, Massachusetts.

Dental Caries

by William H. Bowen, BDS, Ph.D., D.Sc.

Dental caries results from the interaction of specific microorganisms with sugars on a susceptible tooth surface. Although many dietary constituents may affect the onset of dental caries, the overwhelming evidence indicates that fluoride and carbohydrates in the form of sugar are the major nutrients which influence the development of this disease.

Fluoride is now regarded as an essential trace element. Its presence in the drinking water at a level of about 1 part per million during tooth development and continuously after tooth eruption prevents dental caries, particularly on the smooth surfaces, by up to 65%. In areas where the water is not fluoridated, dietary supplements of fluoride can be provided through the ingestion of tablets.

Fluoride may confer protection through one or more of several mechanisms. Enamel formed in the presence of fluoride resists acid dissolution to a greater extent than that formed in its absence. There is also evidence which shows that the presence of fluoride promotes the remineralization of very early carious lesions.

Fluoride appears also to be concentrated in dental plaque. Levels 200 times greater than those found in the surrounding saliva occur in plaque. It appears that fluoride may influence the type of extracellular polysaccharide produced by microorganisms, their ability to synthesize intracellular polysaccharide and their capacity to form acid from sugars.

There is an abundance of evidence accumulated from epidemilogical surveys and animal experimentation, which clearly shows that dental caries does not develop in the absence of fermentable carbohydrate. In an elegant clinical study carried out in Vipeholm, Sweden, investigators showed that the level of dental caries was related more strongly to the frequency of carbohydrate intake than to the total amount consumed. For example, subjects who in one year consumed 94 kg of sugar with meals developed substantially fewer lesions than subjects who consumed 85 kg, 15 of which was taken between meals.

From *Contemporary Nutrition, 2,* (8) 1977. Reprinted by permission of General Mills, Inc.

Dr. Bowen is Acting Chief, Caries Prevention and Research Branch, National Caries Program, National Institute of Dental Research, National Institutes of Health Bethesda, Maryland 20014

The frequent ingestion of carbohydrate may affect the pathogenesis of dental caries through several mechanisms. Carbohydrates and sugars, in particular, may affect the maturation of enamel, a process which normally leads to hardening and increased resistance of enamel to dental caries, post eruptively. The teeth of rats exposed to high sugar diets show delayed maturation and appear to have reduced resistance to carious attack. It has also been observed that rats fed a diet conducive to the formation of severe protein-calorie imbalance have increased susceptibility to dental caries, which has been ascribed to altered tooth size and changes in the protein composition of saliva.

The physical form in which sugar is ingested will also influence its cariogenicity. Sugar taken in powered form is substantially more cariogenic in laboratory animals than that consumed in liquids. In addition, the particle size and adhesiveness of the diet may influence its cariogenicity. In general, the longer sugar remains in the mouth the more cariogenic it is likely to be. An extreme example of the effect of protracted exposure to sugar may be observed in infants who habitually suck on pacifiers or bottles containing sugar solutions. These children develop rampant dental caries and are often edentulous before they are aged 3–4 years.

The constituents of the diet may also influence the nature of flora colonizing the tooth surface. Regular ingestion of sucrose promotes the establishment of organisms such as *S. mutans* and *S. sanguis* on the tooth surface. Both organisms have the ability to synthesize extracellular polysaccharides such as glucan and fructan from sucrose. The formation of these materials enhances the ability of microorganisms to adhere to the tooth surface.

The formation of dental plaque is the first clinical evidence of interaction between microorganisms and diet on the tooth surface. Plaque is a soft, white, tenacious material and consists essentially of a dense aggregation of microorganisms embedded in a matrix of protein (40–45% dry wt) and carbohydrate (10–20% dry wt) and contains approximately 80% water. Following ingestion of fermentable carbohydrate such as sugars, acid is formed rapidly within plaque. Thus, following exposure to sugar, plaque becomes, in effect, an acid sponge in close proximity of the tooth. Each ingestion of carbohydrate is followed by a rapid fall in pH value; values as low (acidic) as 4 are frequently recorded. The tooth begins to dissolve rapidly when a value of 5.5 is reached. The types of acid formed in dental plaque have not been extensively studied; however, all the available information suggests that the predominant acid found is lactic, although propionic, acetic and formic acids are also present.

Plaque can also form acid in the absence of extraneous sources of carbohydrate. Many microorganisms in plaque store polysaccharide similar to amylopectin intracellularly, which is catabolized when dietary carbohydrates are lacking. In addition, a small number of microorganisms have the capacity to catabolize fructan and levan.

Considerable dental benefits are derived by those who reduce the frequency of intake of carbohydrate. For example, children in Hopewood House, Australia, who were not permitted to eat cookies, candies, molasses, honey and similar food Monday through Friday, had substantially fewer carious lesions than their counterparts, who were not subjected to such restriction.

The results of many epidemiological surveys and clinical trials suggest that there is an association between the prevalence of dental caries and the consumption of chewing gum and soft drinks. Recognizing this relationship the National Caries Program, NIDR, NIH, issued the following statement:

"From the evidence, it is clear that how frequently sugar is eaten is even more important than how much is consumed. Eating sugar-sweetened foods between meals is, therefore, particularly dangerous to oral health . . . sugar-sweetened foods should be eaten only at regular meals and only as part of a well-balanced diet."

Sorbitol is a sugar alcohol, which is about 80% as sweet as sugar. It is not readily fermented by oral microorganisms. Primates, which had most of the sugar in their diet replaced by sorbitol, developed only a few very small lesions during a 3-year study. The ability of plaque to ferment sorbitol did not increase during the 3-year study. Results of studies carried out in humans indicate that sorbitol-containing gum is minimally cariogenic. *In vitro* studies have shown that oral microorganisms metabolize sorbitol to carbon-dioxide, ethanol and formic acid.

Recently, particular attention has been focused on xylitol, which is a pentitol. It is as sweet as sucrose and has a pleasant cooling taste. Results of investigations carried out in animals and in humans show clearly that it is non-cariogenic. However, claims that it has a therapeutic effect remain to be substantiated.

Dental caries is a public health problem and as such is unlikely to be completely controlled by individual effort. Public health measures are, therefore, called for and of these, community water fluoridation is by far the most effective and reduces the prevalence of caries by as much as 65%. Recently, representatives of the candy and related industries have stated that people living in fluoridated areas eat all the candy they want and don't get caries. Such statements do a gross disservice to the public. Fluoridation of water supplies is not a license for unrestricted consumption of sugar. Reduction in the frequency of intake of sugar in fluoridated areas will result in even more effective protection against caries.

REFERENCES

1. Bowen, W.H., *Role of Carbohydrates in Dental Caries.* ASC Symposium Series, No. 15, (1975).
2. Gustafson, B.E., et al. *Vipeholm Dental Caries Study.* Acta Odont. Scand. 11:232 (1954).
3. Harris, R.M., *Biology of the Children of Hopewood House.* J. Dent. Res. 42:1387 (1963).
4. Newbrun, E., *Diet and Dental Caries Relationships.* Advances in Caries Research 2:XV, 1974).

6

Food, Nutrition and Health

This chapter provides readings on several topical subjects which have been the focus of health scares or health cures.

The first paper deals with dietary fiber, what our grandmother called roughage or bulk.

The next two papers deal with a very important health issue, that is, dietary fat, cholesterol, and heart disease. This is a subject of controversy even among scientists but the papers presented will hopefully present views which might help to focus on the controversy in your mind.

The fourth paper discusses the possible relationships between food and cancer. Cancer is a feared disease and this topic is an important area for the reader to consider.

The last paper in this section is on weight control. If one views the factors with the highest risk to health, weight is very high.

In fact, we feel the major risk factors are: overweight, cigarette smoking, alcohol consumption, hypertension, and lack of exercise.

It is unfortunate that issues such as the one involving sugar throw up a smokescreen which clouds these real issues. It really isn't fair to the public.

As a nation we spend billions on fad diets. Hopefully, this paper might lessen the cost and increase the probability of controlling your weight.

Dietary Fiber

*A Scientific Status Summary by the Institute of Food Technologists'
Expert Panel on Food Safety & Nutrition and the Committee
on Public Information (January, 1979)*

The role played by fiber (or "roughage" as our grandparents called it) in health and disease has recently become the subject of increased public attention. It has gained so much attention, in fact, that a variety of new "high fiber" foods have come on the market, and the retail sale of bran-fortified cereal products increased 20% in a single year. Strange as it may seem, fiber has been largely ignored by nutritionists, who are accustomed to thinking in terms of digestion of foods and subsequent absorption and metabolism of nutrients, whereas fiber, most of which is not digested by humans to absorbable nutrients, is excreted directly in the feces.

Much of the current interest in fiber results from reports by D.P. Burkitt, a British medical researcher and surgeon, who observed that rural Africans—whose diets are high in fiber-containing foods—have a lower incidence of appendicitis, hemorrhoids, diverticular disease, cardiovascular disease, and cancer of the colon than in the United States and other developed countries where diets are low in fiber (Burkitt, 1973).

WHAT IS DIETARY FIBER?

One of the many factors complicating the interpretation of fiber research lies in the lack of a widely accepted definition of the word. For years, fiber has been discussed in terms of "crude fiber," which is simply the residue after a food sample is treated in the laboratory with a solvent, hot acid, and hot alkali. This chemically inert residue is composed primarily of the lignin and most of the cellulose in the food being analyzed.

"Dietary fiber," on the other hand, is defined as including all the components of a food that are not broken down by enzymes in the human digestive tract to produce small molecular compounds which are then absorbed into the blood stream. Dietary fiber includes hemicelluloses, pectic substances, gums, mucilages, and certain other carbohydrates, as well as the lignin and cellulose. These chemical compounds are found largely in the cell walls of plant tissues, and, as shown in Table 1, their total greatly exceeds that expressed as crude fiber.

The use of "crude fiber" in dietary descriptions is thus of limited value, since it may represent as little as one-seventh of the total dietary fiber of the food. The value of fruit is particularly understated by this method. Even the word "fiber" itself may be misleading, since not all the components of "dietary fiber" are fibrous in the usual physical sense, while foods that do contain recognizable fibers, such as muscle meats, do not yield undigestible residue.

ALLEGED BENEFITS OF DIETARY FIBER

Physiological claims for fiber fall into three categories:

1. **Definite value**—relieving constipation problems by increasing the water content of the feces.
2. **Probable value**—treating (or preventing) diverticular disease.
3. **Possible value**—reducing serum cholesterol, prevention of a variety of disorders such as hemorrhoids, varicose veins, ischemic heart disease, colon-rectal cancer, diabetes, appendicitis, obesity, gallstones, phlebitis, dental caries, irritable bowel, ulcerative colitis, and the harmful effects of some ingested toxic substances.

The evidence underlying these claims varies. Some comes from direct human studies, others from animal experimentation. Some observations have been made on different population groups, and attempts made to correlate various disease statistics with local dietary factors. Still other claims are really theoretical hypotheses derived by combining known physical characteristics of foods and physiology. For example:

Constipation.   Fiber's value for relieving constipation lies in its ability to increase the water content of the feces, producing bulkier, but soft, well-formed stools. This, in turn, leads to a transit time in the gastrointestinal tract which is intermediate between being too rapid, causing diarrhea, and too slow, causing constipation. It has been proposed that the increased volume and softness of the stools, by reducing straining during defecation, is a factor in preventing hemorrhoids and varicose veins. Experimental evidence for this latter claim, however, is limited.

Diverticulosis.   Diverticula are outpouchings which develop in weak areas in the bowel wall. When they are numerous and become inflamed, diverticulitis results. This condition is often accompanied by pain on the lower left side, alternating diarrhea and constipation, and flatulence. Diverticulitis was virtually nonexistent in the early 20th century, but its incidence has grown steadily in industrialized countries. Now, an estimated one-fourth to one-third of the middle-aged and older population in the U.S. and other western countries have the condition, although not all suffer from its symptoms. The incidence of the disease has changed little in populations where the diet is high in indigestible residue (e.g. South African Bantus and Chinese).

Until recently, the standard medical treatment for this malady was a low-residue diet, on the presumption that such a diet would allow healing and cause less irritation to the bowel. Now, however, it is treated with a high-fiber diet with good results. This supports the hypothesis that the disease results from a dietary fiber deficiency, although it obviously does not prove it.

Laboratory studies have shown that rats fed a fiber-free diet develop diverticulosis, while those fed a normal, fiber-containing control diet do not. Also, a fiber-containing diet could be used to cure diverticulosis in rats (Carlson and Hoelzel, 1949).

Cardiovascular diseases. A diet high in dietary fiber may lower blood cholesterol levels by reducing the "transit time" through the gastro-intestinal tract, leading to decreased absorption of dietary cholesterol. It may also decrease the reabsorption of bile salts, although evidence is based more on epidemiological studies (comparisons of population characteristics) than on clinical studies. Bile salts are essential in digestion; they emulsify fats and oils, and thus permit their absorption from the intestine. People on certain high-fiber diets excrete more bile acids, sterols, and fat, implying that the fiber compounds "bind" bile acids, and thereby prevent absorption of cholesterol and fat and also the reabsorption of bile acid, derived from the body's cholesterol (Stanley, 1970). The body then draws on its cholesterol stores to synthesize more bile acid, presumably resulting in a lowering of the blood (serum) cholesterol level.

High serum cholesterol levels have been identified as one of the risk factors in atherosclerosis, although there is disagreement as to whether the actual risk can be reduced by lowering cholesterol levels by means of diet or drugs.

Also complicating any resolution of the role of dietary fiber in cardiovascular disease are the inconsistent effects produced by dietary fiber from different foods. For example, studies have shown that adding rolled oats or barley to the diet reduces serum cholesterol levels in rats; the effect of adding whole wheat is variable. Rolled oats has also been shown to have a cholesterol-lowering effect in man (DeGroot, et al, 1963). Pectin (another dietary fiber component) has been shown to have similar effect in man and experimental animals (Keys, et al, 1961; Leveille and Sauberlich, 1966). Bran does not appear to alter serum lipids, while alfalfa and possilby a lignin component may have a depressing effect (Eastwood, 1977).

Cancer. Some health professionals believe that dietary fiber may provide protection from cancer of the colon and the rectum, based on epidemiological studies of various populations comparing cancer incidence with dietary fiber consumed. The hypothesis relating dietary fiber to cancer pre-

TABLE 1. A Comparison of Crude Fiber and Dietary Fiber in Certain Foods[a]

Food	Crude Fiber g/100 g	Dietary Fiber g/100 g
Breads and cereals		
White bread	0.2	2.72
Whole wheat bread	1.6	8.50
All bran cereal	7.8	26.7
Cornflakes	0.7	11.0
Puffed Wheat	2.0	15.41
Puffed wheat, sugar coated	0.9	6.08
Vegetables		
Broccoli tops, boiled	1.5	4.10
Lettuce, raw	0.6	1.53
Carrots, boiled	1.0	3.70
Peas, canned	2.3	6.28
Sweet corn, cooked	0.7	4.74
Fruits		
Apples, without skin	0.6	1.42
Peaches, with skin	0.6	2.28
Strawberries, raw	1.3	2.12
Nuts		
Brazil	3.1	7.73
Peanuts	1.9	9.30
Peanut butter	1.9	7.55

[a]Crude fiber data from U.S.D.A. Handbook 8, Composition of Foods.
Dietary fiber data from David Southgate. Medical Research Council, Cambridge, England.

sumes that the slow movement of the feces which occurs with a low-fiber diet allows more time for any carcinogens present in the colon to initiate cancer. In addition, according to this hypothesis, the extra water, bile acids, salts, and fat bound by added fiber act as solvents to remove a wide variety of chemical factors which might be carcinogenic.

Also, a high-fiber diet may alter the type and number of microorganisms in the colon, and may possibly inhibit their production of potential carcinogens. A diet high in fiber might also contain less of the materials which are converted by microbial action to carcinogens (Leveille, 1976). One study supporting this theory showed that one class of microorganisms, which produce compounds convertible to carcinogens, is present in the feces of Western populations in significantly greater amounts than in feces from populations in the underdeveloped countries (Aries, et al: 1969).

Theories based on correlations of various population characteristics can, of course, be misleading. For example, the incidence of colon cancer in different countries and cultures correlates much better with the consumption of fat in the diet that it does with the consumption of fiber (Carroll, 1975; Chan and Cohen, 1975). Furthermore, there is no proven relationship between bowel transit times and the incidence of colon cancer. Also, no proof exists that constipation leads to cancer, and none that dietary fiber *per se* has a definable effect on the intestinal flora of man (Mendeloff, 1975).

Diabetes.   Blood-sugar levels of patients taking insulin were significantly higher on a low-fiber diet than on a high-fiber diet (Miranda and Horwitz, 1978). While this preliminary observation is of interest, clearly diabetics should not change to a high-fiber diet without the advice of a physician.

Appendicitis has been linked to low-fiber diets in some epidemiological comparisons, but other data fail to support this hypothesis. For example, the incidence of appendicitis in the U.S. has decreased by 40% in the last 20 years, while fiber intake has been falling.

Weight loss.   Preliminary studies indicate that high-fiber foods, bread, for example, may help promote weight loss although additional studies are required before firm conclusions can be drawn. Pound for pound, such breads frequently contain fewer calories than normal breads, and they could also simply reduce food consumption because of an increased feeling of satiety (Mrdeza, 1978. One can also envision a mechanism whereby dietary fiber would shorten transit time through the intestine, with consequent decreased absorption of nutrients.

In addition to these major health-related areas, certain plant fibers appear to have a detoxifying effect when fed along with various drugs and chemicals (Ershoff, 1974), but further study is required. On the other hand, there is little evidence to link dietary fiber with such disorders as hiatal hernia, deep vein thrombosis, and phlebitis.

In considering possible relationships between specific diseases and diet or changes in diet, based on epidemiological evidence, one must remember that many changes in lifestyle and the environment occur simultaneously with changes in the diet which might themselves cause or influence the course of these diseases. It must be remembered that epidemiological evidence can never *prove* a causal relationship. It is also dangerous to speculate that a specific dietary factor is most significant. Generally, people eating a low-fiber diet are also consuming increased amounts of refined carbohydrates, fats, and animal products, for example. It is just as logical, epidemiologically speaking, to attribute these diseases to the *presence* of these other materials as it is to the absence of fiber. Furthermore, high-fiber diets also may be high in trace elements and other essential nutrients; thus, it could be *their* presence that produces any beneficial effects (Weininger and Briggs, 1976).

DIETARY FIBER NOT A SINGLE ENTITY

As indicated earlier, results of feeding "high-fiber diets" differ from researcher to researcher. One explanation for the conflicting results may be the relatively poor analytical methods available for determining fiber data. Another explanation, however, is that diferent fiber components have very different physiological functions, and—since fiber composition differs with the food source—the physiological effects noted will depend on the predominant type of fiber used in the experimental diet. Some of the differences are in kind, while others are of degree.

One such example—the effect of fiber on the level of serum cholesterol—has already been mentioned. Pectin, lignin, guar gum, oat hulls, and barley have been shown to have some cholesterol-lowering effect in human and/or animal studies, while bran and cellulose have not. This difference may very well be related in differences in the chemical and physical properties of the various fiber components present. Even the size of the fiber particle being ingested affects the results.

Digestion of some components of dietary fiber, especially the hemicelluloses, takes place in the colon as a result of bacterial action. White flour, for example is high in hemicellulose. The volatile fatty acids produced from this soluble fiber in the digestive process attract water from the surrounding tissues by osmosis, and thus may have a cathartic effect. Some fibers, such as bagasse from sugar cane, are very sharp and abrasive to the intestinal tract, while others, such as lignin, may actually be constipating.

There are such great differences in the physiological effects of the various constituents of dietary fiber that it is almost meaningless to talk about high-fiber diets in the abstract. This is not to deny that needs may exist for *components* of dietary fiber with specific properties, but rather that these needs may vary with different physiologic states.

CAN YOU GET TOO MUCH DIETARY FIBER?

Whenever there is a surge of interest in any dietary component, there is a danger that the significance of laboratory research may be exaggerated relative to everyday dietary decisions. Such a danger exists with respect to fiber. Consumption of as much as 10 tablespoons of bran per day, in addition to the regular diet, has been recommended in some regimes. Such large intakes may cause diarrhea and other digestive complaints.

It has been suggested that too much pectin may cause decreased Vitamin B_{12} absorption. This would be an important concern for certain types of vegetarians, whose diets are already low in this vitamin and high in fiber. There may also be a significant loss of minerals, particularly zinc, iron, calcium, copper, and magnesium, due to binding of these minerals by phytic acid, present in certain plant-based foods.

The high-fiber diets of Africa and India, for example, are associated with a high incidence of such mineral deficiencies and kidney stones, especially in areas where rice is the major calorie source. The rate of stomach cancer in some of these areas is high, which should lead to cautious interpretation of epidemiological studies.

Also, fiber, by its sheer bulk, may reduce the total amount of food consumed, thereby resulting in the deficiency of certain nutrients, and even—in some cases—of needed calories, especially in areas where malnutrition is already existent.

Persons with kidney disease, diabetes, or other disease should, without question, obtain permission from their physician before consuming bran or making other drastic changes in their diet. Very large amounts of fiber could even cause enlargement and twisting (or "volvulus") of the sigmoid colon (Eastwood, 1976) and aggravate ulcerative colitis. Both conditions occur in Africa but rarely in Europe.

FOOD SOURCES OF DIETARY FIBER

A wide variety of foods supply significant amounts of dietary fiber, including all of the various components; Table 2 shows the amounts provided by a selected group of foods. In both fresh vegetables and fruits, the *total* dietary fiber appears to be relatively low, because of their high water content, but it represents a substantial proportion of the solids content. Potatoes and starchy vegetables supply significant amounts of fiber if consumed in fairly large quantities. The lignin content of most vegetables is very low, while that of fruits is highest in those containing lignified seeds, such as the strawberry, or lignified cells in the flesh, such as the pear. The non-cellulosic polysaccharides in these foods are usually rich in pectic substances (uronic acids) and in the so-called 5-carbon sugars (pentoses).

Substitution of whole meal flour for white flour provides increased lignin in the diet, as well as a 3-fold increase in total dietary fiber from that food stuff and a 12-fold increase in non-cellulose pentosans (polymers of 5-carbon sugars).

Consumer interest in this subject has prompted a number of bakeries to develop breads which contain from 6 to 8 percent crude fiber. This is roughly four times as much fiber as is contained in whole wheat bread. Powdered food-grade cellulose is the fiber component added to these products. Cellulose is a recognized food additive often used as a thickener or to decrease the separation of fat and water in other products, although its use in bread is new. When added to bread, it must be listed on the ingredient label. Since cellulose and the water it holds dilute other nutrients in normal bread, fiber enriched bread is sometimes promoted as a calorie-reduced product.

TABLE 2. Total Dietary Fiber and Composition in Some Fruits, Vegetables, and Wheat Products[a]

Food	Total Dietary Fiber (g/100g. fresh basis)	Composition of the Dietary Fiber (%)			Composition of the Non-Cellulosic Fraction (%)		
		Non-Cellulosic Polysaccharides	Cellulose	Lignin	Hexoses	Pentoses	Uronic Acids
Cabbage, cooked	2.83	37	63	Tr	16	55	28
Carrots, cooked	3.70	60	40	Tr	20	35	45
Peas, frozen, raw	7.75	69	27	2	48	22	30
Tomato, raw	1.40	47	32	21	14	42	44
Apple, flesh only	1.42	66	33	<1	20	35	40
Banana	1.75	64	21	15	54	19	27
Pear, flesh only	2.44	54	28	19	20	46	35
Plum, raw, flesh and skin	1.52	65	15	19	28	46	25
Strawberry, raw	2.12	46	16	38	22	33	45
White flour (72%)	3.45	80	19	1	80	11	9
Brown flour (90-95%)	8.70	72	18	10	44	45	11
Wholemeal flour	11.0	72	20	8	39	48	13
Bran	48.0	74	18	7	19	60	12

[a]Southgate, D. 1976. The analysis of dietary fiber. In "Fiber in Human Nutrition." G.A. Spiller and R.J. Amen. Plenum Publ. Co., New York City.

HOW MUCH IS ENOUGH?

While dietary recommendations ranging from 6 to 24 grams of crude fiber per day can be found in popular and scientific literature, almost no detailed information is available to serve as a guide for recommending either the quantity or type of dietary fiber. Trends in fiber consumption that have accompanied increases in the incidence of diseases suspected to be fiber-connected may not be meaningful—they certainly do not *prove* anything.

From 1909–13 to 1965, the daily crude fiber content of the average American diet decreased from approximately 7 grams to about 5 grams. Whether increasing daily consumption of crude fiber by 2 grams to get it back to this earlier level could be expected to have the same effect on health as an increase to the higher levels—25 grams—suggested from the difference between African and American diets, is certainly an unanswered question (McNutt, 1976; Heller and Hackler, 1978).

It may be that the increased consumption of fruits and vegetables, coupled with the decreased intake of cereal in the last 50 years, represents more of a shift in the *type* of fiber than a significant decrease in the amount (Spiller and Shipley, 1976).

RECOMMENDATIONS

Recommendations regarding the consumption of any nutrient must be rational and based on reasonable scientific evidence. In the absence of such evidence, *moderation* should be exercised. A variety of whole grain products, fruits, and vegetables will ensure a good mixture of fiber constituents, and make a positive contribution to the overall nutritional value of diet.

If there are beneficial effects from dietary fiber, they must stem from more than one component of dietary fiber. Therefore, adding fiber in the form of bran alone, for example, can be expected to have little effect other than on bowel activity. Likewise, the benefits of adding cellulose alone to bread may be limited to reducing calories. Any generalized statements about the use of dietary fiber as a drug to cure specific diseases should be looked at with reservations.

In short, the feeling of urgency about fiber in nutrition prevalent today should not cause investigators to jump to premature conclusions, nor cause the public to make drastic changes in their diets, without thinking through their specific needs and the options open for filling them.

REFERENCES

Aries, V., Crowther, J.S., Drasar, B.S., Hill, J., and Williams, R.E.O. 1969, Gut 10: 334.

Burkitt, D.P. 1973. Some diseases characteristic of modern Western Civilization, British Med. J. 1: 274.

Carlson, A.J. and Hoelzel, F. 1949. Relation of diets to diverticulosis in the colon of rats. Gastroenterology 12: 108.

Carroll, K.K. 1975. Experimental evidence of dietary factors and hormone-dependent cancers. Cancer Res. 35: 3374.

Chan, P-C, and Cohen, L.A. 1975. Dietary fat and growth promotion of rat mammary tumors, Cancer Res. 35: 3384.

DeGroot, A.P., Lugken, R., and Pikaar, N.A. 1963. Cholesterol-lowering effects of rolled oats. Lancet 2: 303.

Eastwood, M. 1976. Volvulus of the colon, p. 230. In: "Fiber in Human Nutrition," Spillen, G.A., and Amen, R.J., Plenum Publ. Co., New York.

Eastwood, M. 1977. Vegetable dietary fiber. Nutrition and the M.D., 3(11): 1.

Ershoff, B.H. 1974. Anti-toxic effects of plant fiber. Amer. J. Clin. Nutr. 27: 1395.

Heller, S.N. and Hackler, L.R. 1978. Changes in the crude fiber content of the American diet. Am. J. Clin. Nutr. 31 (Sept.): 1510.

Leveille, G.A. and Sauberlich, H. 1966. Mechanism of the cholesterol-depressing effect of pectin in the cholesterol-fed rat, J Nutr. 88: 209.

Leveille, G.A. 1976. Dietary fiber. Food and Nutr. News. 47(3): 1.

Keys, A., Grande, F. and Anderson, J.T. 1961. Fiber and pectin in the diet and serum cholesterol concentration in man. Proc. Soc. Exp. Biol. Med. 106: 555.

McNutt, K. 1976. Perspective—Fiber. J. Nutr. Ed., 8(4): 150.

Mrdeza, G. 1978. Trends in Specialty breads. Cereal Foods World. 29(11): 635.

Mendeloff, A.I. 1975. Dietary fiber. Nutr. Rev. 33(11): 321.

Miranda, P.M. and Horwitz, D.L. 1978. High-fiber diets in treatment of Diabetes mellitus. Ann. Int. Med. 88(4): 482.

Spiller, G.A. and Shipley, E.A. 1976. New perspectives on dietary fiber. Food Prod. Dev., 10(8): 57.

Stanley, M.M. 1970. Quantification of intestinal functions during fasting: estimations of bile salt turnover, fecal calcium and nitrogen excretions, Metabolism 19: 865.

Weininger, J. and Briggs, G.M. 1976 Nutrition update, J. Nutr. Ed., 8(4): 172.

SUPPLEMENTAL MATERIAL

Burkitt, D.P. and Trowell, H.C. 1975. "Refined Carbohydrate Foods and Disease. Academic Press, London and New York.

Hegsted, D.M. (ed.) 1977. "Food and Fiber." Nutrition Reviews 35: 3.

Roth, H.P. and Mehlman, M.A. 1978. "Symposium on the Role of Dietary Fiber in Health." A. J. Clin. Nutr. (31).

Spiller, G.A. and Amen, R.J. 1976. "Fiber in Human Nutrition." Plenum Publ. Co., New York.

Spiller, G.A. (ed.). 1978. "Topics in Dietary Fiber Research." Plenum Publ. Co., New York.

Fats, Diets and Your Health

By Gilbert A. Leveille and Anita Dean

Fat is an important nutrient in the human diet. It is the most concentrated source of energy. On an equal-weight basis, it provides more than two times the energy in carbohydrate and protein—9 calories from a gram of fat, compared with 4 calories from carbohydrate and protein.(1)

FAT IN U.S. DIET

Fat consumption in the United States has increased significantly over the past 65 years. This includes fats and oils, as such, and fats occurring naturally in foods—examples are butterfat in milk, marbling in meat, and oils in nuts and seeds.

The proportion of calories derived from fat in the U.S. diet has increased over the last 70 years as we have increased our consumption of animal products and decreased our consumption of cereal grains and potatoes, which are low in fat. (See chart on page 137).

Today, fat supplies 40 percent or more of total calories in the average American diet. Three food groups—fats and oils; meat, poultry and fish; and dairy products—account for about nine-tenths of the fat in the U.S. diet. Not all of the fat available for consumption is eaten. For example, some fat used in deep-fat frying by industry or in the home may be discarded; fat may be trimmed from meat either before or after cooking.

The vegetable-fruit group (except olives and avocados) and the bread-cereal group are very low in fat.

Fat is part of virtually all foods. Some foods such as butter, vegetable oil and margarine are nearly 100 percent fat. These are called "visible" fats. Those found in whole milk, cream, ice cream, cheese, egg yolk, meat, nuts, pastries and food mixtures are invisible." The milk-and-meat group furnishes about half the fat in the American diet. Even though all visible fat is trimmed

From *Nutrition Viewpoint* Extension Bulletin E–1192, Michigan State University, No. 4, January 1978. Reprinted by permission.

Gilbert A. Leveille is Chairman of the Department of Food Science and Human Nutrition at Michigan State University, and Chairman of the Foods and Nutrition Board, National Research Council, National Academy of Sciences.

Anita Dean is MSU Extension Specialist in Food Science and Human Nutrition.

CONSUMPTION OF FOOD ENERGY, PROTEIN, FAT, AND CARBOHYDRATE

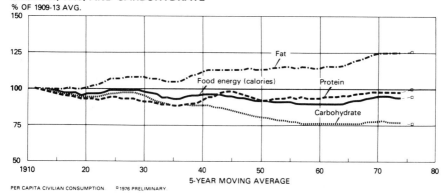

% OF 1909-13 AVG.

PER CAPITA CIVILIAN CONSUMPTION.   □1976 PRELIMINARY

5-YEAR MOVING AVERAGE

Fat Content of Various Foods

Percent Fat	Food
90—100	Salad and cooking oils and fats, lard
80— 90	Butter, margarine
70— 80	Mayonnaise, pecans, macadamia nuts
50— 70	Walnuts, dried unsweetened coconut meat, almonds, bacon, baking chocolate
30— 50	Broiled choice T-bone and porterhouse steaks, spareribs, broiled pork chop, goose, cheddar and cream cheeses, potato chips, french dressing, chocolate candy, butter cream icing.
20— 30	Choice beef pot roast, broiled choice lamb chop, frankfurters, ground beef, chocolate chip cookies
10— 20	Broiled choice round steak, broiled veal chop, roast turkey, eggs, avocado, olives, chocolate cake with icing, french fried potatoes, ice cream, apple pie
1— 10	Pork and beans, broiled cod, halibut, haddock, and many other fish, broiled chicken, crabmeat, cottage cheese, beef liver, milk, creamed soups, sherbert, most breakfast cereals
Less than 1	Baked potato, most vegetables and fruits, egg whites, chicken consomme

off meats, cooked lean meat still contains 4 to 15 percent hidden fat. Choice cuts and higher grades that are well marbled with fat furnish higher amounts of fat.

The type of fat consumed over the past 65 years has also changed. Daily dietary fat from animal sources (mostly saturated)(2) has decreased 8 percent while consumption of vegetable fat (unsaturated)(2) has dramatically increased by 57 percent. Increased consumption of margarine and salad and cooking oils accounts for this increase. Although the increase has come from foods of vegetable origin, animal sources continue to provide the largest proportion of fat in the diet.

ARE FATS NECESSARY IN YOUR DIET?

Fat is a concentrated source of energy. It also makes foods tasty and provides that feeling of satisfaction not available from carbohydrate and protein. Fats are responsible also for many of the characteristic flavors, aromas and textures of foods, and they serve as carriers of vitamins A, D, E and K.

Fats (also called **lipids**) are made up of fatty acids (see Technical Discussion). The body cannot manufacture certain essential fatty acids; and, if these are lacking a skin condition like eczema could develop. Such a condition, however, is extremely unlikely with usual American diets today which provide abundant amounts of fatty acids. In fact, it is unlikely under ordinary circumstances that any human diet will be low enough in fat to produce a critical lack of essential fatty acids. Vegetable oil consumption has increased dramatically in recent years. For example, a tablespoon of most vegetable oils, except peanut and olive oils, will meet the daily requirements for essential fatty acids.

Fats and fat-related substances in the body include (besides fatty acids) **glycerides, pholpholipids**, and **cholesterol**. (For a chemical description of these materials and a discussion of how the body digests and absorbs fats, see Technical Discussion.)

The human body can produce fats (lipids) from a variety of diet sources. Carbohydrate and protein can be transformed into fat in the liver, and this fat can then be transported and stored in the body.

FATS AND YOUR HEART

Fats are transported in the blood and lymph in combination with proteins. The combination is known as **lipoprotein.** Fats cannot be transported in the bloodstream unless they are made soluble. This change occurs in the intestine when fat combines with protein to form a type of lipoprotein known as **chylomicron** (see Technical Discussion). Other varieties of **lipoprotein** are formed in the liver. They differ from one another in their fat and protein composition. Those known as "low-density" lipoproteins have a higher proportion of lipid and less protein than the "high-density" lipoproteins. Generally, the low-density lipoproteins have more **triglyceride** and less **phospholipid** and **cholesterol** than do the higher-density lipoproteins. (See Technical Discussion.)

The amount and kinds of lipoproteins in the blood are important in evaluating the risk category of individuals with regard to diseases of the heart, blood vessels or circulation known as cardiovascular disease.

What Is Atherosclerosis?

Atherosclerosis is a common form of cardiovascular disease. In its earliest stage, fatty deposits build up and infiltrate the artery walls. As the disease progresses, the areas of infiltration become thicker, and fibrous material is deposited along with the fat. These areas eventually become calcified as calcium is deposited. As a consequence, the arteries lose their elastic nature and become ridid. In addition, the artery becomes partially obstructed. (The process is much the same as the buildup of lime in water pipes. The buildup decreases the capacity of the pipe to carry its normal flow of water.) In this latter stage, it is much more likely that a small blood clot may entirely block the vessel. When this occurs in the small vessels feeding the heart, the result is a heart attack or coronary. The blockage of a blood vessel in the brain results in a stroke.

The nature of this abnormal condition and its development is not well understood in spite of many studies. The disease is progressive, beginning in some cases in childhood and advancing through young adulthood, often reaching severe forms in the third to fourth decade of life. The desease is more common in men than in women of childbearing age; however, the incidence has increased in women in recent years.

Risk Factors in Atherosclerosis

Studies over the last several decades have provided a means of identifying persons who are most likely to suffer a coronary or a stroke. The three major risk factors are:

- cigarette smoking,
- hypertension (high blood pressure), and
- high blood cholesterol levels.

An individual having any one of these risk factors has a greater **statistical chance** of suffering a coronary or stroke than a person who is not affected by these factors. Individuals having any two of the risk factors have an even greater chance, and individuals having all three risk factors have the greatest chance of being affected.

One should not, however, conclude from these statements based on medical statistics that **all** individuals having one or more risk factors **will** have a coronary or a stroke, or than individuals free from these risk factors cannot be affected. A number of other factors appear to be important in predisposing individuals to atherosclerotic disease. One is a family history of the disease. Stress also appears to increase the probability of cardiovascular disease. Other contributing factors include overweight and an inactive lifestyle.

Diet and Heart Disease

As indicated, a high blood cholesterol level is a risk factor in the development of cardiovascular disease. Several studies in a variety of countries have shown a higher incidence of heart disease in populations consuming a high proportion of calories from fat, particularly saturated fat, and having relatively high intakes of cholesterol and higher levels of cholesterol in the blood. Studies with animals show that experimentally induced atherosclerotic heart disease is higher in animals fed diets high in saturated fat and cholesterol.

Some studies with humans have shown that high blood cholesterol levels can be reduced through diets lower in actual amount of fat but containing a higher proportion of polyunsaturated fatty acids and less cholesterol (see Technical Discussion).

From these studies, some scientists conclude that the American population and others similar to it would benefit from consuming diets lower in cholesterol and in fat but containing a higher proportion of polyunsaturated fatty acids. But not all scientists agree with this conclusion. Why? It remains to be proven conclusively that lowering the blood cholesterol level by changes in diet will actually lower the incidence of cardiovascular disease. Considerable suggestive evidence has been collected, but not all studies are in agreement. For example, studies have shown that those individuals who had suffered heart attacks did not necessarily have the highest cholesterol and fat intakes in the population under study. So, the matter of dietary change to control cardiovascular disease is not a simple one agreed to by all scientists and physicians. Much controversy still exists. Nevertheless, scientists generally agree that everyone should be examined periodically for abnormal blood lipid profiles and checked for hypertension (high blood pressure).

Some Tests to Take

A blood sample should be taken for lipid analysis, including blood cholesterol and triglycerides; and in many cases, a lipoprotein analysis should be made. From this information, a physician can determine whether an abnormality exists and what it is. If one is found, a corrective diet can be prescribed.

Hypertensive persons should be treated to lower their blood pressure. Patients with elevated blood lipid levels should be treated to lower these levels to normal. In most cases, the treatment to lower blood lipid levels will involve a modification diet.

Usually, two common abnormalities are found in the blood—high cholesterol and/or high triglycerides. The treatment of high cholesterol usually calls for less fat in the diet (approximately 35 percent of calories from fat), a reduction in saturated fat (no more than 10 percent of total calories), and a reduction in cholesterol (to 300 mg per day or less).(3)

Diet change to lower triglycerides in the blood is somewhat different. Those who have this problem usually are overweight, and a lower-calorie diet is recommended to return weight to normal. Also, treatment should call for a reduction in the proportion of calories derived from simple carbohydrates (sugar) and from alcohol. Other abnormalities in blood lipids can exist, but these are rare.

Changes in the General Diet

Although there is no consensus regarding changes in the diet for restricting intake of fat for the general population, most scientists agree that some changes are probably desirable. Because so many Americans are overweight, a reduction in total dietary fat to reduce intake of calories would be desirable, and certainly would cause no harm. If this reduction in total fats could be achieved by reducing saturated fat, the proportion of polyunsaturated fatty acids in the diet would increase automatically. This might also be desirable in controlling heart disease.

As a rule of thumb, it is probably desirable for most Americans to strive for about 15 percent of their calories from protein, 35 percent from fat and 50 percent from carbohydrate. This is moderate and achieveable and is supported by research.

There is much less agreement on dietary cholesterol. Consequently, no general recommendation has been made for the population as a whole. However, everyone should avoid obviously high amounts of cholesterol. A balance of all nutrients in the diet requires a wide variety of basic foods—ample amounts of fruits and vegetables; dairy products; meat, fish, poultry and eggs; whole grain and enriched cereals. This variety of foods will also ensure that the carbohydrate in the diet comes largely from complex sources such as starches in cereal and potatoes, which furnish other nutrients as well, rather than simple sugars (table sugar and soft drinks, which contain little or no other nutrients) and sweet desserts such as rich pies and cakes. Current research findings suggest that increased intakes of complex carbohydrates may be desirable.

Such a change in diet need not involve a drastic change in eating habits. For example, the fat content of the diet can be significantly reduced by simply substituting low-fat milk for whole milk or ice milk for ice cream, or by trimming the fat from meat and selecting leaner cuts of meat. This does not require us to become compulsive about our eating habits; but a few relatively simple changes in the types of food products we eat can make a significant difference in fat consumption.

SOURCES OF INFORMATION

Patients on special diets can gets specific information about diets and heart disease by consulting a dietitian recommended by their physician. In many communities, dietitians provide a service entitled "Dial-a-Dietitian." In some communities, public health nutritionists can be contacted through the Department of Public Health. State Cooperative Extension Services can also be of assistance through nutrition specialists and home economists. Although these nutritionists are not allowed to prescribe diets, they can assist individuals in meeting the recommendations prescribed by their physicians.

TECHNICAL DISCUSSION

What Are Fats or Lipids?

Fats (also called **lipids**) are organic chemical compounds. They will not dissolve in water but are soluble in other organic compounds such as alcohol. Fats are made up of **fatty acids**. Cholesterol and fat-soluble vitamins A, D, E and K are generally grouped with fats.

All fatty acids contain carbon, hydrogen and oxygen. They vary in how much of these three elements they contain. The most common fatty acids in foods have 16 or 18 carbon atoms. Others have fewer than 12.

Fatty acids vary also in the amount of hydrogen they contain. **Saturated** fatty acids contain more hydrogen than the **unsaturated.**

In each molecule of an unsaturated fatty acid, there is a double bond between two carbon atoms. The number of double bonds between carbon atoms determines the degree of unsaturation. A **mono-unsaturated** fatty acid has a single (mono-) double bond between carbon atoms, and a **polyunsaturated** fatty acid has two or more (poly-) double bonds.

Both the number of double bonds and the number of carbon atoms in a molecule of a fatty acid are of special importance: together they influence the nature of fatty acids by altering their melting points. This has very practical applications. Fatty acids with fewer carbon atoms tend to be liquid at room temperature. Those saturated fatty acids with more carbon atoms are solid at room temperature. The more-unsaturated fatty acids (those with less hydrogen) have lower melting points and tend to be liquid, whereas the saturated fatty acids (with more hydrogen) are solid at room temperature.

The naturally unsaturated (lower-hydrogen) fatty acids, such as those found in vegetable oils, can be "hydrogenated;" that is, the double carbon bond can be broken, and hydrogen can be added. This process converts liquid vegetable oils into solid fats, such as margarines and shortenings.

What Are Glycerides?

Glycerides are the major form of fat found in nature. They are made up of fatty acids and **glycerol**, which is a type of alcohol. A molecule of glycerol can be attached to one, two or three molecules of fatty acids. These can be mono-, di- or tri- glycerides. Most animal and vegetable fats are triglycerides.

The characteristics of a fat are determined by the kinds of fatty acids in its makeup. Liquid vegetable oils contain larger amounts of the unsaturated fatty acids, whereas the saturated fats, such as beef tallow, contain more saturated fatty acids. All fats, whether liquid or solid, are glycerides containing both saturated fatty acids. They differ only in the proportions of each.

What Are Phospholipids?

Phospholipids are abundant in nature and are found in such foods as egg yolk and liver. They are a group of complex fats containing glycerides (glycerol and fatty acids) and phosphorus and nitrogen compounds. Lecithin is a phospholipid found commonly in nature and in foods such as egg yolk, beef liver, meats, whole grains, legumes, milk and vegetables, and is also available as a commercial product. Phospholipids serve to emulsify the triglycerides in digestion and absorption (breaking them up into small particles) so the blood can carry them. This process is discussed in more detail in a following section.

Phospholipids are added in the commercial processing of certain foods because of their emulsifying property; examples are egg yolk in preparing mayonnaise, soya lecithin in chocolate candy and some commercial baked products.

What Is Cholesterol?

Cholesterol is an alcohol compound found in animal tissues. Similar compounds found in plants are quite different and are of no concern in the diet. Cholesterol is derived from a variety of animal foods and can also be manufactured by the body. It is abundant in eggs, organ meats (liver, kidney) and in nervous tissues such as brain. Cholesterol is an important part of nervous tissue and cell membranes. It is essential for the development of sex hormones and bile acids. The latter are important in the digestion and absorption of fats from the intestine.

Digestion and Absorption of Fats

Let us follow a fat through the digestive process. It will pass through the mouth and stomach virtually unchanged. In the intestine it is mixed with liver bile which emulsifies it, breaking it up into extremely small particles. The tiny fat particles are then attacked by lipase, an enzyme secreted from the pancreas. This enzyme breaks down the fat particles into free fatty acids and glycerol (the two components of glyceride). Certain fatty acids (those with fewer than 12 carbon atoms) are absorbed through the intestinal wall directly into the bloodstream and are carried to the liver. Other fatty acids and monoglycerides are absorbed into the intestinal cells of the intestinal wall where they are recombined into triglycerides. The triglycerides then combine with protein to form larger fat particles called **chylomicrons**, a form of **lipoprotein**. These enter the lymphatic system and eventually enter the bloodstream and are carried to body fat. In the adipose tissue they are recombined as a triglyceride for storage. Both in the bloodstream and in adipose tissue, they are available to other tissues as a source of energy.

Some fat in the diet is essential as a carrier of the fat-soluble vitamins and to insure their proper absorption. During the process of fat absorption, the fat-soluble vitamins are transported directly into the bloodstream from the intestine. A totally fat-free diet would likely not only be low in fat-soluble vitamins but would also lead to impaired absorption of these vitamins.

GLOSSARY OF TERMS RELATED TO FATS AND OILS

Adipose tissue (ADD-uh-pose)—Body fat.

Arteriosclerosis (ar-teer-eo-skluh-RO-sis)—Hardening of the arteries.

Atherosclerosis (ATH-uh-ro-skluh-RO-sis)—Condition where fatty deposits decrease the inside diameter of arteries and interfere with blood circulation.

Blood lipid profile (lip-ud)—Common clinical laboratory test to determine the level of special lipids (triglycerides and cholesterol) in blood.

Cardiovascular disease (CARD-eo-VASS-kyuh-ler)—Diseases related to the heart and the blood vessels.

Cholesterol (ko-LES-ter-awl)—Substance manufactured by the body which is also found in foods of animal origin.

Chylomicron (ki-lo-MY-cron)—Very low-density lipoprotein (high in lipid).

Emulsify (e-MULL-suh-fy)—To convert into an emulsion (small particles of fat dispersed in liquid).

Essential fatty acid—Polyunsaturated fatty acid which the human body requires but cannot manufacture.

Fat-soluble vitamins—Vitamins A, D, E, K.

Fatty acid—Basic unit (building block) of fat. Each fatty acid molecule consists of a string of carbon atoms to which are attached hydrogen and oxygen atoms in a specific pattern. There are three families of fatty acids: polyunsaturated, monounsaturated and saturated.

Glyceride (GLISS-uh-ride)—Chemical compound formed from glycerol and one or more fatty acids.

Glycerol (GLISS-uh-rawl)—A water-soluble alcohol capable of combining chemically with up to three molecules of fatty acid to form compounds known as glycerides and with a nitrogenous base and phosphorus to form phospholipids.

Lecithin (LESS-uh-thin)—A phospholipid. These naturally occurring glycerides containing phosphorus and nitrogen mix well with both fat and water. They are useful emulsifying agents.

Lipase (LIE-paze)—Fat-splitting enzyme in the blood, pancreatic secretion and tissues.

Lipid (LIP-ud)—Class of chemical compounds that contain fats, sterols and phospholipids. (The word scientists use when they talk about fat.)

Liproprotein (lip-o-PRO-tee-in)—Chemical form in which fat is transported in blood (composed of fat and protein).

Monoglyceride (mah-no)—Glycerol combined with one fatty acid. Monoglycerides are formed during the digestion of triglycerides in the intestinal tract and may also be produced commercially from fat. Monoglycerides are more soluble in water than triglycerides and, therefore, are frequently used as emulsifying agents to prevent the separation of fat and water mixtures.

Mono-unsaturated (mah-no-un-)—Fatty acid with space for one molecule of hydrogen.

Obesity (oh-BEE-sitee)—Excessive accumulation of body fat.

Phospholipid (FAHSS-fo-lip-ud)—Class of lipids containing nitrogen and phosphorus. They are important components of most plant and animal cells.

Polyunsaturated (polly-un-SATCH-uh-rated)—Fatty acid having space for two or molecules of hydrogen.

Saturated (SATCH-uh-rated)—A fatty acid with hydrogen at every available spot in the molecule.

Triglyceride (try-GLISS-uh-ride)—The chemical compound formed from glycerol and three fatty acids. All fats and oils are mixtures of triglycerides and very small amounts of other lipids.

Unsaturated—A fatty acid lacking some hydrogen.

NOTES

1. Alcohol contributes 7 calories per gram.
2. See Technical Discussion, beginning on page 142.
3. See suggestion in "Sources of Information."

Nutrition and Health

by H.J. Sanders

In the past 20 years, few subjects in the nutrition field have attracted as much public attention as cholesterol. Today, everything from margarine and vegetable oils to egg substitutes and meat analogs are advertised on the basis that they contain little or no cholesterol.

CHOLESTEROL AND CARDIOVASCULAR DISEASE

Cholesterol is believed to be a primary factor in the development of atherosclerosis, coronary heart disease, and stroke. As the leading cause of death in the U.S., heart attack and stroke togehter take about 840,000 lives a year.

The disorder underlying both heart attack and stroke is atherosclerosis, characterized by the buildup of deposits (plaques) on the inner surfaces of arteries. If a blood clot forms in such a constricted artery leading to the heart or brain and causes a complete stoppage of blood flow, a heart attack or stroke occurs almost instantly.

In atherosclerotic plaques, the lipid in highest concentration is cholesterol. Present in lower concentrations are two other types of lipids—phospholipids and triglycerides.

Scientists generally agree that elevated cholesterol levels in the blood, as well as high blood pressure and cigarette smoking, are associated in humans with an increased risk of heart attack. A long-term investigation by NIH's Framingham Heart Disease Epidemiology Study in Framingham, Mass., has shown that, among men aged 30 to 49, the incidence of coronary heart disease was five times greater if their cholesterol level was 260 mg per 100 ml of serum or more, compared to the men whose level was 200 mg per 100 ml of serum or less.

What has not been entirely proved say many scientists, is that a lowering of serum cholesterol levels in humans by the use of diet or drugs will reduce the incidence of coronary heart disease. However, such a reduced incidence seems likely on the basis of animal studies.

Some scientists, on the other hand, believe that research in humans already has demonstrated that a lowered cholesterol level does reduce the risk of coronary heart disease. Robert S. Lees, director of MIT's Arteriosclerosis Center, says that research reported in 1972 by Osmo Turpeinen and coworkers at the University of Helsinki has shown that people who reduce their cholesterol level by eating diets low in saturated fat and low in cholesterol have a noticeably decreased incidence of coronary heart disease.

Lees acknowledges that proving this is exceedingly difficult because large numbers of people must be studied over long periods of time. Useful data can be obtained only by a slow, laborious process, partly because only a small percentage of any group will die of coronary heart disease in any given year.

Cholesterol, a waxlike substance found in all body cells, is essential to normal body function. This compound, a steroid alcohol (sterol), is a precursor of adrenal and sex hormones. It also is a precursor of bile acids and vitamin D.

In the human body, cholesterol is synthesized primarily in the liver. The body also obtains it from food of aminal origin, such as eggs, dairy products, and meat. Generally, the more cholesterol a person eats, the less his body synthesizes.

Because lipids such as cholesterol are not soluble in water, they cannot be transported in the blood (an aqueous medium) unless complexed with water-soluble proteins. These complexes, which have a wide range of properties, are known as lipoproteins.

Lipoproteins generally are classified according to their density and origin. There are four broad categories: chylomicrons (density of less than 1.006 gram per ml and made in the intestine), very low-density lipoproteins (density of less than 1.006 and made mainly in the liver), low-density lipoproteins (1.006 to 1.063), and high-density lipoproteins (1.063 to 1.21).

The chylomicrons contain up to 99% by weight of lipids, and the very low-density lipoproteins (VLDL's) contain up to about 95% lipids. The low-density lipoproteins (LDL's) contain about 75% lipids, and the high-density lipoproteins (HDL's) only about 50%.

In research on cholesterol and its role in heart disease, the types of lipoproteins that have received the greatest attention in recent years have been the LDL's and HDL's. The reason is that they almost always contain a higher percentage of cholesterol than do the chylomicrons or the VLDL's.

HDL, THE GOOD CHOLESTEROL

One of the most fascinating discoveries in this field is that, contrary to what might be assumed, cholesterol in the form of HDL reduces (not increases) a person's risk of developing coronary heart disease. For this reason, HDL has come to be known as "good cholesterol." On the other hand, cholesterol in the form of LDL increases a person's risk of developing coronary heart disease and thus sometimes is referred to as "bad cholesterol."

Back in 1954, John W. Gofman and coworkers at the University of California, Berkeley, reported that atherosclerosis and coronary heart disease are associated with elevated levels of serum LDL's rather than with serum lipoproteins in general. They also reported that the level of serum LDL's was a better predictor of coronary heart disease risk than was the level of serum cholesterol.

Initially, the findings of Gofman and associates were not taken very seriously by many scientists studying coronary heart disease because they tended to think solely in terms of serum cholesterol levels rather than of whether the cholesterol was present as LDL's or HDL's. Now, scientists recognize that, even if the total cholesterol level is high, the risk of coronary heart disease may be only moderate if the level of LDL is low and that of HDL is high.

Low-density lipoproteins contain an unusually high proportion of cholesterol—40 to 45%. High-density lipoproteins contain only about 15 to 20% cholesterol.

LDL's are believed to promote coronary heart disease by first penetrating the coronary artery wall, where they are broken down enzymically to cholesterol, cholesterol ester, and protein. The cholesterol and cholesterol ester are then deposited in the artery wall, becoming major parts of the atherosclerotic plaque.

Robert W. Mahley, head of the comparative atherosclerosis and arterial metabolism section of the National Heart, Lung & Blood Institute, points out that patients who, because of hereditary factors, have high levels of LDL in their blood have a high incidence of coronary heart disease. Often they die from this disease in their teens.

How do HDL's reduce the risk of developing coronary heart disease? No one knows for sure—but there are some fairly compelling theories.

Daniel Steinberg and coworkers at the University of California, San Diego, have suggested that HDL competitively inhibits the uptake of LDL by cells by occupying the binding sites that otherwise might be occupied by LDL. Research by Yechezkiel and Olga Stein, a husband-and-wife team at Hadassah University Hospital in Jerusalem, also supports the view that HDL helps to block the attachment of LDL to the cells. The independent studies of Steinberg and the Steins also indicate that HDL may help to combat coronary heart disease by transporting cholesterol out of the cells.

John A. Glomset of the University of Washington was the first to propose that HDL promotes the removal of cholesterol from cells. He showed that the enzyme lecithin/cholesterol acyl transferase (LCAT) converts the cholesterol in HDL to cholesterol ester, which leaves the surface of the molecule and is transferred to the core of the HDL particle. The HDL then can pick up additional free cholesterol from the cells and carry it to the liver, where it is converted to bile acids. These acids pass into the intestine and are excreted.

According to Robert J. Nicolosi, a biochemist at the New England Regional Primate Research Center, HDL's ability to remove cholesterol from tissue, at least in vitro, may depend on the nature of the specific protein-phospholipid complexes present in the HDL. These complexes act as substrate for the LCAT enzyme.

Assuming that HDL helps to protect the body against coronary heart disease, what can be done to increase serum levels of this lipoprotein?

One way, for reasons not now known, is by exercise. Last year, G. Harley Hartung of Houston's Methodist Hospital reported that the group of marathon runners he studied had a decidedly higher average HDL level than did a group of sedentary men. He believes that the difference in HDL levels of the two groups was related to their degree of physical activity and was not significantly related to their diet.

Lees of MIT has shown that HDL levels also can be increased by losing weight. He recommends that a person's weight be held to within a few pounds of his or her so-scalled "ideal weight."

Christian Gulbrandsen and coworkers at NIH's Hawaii Heart Study have reported that HDL levels in the blood can be increased by drinking alcohol in moderation. The amount of alcohol used in their research project per person was equivalent to about three 12-oz bottles of beer a day.

Actually, not everyone agrees that raising HDL levels in the blood is an effective way to combat coronary heart disease. Mahley of the National Heart, Lung & Blood Institute declares, "It is premature to say that all HDL-cholesterol is beneficial. We really do not know enough about the different types of lipoproteins that, in general terms, are referred to as HDL. Contrary to what other investigators have implied, our research group finds that more than 90% of the HDL does not interact with the cell receptor sites and thus does not block the attachment of LDL. However, a minor subclass of HDL is capable of binding to the receptor. From these findings, we have concluded that HDL represents a mixed group of lipoproteins with at least two distinctly different metabolic roles."

A reduction of low-density lipoprotein levels is believed by many scientists to be desirable. This may be accomplished by eating a diet low in cholesterol and low in saturated fat. And some physicians recommend that overweight people go on reducing diets to achieve their recommended weight.

Food and Cancer

The relationship between food and cancer was the subject of the Sixth Annual Marabou Symposium in Stockholm, Sweden, on June 16–17, 1978. The following statement summarizing papers presented and discussions taking place during the symposium was prepared by Professor A. Stewart Truswell, University of Sydney, Sydney, Australia; Dr. Nils-Georg Asp, University of Lund, Lund, Sweden, Dr. W. Philip T. James, Dunn Clinical Nutrition Center, Cambridge, England; and Professor Brian MacMahon, Harvard University, Boston, Massachusetts, USA.

Of the potential sources of harm in foods the largest by far are, first, microbiological contamination and, next, nutritional imbalance. Risks from environmental contamination are about 1,000 times less and risks from pesticide residues and food additives can be estimated as about a further 100 times smaller again. Naturally occurring compounds in food are far more likely to cause toxicity than intentional food additives.

Food and nutrition have frequently and for many years been associated with cancer but our knowledge of the causes of cancer is incomplete. It is derived partly from epidemiological studies of the frequency of cancer of different organs in various populations and partly from animal experiments. Epidemiological studies are showing environmental factors which appear to predispose to cancer while animal studies help to elucidate mechanisms by which these environmental factors lead to the development of cancer (carcinogenesis). It should be emphasized that the different types of cancer have no single cause. Environmental factors are more important causes of most types of cancer than inheritance. In the environment, different dietary factors appear to be associated with cancer of the gastrointestinal tract (mouth, oesophagus, stomach, colon and rectum), of the liver and possibly the urinary bladder. There is also evidence for an indirect association between the level and type of nutrition and cancers of the breast and uterine endometrium. It is difficult to establish whether there is a threshold level for a carcinogen (cancer-producing stbstance) in the environment below which there is no risk. At low levels of an environmental hazard the spontaneous rate of cancer development and variations in individual susceptibility complicate the picture.

From *Nutrition Reviews,* *36* (10), 313–314, October, 1978. Reprinted by permission of the Nutrition Foundation.

Cancer of the breast shows geographical variations of incidence which suggest there is a nutritional component in the aetiology (causation). Animal experiments have shown that high fat diets predispose. The human epidemiological data are consistent but do not make clear which type of overnutrition is important. Girls who grow fast and start menstruating early have a slightly greater chance of developing breast cancer. In Japanese migrants the rate of breast cancer did not increase to the level in the USA until the second generation. The level of nutrition and/or dietary fat are thought to predispose to breast cancer by changes in the balance of hormones, e.g., production of different proportions of oestrogens. Non-nutritional factors are clearly important as well as the lower rate in women who have their first child at a young age.

Cancer of the large intestine is associated with the "western" diet. Its incidence is correlated epidemiologically to the total fat intake with Finland and a notable exception (high fat intake but intermediate incidence of large intestine cancer). Migrants have been found to acquire the incidence of the host community in a relatively short time and in the same generation. A possible hypothesis is that dietary fat increases production of bile acids. Degradation products of these could favor carcinogenesis. Dietary fibre may be protective but animal experiments give varying results and it is known that not all types of fibre have the same biological properties. There is some epidemiological evidence in international comparisons suggesting that beef consumption is correlated with cancer of the large intestine. It is claimed that frying or broiling could produce a carcinogenic product but this evidence is not firm enough to justify recommendations to the general public. Cancer of the rectum should be distinguished from the more common site in the colon. Evidence associating cancer of the rectum with beer consumption is inconsistent.

Cancer of the oesophagus varies more strikingly in different communities than that of any other part of the body. The highest rates in the world are seen in N. Iran (where the people eat a coarse wheat, little fruit or vegetables and follow the Moslem prohibition of alcohol) and in parts of E. and S. Africa (where there appears to be a relationship to home-brewed beers made from maize).

Cancer of the stomach has shown a downward trend in all the industrial countries. The highest rates are in Japan, Iceland and eastern Europe. Salt-cured and smoked foods could lead to this cancer by formation of nitrosamines by conversion in the stomach from nitrites. Epidemiological studies have shown a protective effect of vegetables and fruits, possibley because of the anti-oxidant action of vitamin C. Reduction of nitrate-cured and less bacterial amine production because of refrigeration, and longer availability of fruits and vegetables throughout the year might explain the decline in incidence of cancer of the stomach.

The participants agreed that there is a need for more and better retrospective and prospective measurements of food intake in human studies on cancer incidence. Weaknesses of earlier dietary methods were discussed; biochemical tests for independent validation of the dietary history should be sought. This symposium should help to lead to better and more relevant designs of food intake methods.

As to recommendations to the general public, avoidance of obesity, lower consumption of total fat and a larger intake of fibre are already part of the Swedish Diet and Exercise program. Conceivably this program could help reduce cancer of some organs. Mouldy food contaminated with fungal toxins such as aflatoxin can be carcinogenic, although this is less of a factor in countries with an efficient food industry. Other factors discussed need more research before thay can serve as a basis for dietary recommendations to the general public.

What's New in Weight Control?

Summary

A better understanding of the multifaceted etiology and types of obesity undoubtedly will suggest the appropriate approach for its control. While prevention offers the only foolproof answer, various means of treatment have been medically or self-prescribed for those with excess body fat. These means fall into the categories of dietary management, excerise, drug therapy, surgical procedures, and behavior modification. Their effectiveness and implications to overall health have been the subject of considerable interest and controversy in the medical, scientific and lay communities. Gaining recognition as the best available effective approach to weight reduction and maintenance is the three-pronged program consisiting of an appropriate dietary regimen, regular exercise, and behavior modification directed at the first two components.

Obesity can be considered justifiably as a national health problem. Estimates of its prevalence in the U.S. differ, however, depending on the source of data and the criteria used in its assessment. Prevalence figures have been provided by life insurance companies, national health surveys, prospective studies of the etiology of chronic diseases, and smaller clinical series reported by practitioners (1–3). The lack of differentiation between "overweight" and obesity likewise has contributed to the differences in estimates reported. Obesity is a condition wherein there is an excess of body fat when compared with some standard or range of acceptable degrees of fat for a particular population under study (1). Not synonymous with obesity, overweight denotes a body weight which exceeds some standard weight usually related to height, sex, and age (1). Thus, while it is fair to say that obese people usually are overweight, some overweight people such as professional athletes are not obese. For practical purposes, however, the two terms will be used interchangeably in this review.

Dieting or the attempt to lose weight by modifying food intake has become a national preoccupation because of the social, psychological, and economic rewards derived from having a trim figure. Unfortunately, most people tend to be more preoccupied by their appearance than by the ultimate health benefits of slimness (1,2,4,5).

From *Dairy Council Digest, 49* (2), 7–12, March-April 1978. Reprinted by permission of the National Dairy Council.

Such preoccupation has given rise to the revival or variations of some century-old weight-reducing dietary regimens as well as a multitude of different approaches to control obesity. This *Digest* will attempt to briefly discuss the effectiveness and potential hazards to health of some of these methods which are categorized under the following headings: (a) dietary management, (b) exercise, (c) drug treatment, (d) surgical treatment, and (e) behavior modification. Space limitation will not permit discussion of the less commonly employed methods such as jaw wiring (6,7), acupuncture (8), and hypnosis (1).

DIETARY MANAGEMENT

A rather large number of "diets"—techniques for modifying food intake which will achieve weight loss—has been listed in the scientific literature as well as in the popular press (9–12). These diets, ever-increasing in number, can be grouped according to the number of calories recommended and the components of which that caloric intake is to be comprised. Thus, there are starvation or fasting diets, one-emphasis diets, and any combination of low or high carbohydrate-protein-fat diets.

Fasting or starvation has been reported to be effective in the treatment of refractory obesity and to pose no serious metabolic disturbances when short in duration (13,14). Prolonged fasting, however, has some serious drawbacks, the loss of lean body mass being of primary significance. Barrett (15) noted among fasting patients an increase in serum bilirubin concentration, a widely used index of hepatic dysfunction. Other complications noted include anemia, hyperuricemia, postural hypotension, ketosis, and electrolyte disorders (2,14,16–18). Deaths during and after prolonged fasting, presumably as a result of cardiac complications, have been reported (2).

Even short-term fasting is contraindicated for patients within six months of an episode of cardiac failure because of the danger of inducing ventricular fibrillation and cardiac arrest (17). Oster (19) likewise reported severe complications such as reversible cerebral ischemia and cardiac arrhythmias in fasting individuals with clinical signs of atherosclerosis.

An insight into the permanence of weight loss effected by fasting can be gleaned from a 7.3 year follow-up period in 121 patients by Johnson and Drenick (20). They reported that while the reduced weight was maintained during the first 12 to 18 months, 50% of the patients regained their original weight within two to three years. Of the 121 patients only seven had maintained reduced weights over the entire follow-up period.

Supplemented fasting regimens to minimize the incidence and severity of the complications of fasting while achieving the desired weight loss have been described. Genuth and co-workers (21,22) described a regimen providing a mixture of casein and glucose supplying about 300 kcal/day as the first phase in a total program of long-term weight reduction for the grossly obese.

Another type of supplemented fasting is what is commonly termed the protein-sparing modified fast or PSMF (23–25). Supplying 400 to 600 kcal, it consists of 1.0 to 1.5 kg of protein per kilogram of ideal body weight daily, water, and some supplementary vitamins and minerals. It has produced rapid weight loss among diabetics and patients with Prader-Willi obesity under close medical supervision (24,26).

Recently, a consumer-oriented version of the protein-sparing diet, prescribing liquid protein solutions or powders to be reconstituted, was promoted. The protein supplements used are derived from whole protein sources or are hydrolysates of proteins, most of which are of low nutritional value, such as collagen or gelatin (27). While some of the products are fortified with various essential amino acids, vitamins, and minerals, many do not supply a complete spectrum of nutrients necessary for sustaining normal body functions during extended periods of usage (27).

Popularly advertised as the "last chance" diet (28), it has received notoriety after reports of death and a number of serious complications were associated with the extended use of the diet with and without medical supervision (29). The American Medical Association (AMA) identified the potential problems associated with this diet including nausea, vomiting, constipation, electroylte imbalance, dehydration, hyperuricemia, and postural hypotension (30). Roberts (31) also reported the development of acute or recurrent thrombophlebitis of the lower extremities, with or without pulmonary embolism, in patients within one to three weeks after starting the liquid protein diet. As a consequence of these reports, the Food and Drug Administration (27,29) has proposed mandatory warning labels and is exploring possible ways to ban these liquid "predigested" protein supplements.

Prolonged or modified fasting may be ill-advised since the patient does not learn good food habits and such a regimen may result also in a pattern of repeated food restriction—refeeding. The effects of such intermittent feedings observed in experimental animals include, among others, reduced caloric efficiency, stimulation of lipogenesis and glucose oxidation, and, most significantly, a relative excess of body fat or faster than normal growth rate (32,33). If these findings were extrapolated to man, they would suggest that periodic fasting (or crash dieting) is an unproductive approach to the long-term control of obesity. The individual whose weight has fluctuated numerous times is regarded as worse off than a patient with excessive but stable weight (34,35).

The *one-emphasis diets* are numerous and are based on the premise that the one food they feature can lead to weight loss (10). One of the most popular of these diets is the grapefruit or Mayo diet (no association with the Mayo Clinic). While this diet consists of other foods, it promotes grapefruit on the premise that it has an enzyme that breaks down fat faster. No food is known to have such a property (36).

The *low carbohydrate diet* is the recurring phenomenon of the last century. In the 1860s and 1870s it was the Banting Diet. In the 1950s and early 1960s it resurfaced as the Calories-Don't Count Diet, the Dupont Diet, the Air Force Diet, and the Drinking Man's Diet (37). More recently, it was disguised as the Doctor's Quick-Weight-Loss Diet (38) and as the Dr. Atkins' Diet Revolution. (39).

The low carbohydrate diets, however, differ in the amounts of protein and fat they allowed. For example, the Doctor's Quick-Weight-Loss Diet prescribed no fat other than that inherent in the protein foods allowed (38). The Dr. Atkins' Diet Revolution (39), on the other hand, advocated not only high levels of protein, but also high levels of fat in the diet. These diets, in particular, have received close scrutiny from the medical community because of the potential harmful effects that may occur from adherence to such ketogenic diets. The use of the Doctor's Quick-Weight-Loss Diet was questioned because its resultant hypercholesterolemia presents potential risks, particularly to patients with overt or subclinical coronary artery disease (41).

These and other concerns were raised by the Council on Foods and Nutrition, AMA, in their critique of the low-carbohydrate ketogenic weight reduction regimens with special attention to Dr. Atkins' Diet Revolution (37). The AMA concluded that weight loss resulting from these diets was due principally to the spontaneous consumption of fewer calories. Apparently, the obese individuals, in reducing their carbohydrate intake drastically, are unable to make up the ensuing deficit through an appreciable increase in protein and fat (37).

While protein is certainly an important dietary constituent, the great emphasis it receives in weight reducing diets because of its alleged higher specific dynamic action (SDA) or thermic effect is not supported by current scientific knowledge. Although when single nutrients are ingested under laboratory conditions, there are differences between the SDA of protein, carbohydrate, and fat (42), the SDA of mixed meals varies within narrow limits and is relatively insensitive to wide variations of protein content. The effects of very restrictive high protein diets have been described by Apfelbaum (43). Bradfield and Jourdan (44) found no advantage in selecting a high-protein diet in weight reduction among obese women.

On the other end of the spectrum are the low-protein diets which do not restrict carbohydrates. The most popular of these is the Doctors' Quick-Inches-Off Diet (45), basically a vegetarian diet.

Claims for success have been made for the different reducing diets but it is not as yet possible to account for the marked variability in weight loss that can occur in different people on different diets for several reasons (46). First, there are different constituents that contribute appreciably to weight loss over the short-term; these include water, fat, protein, and glycogen. In longer-term situations, deficits of minerals from both bone and soft tissues can contribute to weight loss. Second, the composition of the weight loss varies widely depending on the nature of the diet, the pre-existing nutritional state (morbidly or mildly obese) of the subject, as well as the short-term and longer-term adherence to a given weight reduction regimen (46).

Thus, the formulation of an ideal reducing diet regimen must be individualized by considering factors such as the degree of overweight of the patient, his age, his state of physical fitness, his normal level of physical activity, and the presence of associated illness (47).

For ambulatory adult patients, Van Itallie and Hashim (47) defined a calorie-restricted reference diet that could serve as a lower limit in food restriction. Such a diet would provide enough carbohydrates to reduce or largely prevent ketosis and to minimize wastage of protein and electrolytes. It would contain enough protein to replace wear and tear tissue losses and to maintain reasonable reserves. It provides all other essential nutrients in recommended amounts (47). In short, a calorie-restricted diet must provide fewer calories but adequate amounts of essential nutrients.

At the present time, there is conflicting evidence regarding the effect of the frequency of feeding on the incidence of obesity. Experimental data (48) as well as clinical evidence cited by Bray (1) negatively correlated frequency of feeding with the incidence of obesity, hypercholesterolemia, and abnormal glucose tolerance. Stern (9) cited studies wherein frequency of feeding did not appear to influence the amount of weight loss.

EXERCISE

The lack of regular exercise or physical activity may encourage the development of obesity in two ways: (a) in the absence of sufficient exercise, only a small fraction of generously consumed food calories is used up and the unused calories are incorporated into fat storage deposits, and (b) recent evidence shows that the normal internal mechanism which regulates appetite and satiety does not operate properly at low levels of physical exertion (48).

Traditionally, physical activity has been ignored or discredited in weight control because of two misconceptions (48). First, it has been believed that exercise plays an insignificant role in total body energy requirements and that increases in exertion will not appreciably increase the body's calorie requirements. Second, it has been believed that increases in exercise always result in increased appetite and, hence, increased food consumption. Stuart and Davis (49) and Bray (1) provided evidence contrary to the above concepts.

It is likewise important to recognize the metabolic and endocrine effects observed after physical training in order to understand risks which may be associated with this regimen (50,51). Björntorp (51) reported lethal arrhythmia following physical training in subjects with cardiovascular disease.

Because exercise may be contraindicated for certain individuals, Stuart (52) found it essential that every "exercise candidate" have a thorough physical examination prior to a program of exertion which should be followed by a supervised activity stress test in order to determine the appropriate starting and target intensities of the exercise program.

DRUG TREATMENT

Numerous drugs have been used in attempts to promote weight loss. They include drugs producing anorexia and nausea, drugs preventing gastrointestinal absorption, hormones increasing metabolism and lipolysis, tranquilizers, and diuretics (53). A comprehensive discussion of these agents—their chemistry, mechanism of action, metabolic and pharmacologic effects, clinical use and safety—is available (1) and thus will not be discussed in length in this review.

Only a few of the various drugs used in the treatment of obesity have been reported to be more effective than placebos (53). Thyroid hormone is reported to increase basal metabolism and energy output and theoretically promote lipolysis by potentiating the effect of epinephrine (53). It, however, may increase lean tissue losses to an unacceptable degree.

In selected cases, the amphetamines and related sympathomimetic amines have been found to be useful adjuncts to a calorie-restricted diet. Other anorexiants with actions differing from that of the amphetamines have been evaluated (1,54,55). However, it was emphasized that no one anorexiant consistently has been demonstrated to be substantially more effective than any other. While the weight loss is greater than that which can be achieved with caloric restriction without the aid of an anorexiant, the total amount lost remains modest.

Because they swell in the stomach, bulk fillers also have been used for the suppression of appetite (1). The effectiveness in diminishing appetite of one such agent, methylcellulose, has been questioned on the basis that it swells relatively slowly in the stomach, thus acting more as a laxative than as an anorexiant (1). There are reports, however, that treatments with bulk-producing tablets and diet are significantly more effective than diet alone in reducing the patient's feeling of hunger intensity and mean daily caloric intake. While significant weight losses accompanied these reductions in hunger intensity and caloric intake, it was stressed that the tablets can be useful only as a means to reduce hunger intensity and not weight itself (56).

Because of potential danger of psychological dependence, abuse or other undesirable side-effects, anorexiants and bulk fillers probably should be prescribed, if at all, only as short-term adjuncts (four to six weeks) in an overall program of weight reduction particularly for those who have difficulty adhering to a prescribed calorie-restricted diet (55).

Drugs are used not only to suppress appetite but also allegedly to break down fat. This is the rationale behind the Simeons regimen, which consists of daily intramuscular injections of 125 I.U. of human chorionic gonadotropin (HCG) six times a week until a total of 40 injections have been given, accompanied by a 500-calorie diet given in two daily meals (57).

This regimen was reported first in 1954 by Simeons (58) who claimed that although HCG alone does not reduce weight, it renders so-called "abnormal" fat deposits readily available, enabling the obese to adhere to and live comfortably on 500 calories per day for several days. Simeons' findings were substantiated by Lebon (59,60) and more recently by Asher and Harper (61). The results of the latter study were questioned and criticized by Hirsch and Van Itallie (62) on the basis of the experimental design and analysis of data although a rebuttal to this was subsequently made (63). Moreover, two clinical trials designed to retest the efficacy of HCG on weight reduction have indicated that this hormone is no more effective than the injection of a placebo (64,65).

The Departments of Drugs and of Food and Nutrition, AMA (57), in their review of the Simeons regimen from a pharmacologic, clinical, and nutritional standpoint, found no convincing scientific evidence that HCG has any pharmacologic effect in weight reduction or that it causes preferential mobilization of "abnormal" fat. The weight loss under this regimen was attributed solely to the semi-starvation required and the 500-calorie diet was regarded as unphysiological and unsafe especially under conditions where medical supervision is minimal. A review of the clinical literature regarding HCG by the Food and Drug Administration (66) provided similar conclusions.

SURGICAL TREATMENT

For morbidly obese individuals who are refractory to traditional approaches to weight control, certain surgical procedures have been regarded as effective alternatives (1). Currently the most widely performed procedure, jejunoileal bypass surgery, was first proposed 25 years ago for the treatment of obesity and has been the subject of a recent multidisciplinary conference (67). While weight loss following jejunoileostomy in animals was attributed originally to the resulting malabsorption of nutrients (68,69), current available data reveal that malabsorption alone cannot account for the magnitude of weight loss achieved (67,69–72).

Instead, the postoperative decrease in food intake was reported to account for much of the weight loss. This was considered a most significant finding because it implied that such operations effected weight loss by suppressing the appetite (70) as well as suggested a role for taste or other gastrointestinal factors in food intake regulation (71). Food intake may be restricted or altered voluntarily to reduce the frequency of diarrhea in the early postoperative period or to avoid intestinal distention (71).

While weight loss is the most consistent benefit to be derived from jejunoileal bypass, there also is improved psychosocial function (enhanced self-respect, improved chances for employment, feeling of new independence), reduced risk factors for cardiovascular disease (consistent lowering of serum cholesterol, decreased blood pressure, reduced hyperglycemia) among postoperative patients (1,73).

It is equally worth noting the complications following this surgical procedure (70,73,74). Mortality has resulted from the surgery itself or from postoperative complications such as liver failure, pulmonary embolism, cardiac failure, pancreatitis, and suicide. Gastrointestinal complications include intractable diarrhea, hemorrhage, and "bypass enteritis". Metabolic side effects result from severe loss of minerals associated with diarrhea as well as hypoproteinemia and anemia.

Appropriate postoperative treatments for some of the metabolic side effects have been described (74–78). For example, because of the incidence of hyperoxaluria and nephrolithiasis among postoperative patients, adequate nutritional management must include a relatively high intake of calcium to reduce oxalate absorption as well as reduced oxalate intake (74–76). Because protein malnutrition after bypass surgery contributes to hepatic dysfunction, postoperative amino acid supplementation has been recommended by Moxley et al (77). The intestinal malabsorption resulting from bypass surgery has been reported to affect bone status adversely and consequently the doses of vitamin D and calcium ordinarily given to these patients may be inadequate (78). The patient also needs replacement with certain vitamins, particularly vitamin B_{12}, as well as potassium supplements. As the intestines adapt and weight loss tapers off at the new equilibrium, the need for special therapeutic supplements may diminish (74).

Gradually assuming increasing importance in the management of morbidly obese individuals is the gastric bypass procedure (79). Because gastric bypass limits food intake but allows a more normal digestion and absorption, patients can lose fat without a great risk of malnutrition as is associated with intestinal bypass (80). Loss of lean body mass is minimal (15%) in direct contrast to that seen in jejunoileal bypass, where 50% of initial weight loss consists of lean tissue. Moreover, no hepatic or metabolic complications are observed with gastric bypass (79).

Bypass operations for obesity remain investigational. There is much need for an evaluation of its long-term effect on appetite, food intake, and maintenance of weight loss along with the assessment of its psychological, nutritional, medical, and economic hazards and benefits.

BEHAVIOR MODIFICATION

Previously utilized in psychiatry and psychology to treat numerous conditions, behavior modification techniques have been applied to the treatment of obesity during the last decade and appear to constitute one of the most promising avenues for weight control.

One of the basic assumptions in the behavioral treatment of obesity is that the connection between a stimulus in the environment and the consequent response of eating is learned. As such, it can be unlearned (49,81,82). Thus, given the observation that the obese person is triggered to eat more by environmental stimuli than by normal internal mechanisms regulating appetite and satiety, the intake and consequently body weight can be altered by changing patterns of these external cues (49,81).

Various behavior modification techniques have been described and can be grouped into self-control, reinforcement, stimulus control, and cognitive procedures (49,81,83,84). Self-control procedures (85) involve the patient's structuring those situations which influence eating (49), and reinforcing himself for behavior change (as well as weight change) (86). Reinforcement is crucial in behavior programs, and every attempt is made to provide rewards for positive behavior changes so that their likelihood of maintenance is maximized (49,81,82). The cognitive procedures (83,84,87) are used to provide a more positive atmosphere in the dieter's mind so that self-defeating thoughts do not hinder progress.

Behavior modification programs for weight reduction basically consist of several phases (81,83,84). The behavioral approach necessarily begins with a base line "diagnostic" period of a week or two during which no changes in behavior are attempted but rather an elaborate food intake diary is kept. In addition to amount and kind of food eaten, the patient records the intensity of hunger, type of mood, place of eating, companions, etc. The goal of this phase is to identify those classes of behavior that are maladaptive for a particular patient and then seek out these specific environmental determinants. Only then is an attempt made to institute appropriate behavioral changes.

The clinician and patient initiate these changes toward more adaptive behavior gradually through a process of step-by-step approximation known as "shaping". This treatment phase, lasting 12 to 16 weeks in most programs, emphasizes changing behavior rather than reducing caloric intake or losing pounds per se (83,86,88). The rationale is that weight loss will eventually follow after the determinants of overeating are dealt with.

Behavior treatment for obesity consists of a multifaceted treatment program (49,81,82,89) which appears to be the most effective form of treatment for mild to moderate obesity (81,82). However, when a combination of several different techniques is used, the question always arises as to which technique is most potent in producing weight loss (90).

The rationale for behavioral approach to the treatment of obesity appears very sound but the final justification will be in the end result—successful weight reduction with the maintenance of loss over time. The initial reports are encouraging. Stunkard (81) reviewed 30 different studies where the superiority of the behavioral approach was demonstrated over other methods of weight reduction and reported on a one-year follow-up in which the proportion of obese people who initially lost substantial weight remained the same. Behavior modification used in self-help groups also has shown some notable success (89).

Despite the progress achieved in this field, there are still methodological shortcomings that need to be addressed (81,82,91). Long-term follow-up studies are needed before reasonable conclusions can be drawn about the relative value of the behavioral approach to weight reduction.

MULTIDISCIPLINARY APPROACH

A common feature of the several treatment methods described seems to be the failure of any one of them to effect weight loss in all obese individuals, although each has had some major success in some individuals. Why or how this success is effected is at present poorly understood. It is hoped that through increased research efforts an understanding of the multifaceted etiology and types of obesity can provide a key to determining the success or failure of treatment.

At the present time, however, regardless of the etiology or classification of obesity, the rational approach to treatment should aim to effect a change in energy intake and/or expenditure in order to reverse the process. However, many of the treatment programs described usually demanded drastic changes in lifestyle that cannot be continued on a permanent basis.

Currently, the best available approach to weight reduction and maintenance seems to be a three-pronged program consisting of nutritionally sound dietary management, exercise, and behavior modification directed at the first two aspects (1,9). Stuart and Davis (49) described a comprehensive step-by-step program embodying this approach but cautioned that while this offers a realistic opportunity, it should not be considered a panacea for weight reduction. The only foolproof approach remains to be that appropriately conveyed in the popular cliche, "an ounce of prevention is worth a pound of cure". A multidisciplinary effort toward prevention involving among other things nutrition education and behavioral sciences must be launched to minimize or eliminate the occurrence of this hard-to-control malady.

REFERENCES

1. Bray, G.A. *The Obese Patient*. Vol. 9. Series of Major Problems in Internal Medicine. Philadelphia: W.B. Saunders Co., 1976.
2. National Institutes of Health. *Obesity in Perspective*. G.A. Bray, ed., Fogarty International Series on Preventive Medicine, Vol. II, Part 2, DHEW Publication No. (NIH) 75–708, 1975.
3. Van Itallie, T.B. Statement to the U.S. Senate Select Committee on Nutrition and Human Needs, Hearings on Diet Related to Killer Diseases, II—Obesity. Feb. 1–2, 1977.
4. Mann, G.V.N. Engl. J. Med. *291*:178, 1974.
5. Mann, G.V.N. Engl. J. Med. *291*:226, 1974.
6. Rodgers, S., R. Burnet, A. Goss, P. Phillips, R. Goldney, C. Kimber, D. Thomas, P. Harding, and P. Wise. Lancet *1*:1221, 1977.
7. Garrow, J.S. Proc. Nutr. Soc. *33*:29A, 1974.
8. Mok, M.S., L.N. Parker, S. Voina, and G.A. Bray. Am. J. Clin. Nutr. *29*:832, 1976.
9. Stern, J.S. In: *Current Concepts in Nutrition* 5:137, 1977.
10. Berland, T. *Diet '78*. Consumer Guide, 1978.
11. Goldbeck, N., and D. Goldbeck. *The Dieter's Companion*. New York: New American Library Inc., 1975.
12. Goldberg, L. *Goldberg's Diet Catalog*. New York: Collier Books, 1977.
13. Stunkard, A.J., and J. Rush. Ann. Intern. Med. *81*:526, 1974.
14. Lawlor, T., and D.G. Wells, Am. J. Clin. Nutr. *22*:1142, 1969.
15. Barrett, P.V.D. *JAMA 217*: 1349, 1971.
16. Vertes, V., S.M. Genuth, and I.M. Hazelton, JAMA *238*:2151, 1977.
17. Runcie, J., and T.E. Hilditch. Compr. Ther. *3*:29, Oct. 1977.
18. Spencer, H., I. Lewin, J. Samachson, and J. Laszlo. Am J. Med. 40:27, 1966.
19. Oster, P. Schweiz. Med. Wochescher *107*:1313, 1977 (Abstract In: JAMA *239*:654, 1978.
20. Johnson, D., and E.J. Drenick. Arch Intern. Med. *137*:1381, 1977.
21. Genuth, S.M., J.H. Castro, and V. Vertes. JAMA *230*:987, 1974.
23. Bistrian, B.R., J. Winterer, G.L. Blackburn, V. Young, and M. Sherman. J. Lab. Clin. Med. *89*:1030, 1977.
24. Bistrian, B.R., G.L. Blackburn, and J.P. Flatt. Diabetes *25*:494, 1976.
25. Bistrian, B.R., G.L. Blackburn, and J.B. Stanbury. N. Engl. J. Med. *296*:774, 1977.

Acknowledgments: The National Dairy Council assumes the responsibility for writing and editing this publication. However, we would like to acknowledge the help and suggestions of the following reviewers in its preparation: K.D. Brownell, Ph.D., Assistant Professor of Psychiatry and A.J. Strunkard, M.D., Professor of Psychiatry, University of Pennsylvania, Philadelphia, Pennsylvania, and T.B. Van Itallie, M.D., Professor of Medicine, Columbia University. College of Physicians and Surgeons, St. Luke's Hospital Center, New York, New York.

26. Lindner, P.G., and G. L. Blackburn. Obesity/Bariatric Med. *5*:198, 1976.
27. Food and Drug Administration. Federal Register *42*:61285, 1977.
28. Linn, R., and S.L. Stuart. *The Last Chance Diet.* New York: Bantam Books, Inc., 1976.
29. Food and Drug Administration Talk Paper. Nov. 9, Dec. 1, Dec. 7, 1977.
30. Anonymous. American Medical News, May 23, 1977.
31. Roberts, H.J. N. Engl. J. Med. *298*:165, 1978.
32. Goldman, J.K. Nutr. Metabol. *14*:325, 1972.
33. Szepesi, B., and M.G. Epstein. Am. J. Clin. Nutr. *30*:1692, 1977.
34. U.S. Public Health Service. *Obesity and Health.* Department of Health, Education, and Welfare, Washington, D.C., 1966.
35. Paulsen, B.K., and W.T. McReynolds. Baroda J. Nutr. *3*:156, 1976.
36. White, P.L. Today's Health *49*:59, Sept. 1971.
37. Council on Foods and Nutrition, American Medical Association. JAMA *224*:1415, 1973.
38. Stillman, I.M., and S.S. Baker. *Doctor's Quick Weight Loss Diet.* Englewood Cliffs, New Jersey: Prentice-Hall, Inc., 1967.
39. Atkins, R.C. *Dr. Atkins' Diet Revolution.* New York: David McKay, 1972.
40. Chlouverakis, C.S. Obesity/Bariatric Med. *4*:98, 1975.
41. Rickman, F., N. Mitchell, J. Dingman, and J.E. Dalen. JAMA *228*:54, 1974.
42. Mayer, J. *Human Nutrition: Its Physiological, Medical and Social Aspects.* Springfield, Ill.: C.C. Thomas, 1972, p. 18.
43. Apfelbaum, M. Clin. Endocrinol. Metabol. *5*:417, 1976.
44. Bradfield, R.B., and M.H. Jourdan. Lancet *2*:640, 1973.
45. Stillman, I.M., and S.S. Baker. *The Doctor's Quick Inches-Off Diet.* Englewood Cliffs, New Jersey: Prentice-Hall, Inc., 1969.
46. Van Itallie, T.B., and M.U. Yang. N. Engl. J. Med. *297*:1158, 1977.
47. Van Itallie, T.B., and S.A. Hashim. Mod. Med. p. 89, Nov. 30, 1970.
48. National Institutes of Health. *Facts About Obesity.* Washington, D.C., 1976.
49. Stuart, R.B., and B. Davis. *Slim Chance in a Fat World.* Champaign, Ill.: Research Press Co., 1972.
50. Goodman, C., and M. Kenrich. Obesity/Bariatric Med. *4*:12, 1975.
51. Björntorp, P. Clin. Endocrinol. Metabol. *5*:431, 1976.
52. Stuart, R.B. Obesity/Bariatric Med. *4*:16, 1975.
53. Gershberg, H. Posgrad. Med. *51*:135, 1972.
54. Wallace, A.G. Med. J. Aust. *1*:343, 1976.
55. Dykes, M.H. JAMA *230*:270–272, 1974.
56. Marquette, C.J., Jr. Obesity/Bariatric Med. *5*:84, May-June 1976.
57. Department of Drugs and Department of Foods and Nutrition, American Medical Association, JAMA *230*:693, 1974.
58. Simeons, A.T.W. Lancet *2*:946, 1954.
59. Lebon, P. Lancet *1*:268, 1961.
60. Lebon, P.J. Am. Geriatr. Soc. *14*:116, 1966.
61. Asher, W.L., and H.W. Harper. Am. J. Clin. Nutr. *26*:211, 1973.
62. Hirsch, J., and T.B. Van Itallie. Am J. Clin. Nutr. *26*:1039, 1973.
63. Asher, W.L., and H.W. Harper. Am. J. Clin. Nutr. *27*:450, 1974.
64. Stein, M.R., E.R. Julis, C.C. Peck, W. Hinshaw, J.E. Sawicki, and J.J. Deller. Am. J. Clin. Nutr. *29*:940, 1976.
65. Young, B.L., R.J. Fuchs, and M.J. Waltjen. JAMA *236*:2495, 1976.
66. Food and Drug Administration. Federal Register *39*:42397, Dec. 5, 1974.

67. Symposium on Jejunoileostomy for Obesity. Am. J. Clin. Nutr. *30*:1–129, 1977.
68. Condon, S.C., N.J. Janes, L. Wise, and D.H. Alpers. Gastroenterology *74*:34, 1978.
69. Mills, M.J. and A.J. Stunkard. Am. J. Psychiatry *133*:527, 1976.
70. Benfield, J.R., F.L. Greenway, G.A. Bray, R.E. Barry, J. Lechago, I. Mena, and H. Schedewie. Surg. Gynecol. Obstet. *143*:401, 1976.
71. Bray, G.A., R.E. Barry, J.R. Benfield, P. Castelnuovo-Tedesco, and J. Rodin. Am. J. Clin. Nutr. *29*:779, 1976.
72. B. Zachary, W.T. Dahms, R.L. Atkinson, and T.H. Oddie. Bray, G.A., J. Am. Diet. Assoc. *72*:24, 1978.
73. Bray, G.A., A.I. Mendeloff, F.I. Iber, H.P. Roth, and W.W. Faloon. Am. Fam. Physician *15*:111, March 1977.
74. Bray, G.A., R.E. Barry, J.R. Benfield, P. Castelnuovo-Tedesco, E.J. Drenick, and E. Passaro. Ann. Intern. Med. *85*:97, July 1976.
75. Fisler, J.S., G. McGhee, Jr., and E.J. Drenick. Fed. Proc. *37*:593, 1978.
76. O'Leary, J.P., and E.R. Woodward. Abstract Presented at Second International Congress on Obesity, Washington, D.C., Oct. 23–26, 1977.
77. Moxley, R.T., T. Pozefsky, and D.H. Lockwood. N. Engl. J. Med. *290*:921, 1974.
78. Frame, B., M.J. Miller, and A.M. Parfitt. Abstract Presented at Second International Congress on Obesity. Washington, D.C., Oct. 23–26, 1977.
79. Maine, B.S., G.L. Blackburn, P. Reinhold, B.R. Bistrian, and C. Maletskos. Abstract at Second International Congress on Obesity, Washington, D.C., Oct. 23–26, 1977.
80. Questions and Answers. JAMA *223*:1281, 1973.
81. Stunkard, A.J. Psychosom. Med. *37*:195, 1975.
82. Stunkard, A.J., and M.J. Mahoney. In: H. Leitenberg (Ed.). *The Handbook of Behavior Modification.* Englewood Cliffs, N.J.: Prentice Hall, 1976.
83. Mahoney, M.J., and K. Mahoney. *Permanent Weight Control: The Total Solution to the Dieter's Dilemma.* New York: Norton, 1970.
84. Brownell, K.D., and A.J. Stunkard. Am. J. Dis. Child. *132*:403, 1978.
85. Thoresen, C.E., and M.J. Mahoney. *Behavioral Self-Control.* New York: Holt, Rinehart, and Winston, 1974.
86. Mahoney, M.J. Behav. Ther. *5*:48, 1974.
87. Mahoney, M.J. *Cognition & Behavior Modification.* Cambridge: Ballinger, 1975.
88. Leon, G.R. Am.J. Clin. Nutr. *30*:785, 1977.
89. Levitz, L.S. and A.J. Stunkard. Am. J. Psychiatry *131*:423, 1974.
90. Romanczyk, R.G. Behav. Ther. *5*:531, 1974.
91. O'Leary, K.D., and G.T. Wilson. *Behavior Therapy: Application and Outcome.* Englewood Cliffs, N.J.: Prentice Hall, 1975.

7

Population

This book is principally aimed at food—its quality, safety and availability. Yet it is obvious that food availability and population cannot be treated as separate entities. They have to be considered together since a population growth rate which outstrips food supply will soon lead to disaster. This may seem like a paradox since obviously if food is not available, the people would not be there. What does happen is that in time of good harvests, the population may increase only to suffer famine when crops are less abundant.

The population growth rate is shown in Table 1. It is obvious that this rate of growth cannot be sustained so the question becomes not, if it will change, but how it will change. A simplistic version of the possibilities are presented in Fig. 7.1, 7.2, and 7.3. In Fig. 7.1, the crude birth rate and crude death rate are plotted for a typical developed country. Excluding population movement between countries, the population growth is the difference between the two curves. Since the two curves roughly parallel each other, the population growth is slow and relatively stable. Fig. 7.2 shows the same data for a typical undeveloped country. The data for the earlier years are relatively similar, but the crude death rate started downward about 1925. This was due in part to the public health efforts of the League of Nations and later to the United Nations. Both were very proud, and rightly so, of their efforts in death control, but birth control was a forbidden word. Birth control efforts as a public health concern are relatively new around the world. Consequently, this crude birth rate remained high and resulted in the "population bomb." The question today is whether the crude birth rate will come down sufficiently rapidly to stabilize the population at the low death rate. It is more likely that the scenario in Fig. 7.3 will prevail but hopefully to a lesser extent. Population growth may outstrip resources to the point where the death rate rises precipitously. This situation is morally economically and politically unacceptable, so it is to be hoped that mankind will be capable of creating the scenario in Fig. 7.2 or something close to it.

The first paper in this chapter is a realistic description of the population situation as it exists today. The second paper presents a pessimistic view of mass utilization of resources as applied to population growth. The third paper presents a more optimistic view. The fourth paper entitled "Populandia" presents a delightful way of dramatizing population growth.

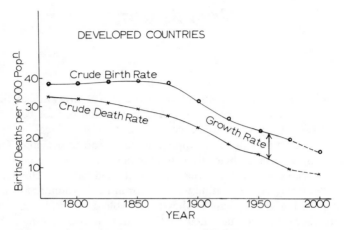

Figure 7.1. Population growth rate as shown by the difference between the crude birth rate and the crude death rate for a developed country.

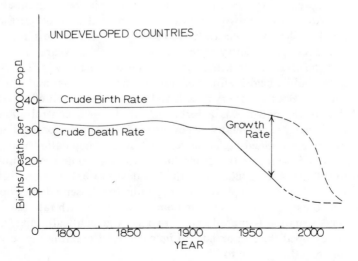

Figure 7.2. Population growth rate for a developing country in which the crude birth rate decreased rapidly.

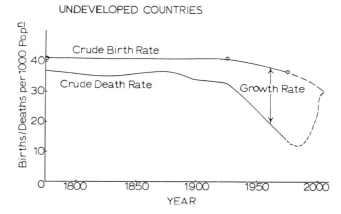

Figure 7.3. Population growth rate for a developing country in which the crude death rate increased.

TABLE 7.1. World Population Growth Rate

Year	Population (billions)	Time to Reach Population at Left (years)
1830	1	2 million
1930	2	100
1960	3	30
1975	4	15
1988	5	13 ?
1998	6	10 ?

Today's Children—Tomorrow's Parents

by Marshall Green and Robert A. Fearey

It took from mankind's earliest beginnings over a million years ago to the early 1800's for the world to reach a population of 1 billion.

Succeeding decades saw a substantial decline in death rates as increasing agricultural and industrial productivity raised living standards, as public sanitation improved, as scientific medicine developed and became increasingly available (notably smallpox vaccination), and as better communications and transportation permitted more effective action against famine. The world reached its second billion in 100 years—by 1930.

With accelerated advances in medicine, including the discovery and widespread use of antibiotics, with malaria control programs in effect in many areas of the world, and with further improvements in the production and distribution of food, the third billion was reached in 1960—30 years.

The fourth billion was added in 15 years, by 1975. It had taken only 45 years for world population to double, from 2 billion to 4 billion.

The rate of world population growth is believed to have peaked at about 2% around 1970, declining to about 1.8–1.9% by 1977. At this rate world resources and national economies are called upon to support nearly 80 million additional persons every year. Barring widespread famine, nuclear holocaust, or other disaster, world population is expected to number about 6 billion by the year 2000.

The level at which mankind's total number ultimately will peak appears to lie between 8 and 11 billion, depending on the determination and skill with which the world addresses the problem. With the ecosystems of the world already heavily burdened at 4 billion, there is urgent need for nations, especially those with high population growth rates, to deal with this problem more effectively.

How will mankind's growing numbers be distributed in the year 2000?

The share of people in developing countries, the least able to support larger populations, will continue to rise in the remainder of this century— from 66% in 1950 to nearly 80% in 2000, according to the U.N.

From *Agenda,* 2 (1) January–February 1979, 1–5. Agency for International Development, Washington, DC.

Ambassador Marshall Green, Department of State's Coordinator of Population Affairs, and Robert A. Fearey, Special Assistant to Ambassador Green. Excerpted from "World Population: The Silent Explosion—Part I," Department of State Bulletin, October, 1978.

Developed countries have many more people of labor-force age (15–64) than they have children less than 15 years old. In developing countries the age-sex pyramid is much broader at the base, and the proportion of dependent children (less than 15 years old) usually runs between 40% and 45% of the total population, compared with 25% in the developed countries (1975 estimate). Put another way, there is only about one adult of working age for each child under 15 in the developing world compared with nearly three adults of working age per child under 15 in the developed countries.

There are three major disadvantages to the heavily youth-oriented age distribution of most developing countries.

The large number of dependent children relative to the size of the labor force increases the burden of child dependency, promotes spending for immediate consumption, restricts private and public saving, and inhibits investment.

When the excessive number of children reach working age, they swamp the rural and urban labor markets. Large numbers of unemployed and underemployed are both economically wasteful and a potential source of social and political instability.

The number of young men and women entering the years of fertility is much larger—perhaps by three times—than the number of older people growing out of the age of fertility. This is a key factor underlying the high rate of population growth in the developing countries and is certain to accentuate overpopulation problems in the decades ahead.

Even if it were possible to attain in the next few decades an average level of fertility worldwide which would merely replace the parental generation, population would continue to grow for some 50–70 years thereafter. The size of the eventually stabilized (nongrowing) population would be far larger than at the time fertility dropped to replacement level.

The projections are not intended to predict the actual course of world population growth but only to illustrate the enormous potential for growth built into the current youthful age structure of much of the world's population

It is conceivable that at some future point average family size in particular countries or regions, or in the world as a whole, may be less than two children (i.e., that fertility may stabilize at a level below replacement of the parental generation). This would, of course, speed up the cessation of growth and bring stabilization at a small absolute size. A sustained fertility level below replacement would eventually lead to a decline in the absolute size of a population. This is not an objective of any government's current population policy, but this situation may change.

Mexico illustrates the awesome potential for population growth in a developing country.

In 1970 Mexicans numbered 51 million. Of this number, 46% were under 15 years of age and 65% were under 25 years. Under assumptions of linear fertility decline, leveling off at replacement level, Mexico's population would reach the following levels.

If replacement-level fertility is reached by 2000, the population will stop growing at about 174 million, or 3.4 times its 1970 size.

If replacement-level fertility is reached by 2020, the population will stop growing at about 269 million, or 5.3 times its 1970 size.

These figures should be modified by net emigration of undetermined magnitude, a large proportion to the United States.

Mexico's demographic situation is typical of dozens of developing countries where, even under optimistic assumptions of fertility decline, the momentum of growth is bound to double or triple present population levels.

In 1972 the Mexican Government initiated a family planning program. By the end of 1977, the birth rate was believed to have declined to below 40 per 1,000 population. President Lopez Portillo has recently indicated a national goal of reducing the rate of growth to 2.5% by the end of his term in office in 1982 and to 1% by the year 2000.

One way to grasp the implications of a particular rate of population growth is to consider how long it will take a population to double at that growth rate.

When a sum of money grows at compound interest, the interest rate is applied to both the original principal and to the proceeds of past interest payments, making total growth significantly faster than growth at simple interest. Thus, $1 at 1% simple interest takes 100 years to double, while $1 at 1% compound interest will double in 69 years.

In the same way, when population grows both the original number of people and the numbers accruing from past growth increase. Thus a population growing at 1% per year will take not 100 years but 69 years to double. A population growing at 2% per year will double in only 35 years.

The concept of a population "explosion," with the developing countries' populations heading sharply upward, derives from the combination of an unprecedentedly rapid drop in death rates, and the compound, or geometric, arithmetic of the resulting population growth.

Before the onset of the Industrial Revolution in the late 18th century. European mortality and fertility rates were both high. By the middle of the 1930's, death rates and birth rates throughout the West had plummeted. Demographers have sought ever since to clarify the sequence of this transition from high to low vital rates and the means by which it was accomplished.

One of the resulting theories of demographic evolution, known as the demographic transition theory, postulates that economic development brings about a fall in mortality, followed—after some time—by a fall in fertility.

Annual Growth Rate (%)	Years to Double Population
1.0	69
1.5	46
2.0	35
2.5	28
3.0	23
3.5	20
4.0	17

	Annual Av. Growth Rate (%)			Share of Population(%)		
	1950—55*	1970—75**	1995—00**	1950*	1970*	2000**
World total	1.7	1.9	1.6	100.0	100.0	100.0
Developed regions	1.3	0.9	0.6	34.3	30.0	21.7
Developing regions	1.9	2.3	1.9	65.7	70.0	78.3
Northern America	1.8	0.9	0.7	6.6	6.3	4.7
Europe	0.8	0.6	0.5	15.7	12.7	8.6
U.S.S.R.	1.7	1.0	0.7	7.2	6.7	5.0
Africa	2.1	2.6	2.8	8.7	9.7	13.0
Latin America	2.7	2.7	2.4	6.6	7.8	9.9
China	1.6	1.7	1.0	22.3	21.4	18.4
India	1.7	2.4	1.8	14.1	15.0	16.9
Other Asia	1.9	2.4	2.0	18.3	19.8	22.9
Oceania	2.25	2.0	1.45	0.5	0.5	0.5

*Estimated
**Projected

During the period of transition from high to low death and birth rates, the pace of population growth accelerates markedly.

The initial state of high population growth potential evolves from a backdrop of high death and high birth rates. The former reflects the harsh struggle for existence and the latter the need to compensate for high mortality. During this stage, death rates begin to fall under the influence of modernization, including rising levels of living and new controls over disease. Birth rates remain high, causing a rise in the rate of population expansion.

During the subsequent transitional stage, the rate of growth of the populations is still relatively high, but a decline in birth rates becomes well established. The new ideal of the small family arises typically in urban, industrial settings.

The stage of incipient decline is reached when mortality is low and fertility levels hover around replacement level. A stabilization of fertility below replacement level would, of course, lead in the absence of net immigration, to an eventual decline in the absolute size of a country's population.

The demographic transition theory, particularly its concepts of more or less automatic decline in fertility subsequent to mortality reduction and economic development as the motive power for both declines, has shaped much of the thinking about population problems in today's developing countries. It

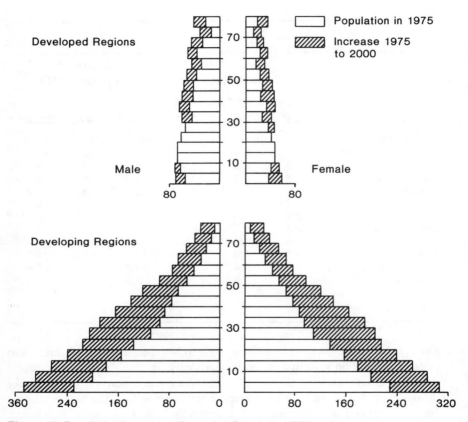

Figure 1. Population by age and sex for the years 1975 and 2000. The developed regions had a population of 1.1 billion in 1975 and the estimates for 2000 is 1.3 billion. The developing regions had a population of 3.0 billion in 1975 and the estimate is 5.0 billion in 2000. (Source U.S. Bureau of the Census. The data projected for the year 2000 represent the Bureau's medium variant.)

has often served as a basis of opposition to government policies and programs aimed at reducing average family size on the premise that economic development will bring a reduction in fertility as a natural consequence of rising levels of living.

The theory's supporters further contend that fertility will not decline in the absence of such prerequisites as rising levels of living and literacy. Family planning services by themselves, it is held, are largely unavailing. "Development is the best contraceptive" was widely proclaimed by Third World government delegations to the 1974 World Population Conference.

The relevance of the classical demographic transition theory for today's LDC's is limited by differences in the population trends of present-day LDC's and those of European countries at comparable periods of their economic development.

The pace of decline from traditionally high mortality levels has been far steeper in the currently developing countries than it was in Europe. Average life expectancy in the West, for example, is estimated to have risen from 41 years in 1840 to 50.5 years in 1900—about 10 years in six decades. The average life expectancy for LDC's as a group has increased from 42 to 51 years in 15 years (between 1955 and 1970). The rapid decline in LDC mortality has been attributed primarily to technological advances in the prevention and control of disease, employed independently of the socioeconomic setting. Marked improvements in the availabiltiy of food also played an important role in sharply reducing death rates.

Birth rates at the beginning of the developing countries' deomographic transition were significantly higher than in preindustrial Europe, due mainly to earlier and more universal marriage. The average birth rate for the LDC's has been estimated at 42.1 per 1,000 population between 1950 and 1955; birth rates in 90 LDC's exceeded this average. By contrast, the birth rate in Western Europe on the eve of the industrial Revolution is estimated at 30–35 per 1,000.

Steeply reduced death rates and generally high birth rates have produced natural growth rates in LDC's up to 3.5% a year or higher, two or three times as high as those experienced during Europe's period of most rapid population growth. At the peak of Costa Rica's fertility (1959–61), for example, the country's natural increase reached 3.8% a year; the rate exceeded 3.5% for more than a decade. In Denmark, by contrast, the rate of natural increase never exceeded 1.5%.

The totally unprecedented disequilibrium between birth and death rates in the developing countries since the end of World War II is the reason for the massive burgeoning of world population.

Reexamination of Europe's historical demographic trends led to the conclusion that the following conditions are necessary for a major fall in marital fertility.

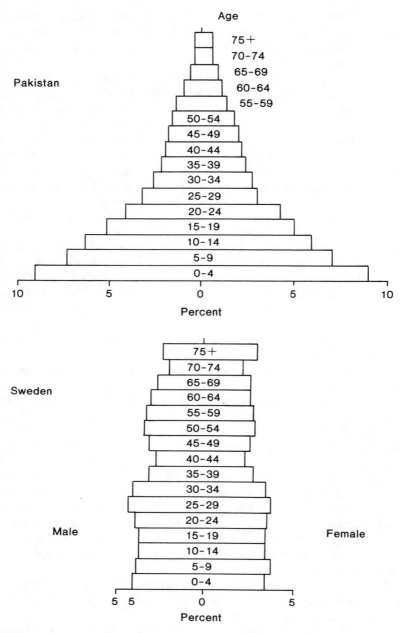

Figure 2. Proportion of population in each age group for Pakistan and Sweden. In a developing country, such as Pakistan, the burden of child dependency weighs heavily. In a developed country such as Sweden, the burden of retirement-age dependence is heavier.

Fertility must be within the calculus of conscious choice. Potential parents must consider it acceptable behavior to balance the advantages and disadvantages of having another child.

Perceived social and economic circumstances must make reduced fertility seem advantageous to individual couples.

Effective techniques of fertility reduction must be known and available, with sufficient communication between spouses and sustained will in both to use them successfully.

Neither the classical demographic transition theory nor its subsequent refinements indicate exactly what combination of social, economic, and political conditions give rise to the "calculus of conscious choice," to the "interest in fertility reduction techniques," or to the "sustained will" or motivation to practice family planning.

The retarding effect of rapid population growth on improvement of the living conditions of the average family in most developing countries renders it highly important for those countries to accelerate in every practicable way the transition from high to low death and birth rates. Effectively organized family planning programs not only provide birth control information and clinical services but also speed up the diffusion of a basic prerequisite for the use of these services, namely making the notion of planned parenthood acceptable.

Birth rate reductions in present day developing countries are often closely correlated with economic and social progress (Singapore, Taiwan, Costa Rica, Hong Kong, South Korea, etc.). Significant declines in birth rates have also taken place, however, in relatively backward economic settings but under conditions of all-out mobilization of political, bureaucratic, and community resources (including womanpower) behind family planning (China and Indonesia).

Since the mid 1960's, some 30 LDC's, containing over two-thirds of the total LDC population, appear to have reduced their birth rates by 10% or more.

Delayed marriages exercise an important role in the reduction of birth rates in many LDC's, particularly in the initial phase of decline. Rising age at marriage is a product of socioeconomic development that provides women with alternatives to an early marriage and motherhood and/or raises a couple's marital requirements for marriage and delays the union until these requirements are satisfied, sometimes with the help of the woman's newly acquired earning power.

Large-scale temporary or permanent migration has also helped to depress the birth rate in a number of LDC's by reducing the proportion of the population in childbearing ages, separating families, delaying marriages, and exposing migrants to cultural values of the receiving (usually developed) countries.

The major cause of the decline in LDC birth rates to date, however, has been reduction in marital fertility, particularly among women over 30 years of age. This decline relates—in various degrees—to a fairly steady growth in the proportion of women of childbearing ages who use modern contraceptive methods. Such use has been significantly accelerated in many LDC's by public provision of family planning information, education, and contraceptive services.

Observed reductions in some LDC birth rates may signal the beginnings of a sustained fertility decline for a large proportion of the LDC population. But this is not assured. The pace of future fertility declines is still unpredictable. The birth rate in Mauritius has risen since 1973; an upward trend in fertility has been observed in Jamaica and Trinidad and Tobago. Nevertheless, there is basis for cautious optimism that fertility will continue to decline in a broad range of LDC's. Unfortunately, this favorable development must be viewed in a context of massively increasing world population totals.

THE HUMAN MISERY, RESOURCE DEPLETION AND FOOD SHORTAGES IN THE THIRD WORLD CAUSED BY POPULATION PRESSURES HAVE A DIRECT IMPACT ON THE DAILY LIVES OF AMERICANS*

There are people today who say that the population time bomb has been "defused." Some recent reports speak optimistically about economic progress in the developing countries and the increased well-being accruing to these people.

The net result of these reports may lead many Americans to believe that solutions to world population problems are on the horizon. This is implicit in a recent editorial in the *Wall Street Journal* which concludes: ". . . It is not pleasant to think that crisis-mongering has become a necessary adjunct to the making of public policy. We would prefer to think that less fear and more rationality would serve better, and there might be fewer vested interests to support after the 'crisis' has been downgraded to a mere problem."

What is implied in this comment, I think, is very unfortunate. If what has been described as a crisis has become just a problem, it is quite a problem.

The World Bank concludes that even with recent encouraging economic trends in the developing world, 600 million people would live in abject poverty by the year 2000. Abject poverty means that they will be hungry, sick, ill-clothed, illiterate, unemployed and without hope. I do not wish to be the one who tells these millions that they have a problem and not a crisis. I seriously

*Excerpts from a speech by John J. Gilligan, Administrator, Agency for International Development at the October, 1978 meeting of the Planned Parenthood Federation of America.

question whether, in our interdependent world, millions of people can live in abject poverty, poverty, and near poverty, without affecting all our lives.

Some recent studies have challenged previous doomsday population projections. But the real issue is not doomsday versus paradise. The real issue is how well the world copes with population growth within these two extremes. The earth's resources are already strained by the present population. Whether that population grows by 2 billion or 3 billion or 4 billion in the next 40 years will have enormous consequences for those additional people and for those who come after them. Just what those figures will be depends upon the seriousness and urgency with which this problem is viewed and what we do about it now.

I would like to describe the extent and ramifications of the population issue and let you decide for yourselves whether it is a problem or a crisis.

To speak of the menace of the population explosion is not to evoke some nightmare world in which people are standing on each other's shoulders because of lack of living space. Rather it is to recognize the significance of statistical reports coming from every continent—reports which detail ecological devastation, the depletion of natural resources, inflation, the avalanche of urbanization, and resultant unemployment, political tensions, and human misery on a scale that defies description.

Today, over 70% of the human race lives in the less-developed countries of the world. By the year 2000 these same countries will contain over 80% of all the people on earth. The total world community today is 4.2 billion—twice as many people as were alive when I was born. By the turn of the century that number will have increased by another 40 to 50%. In other words, if I live to see the year 2000—and I plan to—the population of the world will have tripled in my lifetime.

The demographic predictions of the World Bank and other institutions suggest that Africa, within two decades, must somehow accommodate an additional 390 million people. Latin America must somehow absorb an additional 278 million. And the continent of Asia—already teeming with millions of poverty-stricken people—will have to find room for another billion and a quarter people.

These dry statistics cannot begin to suggest the human misery and seeds of economic and political turmoil that such population increases portend.

The misery will be most evident in the less developed countries where almost half a billion people already exist on diets so seriously deficient as to cause extensive and permanent mental and physical damage.

An estimated 15 million children die each year of malnutrition and related diseases. James Grant, President of the Overseas Development Council, put it this way: "That is the statistical equivalent of detonating a Hiroshima-type bomb every three days among the children of the world."

In many regions of the earth, small farms have been divided and sub-divided, generation after generation, until they are no longer able to provide subsistence to those who till the land. In the crowded cities of the Third World children are abandoned on the streets because their parents can no longer care for them. It is estimated that in Venezuela—one of the richer of the developing countries—half of the children in the country are abandoned.

Many of us in the industrialized West, when brought face to face with these facts, tend to tell ourselves that all that suffering is far away and not part of our own lives. But it is now becoming evident that these population trends affect not only the less developed countries, but threaten the security and stability of the rest of the world as well.

Public opinion polls in the United States indicate that the foremost concern of the minds of most Americans is inflation. This is a complex phenomenon and has many causes. Basically, inflation occurs when demands for goods and services exceed supplies. Since the beginning of history supplies of resources such as arable land, clean water, timber and minerals has far exceeded the number of people dependent on them. But in the past few decades that picture has changed. Today, throughout much of the world, there are more people than resources and in this transformation of our global economy may well lie the seeds of worldwide inflation on a scale and of a character never known before.

Inflation is precipitated when an increasing population places unprecedented demands on the earth's biological systems. These systems provide all of the food for mankind and all of the raw materials for industry, except minerals and petrochemicals.

In one fishery after another the catch now appears to exceed long-term sustainable yield.

Growing populations have also generated a demand for firewood that exceeds the regenerative capacity of our forests, forcing up the price of wood here and abroad.

The changing relationship between resources and the demands made upon them has been developing over a span of decades. But it first became real to most of us in the United States in 1973 when oil prices suddenly skyrocketed and when major crop failures and food scarcities in West Africa, the Soviet Union, and South Asia impacted directly on the American economy. To meet the world-wide demand for food, American food stocks were sold overseas, and the price of food staples rose spectacularly in this country and abroad. It may surprise some of you to know that the production from one out of every three acres of American farmland is sold to other countries.

It is estimated that by 1985, less than seven years from now, there will be a food deficit of one hundred million tons in the Third World—directly attributable to a population growth that increasingly and consistently outstrips agricultural production.

With four billion consumers already in the world and two hundred thousand more being added each day, scarcity-induced inflationary pressures can well become chronic. It is the opinion of an increasing number of economists that without a marked slowdown in population growth, matched by a significant and sustained increase in global food production, the inflation of food prices may not be containable.

As Third World populations increase, and available land is divided and sub-divided into plots incapable of sustaining the increases, millions of people flood into the cities, searching for employment, shelter, and the necessities of life. Urban centers are growing at rates that make our own experience with urbanization seem pallid. Cities throughout Africa, Latin America and Asia are doubling in size every 10 to 15 years. The population of Mexico City is already approximately 13 million. By the year 2000 it is estimated that Mexico City will have a population of 35 million, making it the largest city on earth. Since there is no work and no resources available for most of the illiterate and untrained rural people who flock to the cities, underemployment increases at a dizzying pace, and is already worse than anything Americans have ever known, even during the Great Depression. It has been estimated that in the next two decades it will be necessary to provide more than a billion new jobs in order to accommodate the masses of people who will be entering the global workforce. If an investment of close to ten thousand dollars is required to produce one job, you can readily see the demands that will be made on the world's economy. These problems of urbanization and massive employment will not be resolved without major progress in population control.

The population explosion has other crucial implications. Lester Brown, a widely recognized economist, agronomist, and specialist on Third World problems, has concluded that soon more than half of the world's urban population will be living in slums. Recently Mr. Brown stated: "An increasing percentage of children and youth are growing up in squalid surroundings with little in the way of privacy, amenities, recreation, or education. Theirs is a spiritless world where heat, light and cleanliness are unaffordable luxuries . . . Slum growth can serve as an index of frustration and as an indicator of potential instability, crime, and delinquency. All threaten the traditional concepts of personal security, property rights and the civil order on which they stand. When the core of urban population is socially and economically alienated, not only the urban community itself, but also, inevitably, the national political climate will be affected."

It is inevitable to speak of the population problem in terms of numbers. Actually, it is the relationship between population growth and overall development that is crucial. Nigeria may be able to handle a population three times its present size, but if the size is reached in 50 years instead of 200 years it will have an immense impact on the economic and social development of that country and on the level of opportunity and well-being of millions. In designing programs to bring about a reduction in the population growth rate, we seek to enhance the quality of life.

Some Third World countries have expressed concern that our population programs spring from our fear that we will be a small minority dwarfed by ever increasing numbers. It is not numbers as such that concern us. It is what those numbers mean in terms of the quality of life.

AID is committed to do all in its power to assist in slowing the excessive rate of population growth. In the first two years of this administration the total sum allotted for support of population programs has jumped by 30%. This increase reflects the significance that the President and Congress attach to this problem.

In Western industrial nations the population growth rate has diminished over many generations to a significant degree as a consequence of general economic development. Most LDC's, however, dare not wait for development to bring down their birth rates. Indeed, the danger is that birth rates will bring down development. Therefore, it is urgent that ways be found to reduce the birth rate.

We know that one indispensable component in the accomplishment of this task is family planning services. A substantial portion of U.S. assistance is spent for contraceptive supplies. These commodities are a *sine qua non* for fertility control.

But supply does not automatically mean use. Use is determined, to a significant degree, by the quality of the distribution system. Use also depends on the extent and depth of demand. There are differences of opinion as to how much demand for contraceptives exists in the developing world. AID believes that demand differs from country to country, and region to region and that however large it may be, it is not large enough. To increase demand, we believe that substantial efforts must be made to change attitudes toward family size. When family planning services are readily available and parents want 2 children rather than 3 or 4 or 5, major changes take place in the birth rate.

Ingrained cultural attitudes can be difficult to change, but we believe that it is of utmost urgency that ways be found to influence them. This is a major thrust of AID's population programs. We are working in and with the less developed countries seeking the factors and the combination of factors which will encourage the use of family planning services. We know what some of these factors are.

We know that a government commitment to population programs and its active role in the countryside in promoting them can make a significant difference in the birthrate.

We know that in some countries local groups can be used to influence fellow villagers.

We know that, under certain circumstances, when simple health and nutritional programs are introduced into the villages—enabling a woman to nourish her children properly and keep them healthy thus assuring that they survive to adulthood—fertility rates begin to decline.

These are some of the factors that appear to very quickly effect the number of children a couple will have. But research to date falls far short of supplying us the necessary data and insights. In 1978 AID is spending more than $5 million to further this research. That is a pittance considering the importance and size of the job.

Today the national expenditure of the U.S. government in support of population programs and general economic development in the impoverished countries throughout the world amounts to little more than one-quarter of 1% of our gross national product. By comparison, the Marshall Plan after World War II spent the equivalent of a full 3% of our gross national product on the reconstruction of Europe and Japan.

I leave it to you to judge whether you think our efforts to deal with these massive problems are adequate, or whether we might properly and judiciously and with real determination respond to the challenge to substantially increase our effort to assist the desperate and impoverished people of the earth to attain a higher standard of living for themselves and for future generations.

It is my own conviction that when the American people begin to appreciate the dimensions of the problems that confront the Third World they will respond as they always have in times of national crisis.

A World Gone Mad

by René Dumont

Even if some elements utilized by Meadows in *The Limits to Growth* model are dubious, it would be rash to belittle his report, published in 1972, setting forth the findings of the research project sponsored by the Club of Rome. If the global population's exponential growth persists and industrial production maintains its present rate of expansion, we are told, our civilization faces total collapse as a result of depleted food resources, nonrenewable energy and mineral reserves, and, worse yet, contaminated air and water pollution.

During the United Nations-sponsored talks on population and development, held in Cairo in June 1973, the demographers stressed the difficulties of reducing the birth rate and the inertia vis-à-vis the population problem. Even if birth control measures were rapidly adopted everywhere, we could consider as favourable a prospective global population of approximately 6.5 thousand million by the end of this century, stabilizing at about 11–12 thousand million by the middle of the next century.

This "prospect" strikes me as catastrophic. If the population growth rate does not decline more rapidly and if, at the same time, consumer habits and income distribution systems are not changed, total collapse will undoubtedly be inevitable. This is why at the Cairo meeting I asked that we no longer speak of "prospects" in referring to what is essentially only a series of predictions based on a certain number of premises, which are by no means ineluctable. The basic premise holds that the birth rate can hardly drop unless the standard of living rises and women are better informed. Let us make a distinction between the two factors, then note the results achieved in China and the Democratic Republic of Viet-Nam where, with no marked rise in the material standard of living but with far more security, the birth rate has declined faster than elsewhere, indeed much faster than in India.

Thus, an immense effort must be exerted, first of all, to improve education in this subject which concerns women nearly as much as men. In the Arab and Muslim countries, incidentally, women are given much less instruction. Immense, too, must be the effort to shape political motivation and public

From *Ceres,* 6 (6) November–December 1973, 17–19. Reprinted with permission of the Food and Agriculture Organization of the United Nations.
René Dumont *is a professor at the Institut national agronomique de Paris-Grignon. He has written several books, among them* L'Utopie ou la mort (Utopia or Death).

opinion in favour of the moderate-size family; furthermore, the public authorities must go into action.

Thus, we can justifiably impugn the United Nations "prospects" if we acknowledge our capacity to modify their premises, which seems to me all the more urgent now that we realize the enormous risk in accepting them: the collapse of our civilization. Even if we rectified certain questionable data advanced by the Club of Rome, especially concerning the depletion of mineral reserves, we could only delay not avert the ultimate collapse.

To the population-curbing difficulties deplored by the demographers in Cairo, we have sought persistently to juxtapose another form of inertia—food production in the backward and dominated countries known as the Third World (Group C in the United Nations). FAO's Indicative World Plan proposed a 3.8 percent yearly growth rate in food output from 1963 to 1985 to stamp out the serious incidence of malnutrition and undernourishment by the latter date. By 1970, this rate had not yet been attained. In fact, since 1959, per caput food production in these countries has hardly increased, particularly in view of statistics being exaggerated here and there for propaganda purposes. Moreover, for the Second Development Decade (1970–80), FAO has called for an annual agricultural growth rate of 4 percent. Since the end of 1972, Addeke Boerma, FAO Director-General, has been telling us that real growth in food production failed to exceed 2 percent in 1971 and 1972 taken together, or 1 percent a year; meanwhile, the population swelled by over 5 percent in that period. Barring some miracle, Mr. Boerma concluded, we can assume that the Second Development Decade will not reach its goal in the agricultural sector—a statement portending dire consequences. Malnutrition has not decreased. Indeed, it may well afflict the same proportion of the population as it did 12 years ago, hence a greater number of persons in absolute terms.

RAT HUNTS

The World Health Organization, for its part, points out that millions of children in the poor countires do not get the minimum intake of proteins indispensable to normal brain development. Recently, the person in charge of nutrition at the University of Ibadan in Nigeria called my attention to the grave lack of proteins suffered by the children in the villages of Western Nigeria, most pronounced in those aged from one to five. Infants less than a year old are often nourished with mother's milk; those over five years—and I saw it myself—carry a small sling to hunt rats, mice, and birds, collect various insects and scrounge in refuse. These little hunters are already able to provide at least their own protein complements. But in the one-to-five-year age group, if the protein deficiency is critical, the damage is irreparable.

If we were to list the available proteins suitable for human consumption, we would find them, on the whole, quite adequate. Apart from the standard animal, vegetable and other proteins, there are also those of tens of millions of tons of oil cakes, primarily from the soybean, groundnuts, copra, palm kernel oil, flax (linseed oil), colza and turnsole (sunflower seeds). The quantity of fish ground for flour recently totalled roughly 20 million tons; it could have been used for human feeding—not to mention the millions of tons of powdered skim milk, meat, flour, etc., taken from the mouths of underprivileged children. But nearly all these foodstuffs go to feed the rich countries' livestock—pigs and poultry, milk and meat cattle, sheep and goats—on both sides of the Atlantic, in Japan and Australia. These animals yield "nobler," hence more expensive, proteins, but at considerable protein loss often at a ratio of 6:1 with regard to protein input to output.

The consumption model of the rich countries is a monstrosity for the disparities it fosters and an absurdity for us, the rich. It is monstrous to deprive poor children of the proteins they need for proper brain development only to provide us with more meat than we should eat. The mountains of paper given to aggressive advertising urging greater consumption—already abusive—is unacceptable. The space reserved for advertising in a single issue of the Sunday *New York Times*—90 percent of the whole newspaper—uses up as much paper as all the textbooks, notebooks and manuals on all levels of education in Cameroon require in a whole year. And the schoolchildren are left to do without.

CALIFORNIANIZATION

In India and Bangladesh, the peasant does not always have the money to replace his plough's steel bottom, which weighs hardly a kilogram. Yet, more than a ton of steel and other still more valuable metals are often needed to transport one man from his suburban home to town in his roomy car. Aside from advertising and exaggerated packaging, such as plastic bottles, the automobile strikes me as the most flagrant symbol of our consumption model.

The automobile not only consumes gasoline, which will surely cease to exist—it is scarce even now in the United States—but also metals, some of which are already in short supply. It demands a tremendously costly infrastructure in highways and parking facilities. By 2010, these will cover 40 percent of the entire territory of the Netherlands. By 2020, Netherlands agriculture will be hardly more than a memory, with only several thousands of hectares of greenhouses and a few cattle in her fields to recall a glorious past. The less-populated continent of North America pays cheerfully for this type of land use, but what would happen if such a consumption model were extended to the overpopulated countries?

Ann and Paul Ehrlich tell us that with every thousand new settlers in California, 96 hectares or roughly one square kilometre are lost to agriculture, chiefly because of man's enslavement to his private car. In January 1973, I was studying several purely agricultural Bangladesh villages south of Comvilla, a provincial capital 100 kilometres east of Dacca. With a density of 1 125 inhabitants per square kilometre, each of these villages had no more than 60 hectares for rice cultivation because 40 percent of the land was occupied by houses, streams, schools, ponds and gardens; there was only a single, very narrow road.

A World Bank report on Bangladesh's land and water predicts that the country will count between 140 and 170 million inhabitants by the end of this century. The report also predicts that in those last 30 years of this century, a 30 percent unemployment rate will remain constant; this is termed a "reasonable expectation."

I tremble to think of Mathurapur, one of those villages which by then will have probably doubled in size. With 2 250 inhabitants occupying the same total of 100 hectares, no more than 30 hectares would be left for growing rice; this means that each hectare must feed 75 persons.

All this on the hypothesis that the present standard of consumption is maintained. But let us mentally transfer our California civilization to the Asian deltas, already overpopulated. The agricultural problem there would be extremely simple, to the relief of the agronomists and rural economists, since there would be no more land to cultivate. Even without "Californianization," the World Bank does not say how the 45 to 50 million rural unemployed will manage to feed themselves by the year 2000. In the face of technocratic indifference, I feel rising wrath. A civilization which cannot be expanded on a world scale is morally unacceptable.

The United States justifiably worries about the worldwide population explosion. But when that country counsels universal birth control, for the overcrowded Asian deltas as well as for the sparsely populated Amazon, one is inclined to suspect its motives. The United States utilizes one third of the energy consumed in the world and from 14 to 40 percent of its production of principal raw materials, yet it counts less than 6 percent of the global population. Blessed with land as vast as it is rich in soil, climate and natural deposits, the Americans still are the most massive importers of other people's riches.

They call their agriculture efficient, and so it is—but only because the nation commands more space than China or Europe, since it produces less per hectare. And to achieve this output, it demands not only a disproportionate share of the world's cultivable land but, even worse, an excessive, abusive share of the energy and metals available to the world at large for mechanized agriculture.

In our view, the zero population growth advocated by the Club of Rome thus looms as an absolute, inevitable necessity if we wish to prolong humanity's unparalleled adventure on the surface of the earth.

The United States proposes zero growth to the entire world, to overpopulated Asia as well as the underpopulated regions. Yet an Indian utilizes roughly one twenty-fifth as much energy and scarce materials as a North American does. Five hundred and seventy million Indians waste and pollute one eleventh as much as America's 210 million citizens.

If it is becoming urgent to curb Bangladesh's demographic upsurge sooner than foreseen (otherwise how will she feed her 50 million unemployed, predicted for the year 2000?), it is even more imperative to reduce population growth in the United States if we want to preserve our planet's scant, nonrenewable resources. What deceives us is her vast spaces. By what right, if not the right of her superior wealth—formerly we spoke of her superior strength—does she arrogate to herself an abusive share of our small planet's dwindling resources? By the same token, we could call into question family allowances beyond the second child in the European countries, such as France.

One might well agree with A. Sauvy, who maintains that the danger today lies not in the size of the population but rather in the wasteful consumption model it follows; and this is what must be changed. But we are also aware of the difficulties of such an undertaking and the delays we must expect before persuading the rich to be less voracious. For two thousand years Christianity has presumably been tackling this problem—with a few deviations on the way, notably in favour of slavery—but with only limited results. This is why the proliferation of prodigal populations must be halted.

Meanwhile, a new factor will help us reduce consumption: the looming consequences of air and water pollution threatening the rich countries. No big city has more "breathing space" than Los Angeles, with its 40 inhabitants per hectare, while Calcutta counts 840. Yet few big cities are as badly served by its network of highways ploughing through it in all directions. Indeed, for a quarter century, the city authorities have been vainly fighting the motor car producers in an attempt to reduce the harm they engender.

Nevertheless, no one until now has dared to propose the only valid solution: a ban on private cars, to be replaced by a network of public transportation providing adequate service. No one has dared to propose a prohibitive tax on posters, billboard advertising and radio and television commercials inciting us to consume even more abusively than now and in the process wasting paper and electricity. Only some British ecologists and a few isolated researchers, together with the Club of Rome, have advanced new solutions (albeit too timidly) which we shall soon be obliged to heed.

A heavy tax on fossil fuels, gas and petroleum products would offer an inducement to economize to the maximum, to find substitutes such as animal, windmill, solar, geothermic and other types of energy. This tax could be paid into an international agricultural development fund for the Third World. It would constitute the initial form of an international solidarity levy, which we must surely impose one day if we sincerely hope to avert a global civil war. A tax on metals, higher for those becoming scarce, would encourage recycling and the reutilization of discarded automobile carcasses and other abandoned machines. An amortization tax, higher as the life of commodity is shorter, would encourage the production of more durable goods, motor coaches with a 25-year life span and motors which could last 5000 000 kilometres if used at low speeds.

A special tax on compound foods for domestic animals, especially cattle, utilizing proteins better used for human consumption, could likewise support an international protein bank; the proteins could then be given gratis or at a very low cost to deprived children and mothers.

PEASANT POWER

Our world gone mad has lost control over its demographic growth, its money and its production model, causing fearful unemployment in the backward countries. Our "rich" consumption model has wreaked even more distressing damage. Those who command political or economic power in the Third World want to live like the rich in America and Europe, where many of them have studied, adopted their life style and bad habits.

The backward and dominated countries, first of all, must rid themselves of our economic and cultural influence, which saddles them with a civilization model hindering their authentic development. They will extricate themselves only if they build a more egalitarian society, based on the priority satisfaction of their entire population's needs: food, clothing, housing and health services. Above all, permanent education must be promoted for all, beginning with functional literacy in the local vernacular to instruct them on their economic, social and political problems. This would lead to true development and a consolidation of a strong, oppositional peasant power.

Those who already control the sources of petroleum will hold the fate of the developed economies in their hands on the day they achieve true independence. But if they should take up the cudgels in the interests of the backward countries as well, we would indeed have to submit to their conditions.

This leads us to advocate the establishment of national organizations to control the distribution of goods, also of export offices, to be subsequently federated into world organisms which can protect commodity prices, much as the Organization of Petroleum Exporting Countries (OPEC) now protects petroleum. This could then engender world bodies set up to allocate scarce resources to be shared in proportion to the requirements of each population, rather than according to more or less artificial monetary availability.

Other organisms could progressively assure a rational distribution of the world population by sponsoring massive migrations from the congested Asian regions to the sparsely populated of the Americas, Australia, Siberia and even Africa. They would challenge the problem of proliferating bureaucracy and its abuses, which must be staunchly opposed. All this would require a new man, but we cannot construct him, nor reform humanity in these few pages.

The Trump of Doom Has Not Yet Sounded

by Quentin M. West

Some experts today, like the Reverend Thomas Malthus in 1798, anticipate a final, decisive battle between the forces of plenty and starvation—an Armageddon of Agriculture.

This is just not going to happen; at least according to past and prospective food-people trends.

But world agriculture is going through a very uncertain period; much of this uncertainty was triggered by the 1972 worldwide crop shortfall. At least two factors compound the confusion: energy and affluence. The energy crisis has only recently burst upon the scene, while the effects of growing world affluence have long been building up.

To better understand these and other issues, we should first recognize some basic facts about the past, present, and future relationships between man and his food supply. These facts will not point to a calamitous food Armageddon but they will shed light on some serious problems ahead.

Worldwide, the relationship between people and food has been remarkably stable over the past 20 years. In fact, production in the less-developed countries has increased at about the same rate as in the developed. Production in both regions declined in 1972, but recovered in 1973 with preliminary estimates showing an increase of about 6 percent in each.

But rapid population growth has absorbed most of the increase in production in the developing nations. While Americans approach "ZPG" or zero population growth, there is little sign that population control is taking hold in the less-developed nations. More than 45 million people are added each year in nations unable to feed them adequately. Growth rates can exceed 2.5 percent a year.

Because of rapid population growth, per caput food gains in the less-developed nations have been small compared to those in the developed nations. Nonetheless, there have been advances.

From *Ceres,* 7 (3) May–June 1974, 31–34. Reprinted with permission of the Food and Agriculture Organization of the United Nations.

Quentin M. West *is the Administrator of the Economic Research Service of the U.S. Department of Agriculture. Prior to joining USDA in 1957, he served as a land-use economist with the Organization of American States in Costa Rica and Peru, and was on the staff of Cornell University and Utah State University.*

The long-term growth of affluence has been concentrated in the developed nations where it has resulted in a decided shift toward diets higher in animal protein. The result is unprecedented long-term growth in feed grain and oilseed demand and an acceleration of world trade in these commodities. The impact of this on the food supplies of the poor nations will be discussed below.

FIVEFOLD INCREASE

The steady uptrend in world food production was interrupted in 1972. The U.S.S.R., Argentina, Australia, India, Africa, and Southeast Asia registered sharp production declines. Grain production declined in the United States. The poor Soviet harvest generated the largest world purchases of grain ever. These included 18 million tons from the United States of which over 13 million tons were shipped in 1973. The Soviet purchases, combined with expanded U.S. exports to China and Eastern Europe, spelled a one-year, fivefold increase in U.S. farm exports to these countries.

Dollar devaluation has further strengthened the foreign commercial demand for U.S. farm goods. In the last 2 years, the dollar depreciated on the average by about 10 to 11 percent when compared to the currencies of our major agricultural trading partners.

The net results of short crops, devaluation, and unusual trading between major world economic powers was a tremendous surge in world grain exports in 1973 and a high degree of uncertainty in the world food market.

World crops for 1973/74 look generally better. The United States produced record soybean, wheat, and maize crops last fall. The U.S.S.R. announced a record total grain harvest at 222.5 million metric tons. This compares to 168 million metric tons in 1972.

The 1973/74 world grain crop, including a record rice crop, is about 90 million tons more than the year before. But, high demand and reduced stocks will likely hold prices at high levels. Poor nations are increasingly worried that short supplies and high prices will severely restrict their import plans.

MEETING WORLD IMPORT DEMANDS

In general, our projections to 1977 assume that price and other effects of the 1972 crop shortfall will have been worked out and that world trade will return to a more normal pattern. We look for our 1977 wheat and feed grain exports to fall below current levels. Soybeans, however, will make a continued strong showing in 1977, and rice and cotton exports will also increase.

We have also projected two levels of demand, production, and trade of food grains and coarse grains to 1985. Both indicate steady growth in world demand for livestock feeds. The first assumes continued growth in import demand that will be constrained by high prices and by policies of major importing countries to attain self-sufficiency. This level essentially describes a return to trends established before 1972. The second is a higher demand alternative assuming that animal production will be encouraged in grain-importing countries, leading to accelerated demand for feedstuffs.

The higher demand alternative should translate into a substantial increase in demand for U.S. coarse grains and oilseed meal with some impact on the demand for our wheat. Our projections suggest that the United States could meet nearly all the world's increased import demand for coarse grains. The largest part of the growth in world import demand for oilseed meal probably would be met by the United States, although others such as Brazil would likely play a large part. The developed exporting countries will supply the less-developed importing countries with increasing amounts of wheat, with an important share from the United States.

Our projected production and trade of the less-developed countries indicate that their per caput consumption of grains should increase slightly over the base period. But, their increasing grain imports may severely strain their ability to pay.

A recent study of ours indicates that U.S. farmers have the capacity to substantially increase their output of major farm products to levels consistent with these projections. The study assumes: normal weather; no controls on land use as there were from 1954 to 1973; prices for farm products high enough to encourage farm investments, and sufficient supplies of fuel and fertilizer at reasonable prices.

We believe that a 50 percent increase in feed grain production, a 33 percent increase in wheat wheat and soybean output, and a doubling of rice production over 1973 are possible by 1985. Part of the increase would come from expanded use of cropland, primarily from acreage formerly diverted under government supply management programmes and from cropland pasture. But much of the increases in output would be expected to come from higher yields even with present technology.

We have seen that past food trends show long-term general improvement. And that trend will likely continue. But, serious food problems will continue to plague us and several questions need consideration:

Will there be starvation in the world? Our projections suggest that world per caput food production will increase. But they also indicate that production in the developing countries as a group may not keep up with demand and, in some countries, not even with population. While developing countries with rapidly growing economies may have the foreign exchange to import needed food, others may not. They may have to depend on concessional programmes.

Although per caput supplies are likely to improve, it is still possible for large areas and large numbers of people to be critically short of food. The recent problem in the African Sahel and Ethiopia all too amply demonstrates this.

Policy issues for governments come down to questions of the amounts and kinds of aid, including technical assistance and food aid. U.S. agriculture is now largely free from government supports and controls. Our own markets now interface directly with international commercial markets. With the recent decline of U.S. farm surpluses, the Government must now decide whether or not to produce food specifically for aid purposes. The use of surplus food for aid programmes is not at all the same as the conscious use of resources to produce food to be given away. Those resources may be more productive if used for other purposes, such as for programmes to increase food production in those countries hardest hit by shortages.

Do the affluent preempt food from the poor? The Greek cynic Diogenes once pondered over the proper time to eat: "If a rich man, when you will; if a poor man, when you can." It is the same with world food purchases. The rich nations demand and get high-cost, high-protein, livestock-based diets which soak up vast amounts of feed grains. That is not a problem in plentiful times. But, when world grain supplies are short and the prices are high—like in 1972—the poor nations pay more for less and rich eat what they will.

But agricultural production can, in the longer run, respond very well to increased demands from increasing affluence, and therefore it is possible for us to feed both the affluent and the very poor at increasing levels of nutrition. We now believe U.S. farmers will produce enough this year to alleviate present shortages. However, it does seem that moral issues arise when extraordinary food shortages occur. Should limits be placed on demand, perhaps by rationing?

BRUNT OF THE SURGE

Will prices fluctuate widely or will they be relatively stable? It is impossible to predict a combination of circumstances that could generate the great fluctuations in our farm prices that we experienced in 1973. Foreign demand is the most dynamic element affecting the total demand for U.S. farm products. It is the fastest growing part, and exports now take a large share of our production. Exports are also the most unstable part of demand, since many countries look to imports to fill shortfalls in their own production. One bad year affecting a number of countries greatly increases the demand on world markets. U.S. markets, now closely linked to world markets, feel the brunt of the surge. Prices rise rapidly when stocks decline to very low levels as they did in 1973.

Of course, this situation was greatly influenced by the unprecedented decision of the U.S.S.R. to fill its shortfalls from the international larder. Can we accept Soviet entrance in our food market at any time it chooses? Our market and production news is public information and available to the U.S.S.R. Unfortunately, adequate information does not flow both ways. The recent U.S.-U.S.S.R. agreement will help but much will still be unknown. Many countries use export and import controls, long-run trade agreements, and other devices to insulate their markets against disturbances from foreign sources. However, such devices often conflict with free trade policies.

The Director-General of FAO. Addeke Boerma, has suggested international consultation and agreement on principles of government stockpiles of grain to help stabilize world grain prices. This subject will undoubtedly be an important topic at the World Food Conference next November.

In connection with this Conference, Americans are going to question whether or how much U.S. farm policy should be influenced by international forums and the views of the multilateral agencies. The question is particularly critical at this time, when so many other nations seem to favour independent, unilateral actions or operate in small blocs.

The Conference should provide a forum for determining how much international cooperation—how much sharing of the burden—there is likely to be in resolving some of the world food problems. The United States has long been the principal provider of development assistance and food aid, and has long maintained, at its expense, the grain reserves of much of the world. It is no longer reasonable for the United States to carry so large a share of the burden. Hence, at the FAO Conference of November 1973, we agreed with Mr. Boerma on the need for multinational cooperation to achieve a broader base of food security.

OBSTACLES TO LIBERALIZATION

U.S. policy, in my view, will be guided by evidences of cooperation—particularly by those countries who have recently come into the market to buy large amounts of grain (contributing to scarcity prices for food) and by those who have recently altered the market for oil (contributing to scarcity prices for fuel and fertilizers). It is the poor countries who bear the burden of such shortages and price increases; hence, we are hopeful that the World Food Conference will bring about a new era in cooperation among all the countries in the UN family.

What are chances for, or even the need for, farm trade liberalization? International crosswinds on the trade liberalization issue are blowing even more vigorously than usual. Some Americans, looking at our phenomenal growth in farm exports, are beginning to question whether we even need to worry about the issue. Maybe, they say, demand is sufficiently strong to maintain a healthy growth in our exports without seeking to lower trade barriers. Yet, probably most observers, recognizing that the recent expansion has been caused by short-term developments which may not occur again soon, still feel that liberalization is vital for sustained growth.

The obstacles to trade liberalization have alwys been formidable and they remain so. However, the Trade Policy Research Centre in London holds that high prices in world commodity markets have improved chances for multilateral negotiation. One of the longstanding causes for resistance by the European Economic Community to U.S. efforts to achieve freer trade has been the fear that greater exposure to world markets would seriously injure their agricultural sector because EEC farm product prices have been substantially above world prices. This fear should be reduced if world commodity prices remain strong.

On the other hand, some European spokesmen have recently argued against freer trade. They maintain that the present tight food situation dictates that all-out food production is called for and nothing should be done that might reduce incentives to producers anywhere.

Interestingly, these two contradictory views are in turn contradicted if, as our projections show and as we believe, the tight grain situation eases in the years ahead.

The oil crisis is a serious threat to trade liberalization for several reasons: (*a*) if the oil crisis leads to a general recession with lower profits and higher unemployment, there would be strong pressures for trade protection (while this might affect industrial more than agricultural products, it would undoubtedly affect the negotiating climate); (*b*) the staggering balance of payments deficits that are almost certain to be caused by the high oil prices will also discourage the granting of trade concessions; (*c*) the monetary upheavals caused by the oil crisis will make it more difficult to achieve world monetery reform. The European Community has insisted that monetary reform proceed apace with trade reform.

HOPEFUL THOUGHTS

Will the energy shortage hamstring agriculture? The energy crisis has only recently grabbed our attention. It has already caused us inconveniences and sometimes real problems on our own farms. But, for the poor nations, it can seriously jeopardize food supplies. For one thing, fuel supplies everywhere are short and prices have jumped sharply. And the same is true for fertilizer (nitrogen fertilizer production depends on natural gas). Further, the energy crisis is already slowing economic activity around the world. This can limit incomes and curb the demand for food, thus spoiling incentives to produce food.

The potential impact of the fertilizer and oil crisis on the food balances of countries such as India and China is ominous. Together, they import over one third of the nitrogen in international trade. These and other low-income nations dependent on fuel and fertilizer imports could be drastically hurt. Their ability to improve production and/or food imports will be seriously hampered.

But these and other problems will not produce a sudden widespread food calamity. There will be no Armageddon for agriculture. The world has a great potential for increased food production; the economic and political signals demanding more food grow more apparent day by day. Indeed, if these signals become strong enough, governments, farmers, agribusinessmen, and researchers will respond.

The Birth of a Nation: Populandia

"Then came a terrific explosion, and fire and smoke billowed up from the Pacific's depths. A tidal wave rocked our steamship, nearly swamping her. When the next day finally dawned, we descried to the west a new, mist-shrouded land on the horizon where only ocean had rolled before. We were then at latitude 25°15' South, longitude 179°20' West."

—Captain's log.
the S.S. Interdependence

One of 1977's most celebrated events was the volcanic appearance of a new mini-continent in the Pacific Ocean. The new land consisted of about 160,000 square miles of low, rolling terrain—about the size of California. The ground cooled, and within a few months vegetation began to take root.

Cartographers called the new mini-continent "Populandia," which means "Surprise, surprise" in the dialect of French Polynesia.

Populandia seemed heaven-sent. The new addition to the world's land area lay situated in a pleasant, subtropical climate, surrounded by blue ocean. And, unique among all the continents, the new land was completely unpopulated.

"The population crunch is solved," exulted one international leader as the World League of Countries met in late 1977 to lay claim to the verdant mini-continent. In a special session, the august world body made a historic pronouncement: To ease population pressure on the nations of the world, from January 1, 1978, onward, all the world's natural increase (that is, all the extra people born over and above those needed to replace people who die) would be transplanted to Populandia. Such a move would leave the present continents with their present cozy levels of population. And since the new land, some 400 by 400 miles, was starting off with zero inhabitants, it was reasoned that a long, long time would pass before the world would have to worry about population pressure again.

The practical details of the shift proved somewhat dicey. Suffice it to say that unlimited visiting privileges, and hefty tax incentives were promised to parents willing to let their children become Populandians, while Harvard University generously volunteered to build an extension campus on the mini-continent for its citizens' future education. ("They deserve," a Harvard spokesperson said, "the best.")

From *Intercom,* 6 (1) January 1978, 9; 6 (3) March 1978, 13; 6 (6) June 1978, 6; 6 (9) September 1978, 4; 7 (1) January 1979, 5; 7 (4) April 1979, 6; and 7 (8/9) August/September 1979, 10–11. The International Population News Magazine; a publication of the Population Reference Bureau, Washington, DC.

The first child to become a citizen of Populandia was born at 12:00:01 A.M. (local time), January 1, 1978, in the Tonga Islands. A few hours later, the child, Beverly Ming, was flown to Populandia, where an army of World League nurses and a new temporary city of nurseries and dairy farms awaited her.

The one-thousandth "excess" or natural increase child was born in Fiji about 7 minutes and 14 seconds later. And soon the tropical air was buzzing as every two minutes a jumbo jet carrying 280 more children touched down at Populandia International Airport, the largest, busiest airport in the world.

As the New Year moved west from time zone to time zone, more and more Populandians arrived in the world, culminating in John Cabot Peabody IV, born at 12:00:01 A.M. (local time) January 1 in the Aleutians—24 time zones after little Beverly Ming. A total 200,677 Populandians had been born by this moment, and January 2 had not yet come to Populandia.

POPULANDIA NOW WORLD'S 33RD LARGEST COUNTRY

What has happened to Populandia in the three months since the first child was landed on its shores?

Perhaps the most noticeable fact is that Populandia is now the 33rd largest country in the world. As of March 31, its population was expected to be 18,060,930.

Another Populandian superlative is its international airport—the world's busiest, as wide-body jets land every two minutes with a full passengerload of the newly born. These Populandian babies are met by regiments of WLC nurses and whisked down Myrdal Avenue to the Tots Clinic. There they are fed by WLC wet nurses, while outside an army of workers labors mightily to build new clinic wings to meet the constant need for more space—the equivalent of a new Massachusetts General Hospital (1,084 beds) every seven minutes.

Who are Populandia's tiny citizens? Nearly two-thirds (64 percent) are Asians. This is because some 57 percent of the world's population are Asians; it is also because the rate of natural increase is higher in developing countries (including Asia's) than in the developed nations.

African children make up the next largest contingent of Populandians— 15 percent of the total. Next come the Latin Americans, who make up 12.5 percent, while the developed continents are presently sending relatively small numbers of people—only 2 percent of Populandians come from North America, 2.6 percent from Europe, 3.3 percent from the U.S.S.R., and 0.4 percent from Oceania.

Not only are Asians the Populandian majority, but seven Asian countries—China, India, Bangladesh, Pakistan, Indonesia, the Phillipines, and Thailand—by themselves contribute over half the world's natural increase.

During Populandia's first three months in existence, India has contributed 3,234,000 people to the mini-continent. In the same period, France has contributed only 39,500, while the Federal Republic of Germany and the German Democratic Republic (because of their present negative growth) have yet to send a single child to Populandia.

At midnight New Year's Day, Populandia had a population of zero. But with 200,677 new citizens arriving each day, its population had reached the 1 million mark by January 5. By February 19, Populandia's population was 10 million, and by the end of March, stands at the 18 million mark—giving the island a population density (112 people per square mile) about that of Burma's. And none of Populandia's citizens are over three months old.

INTERCOM will give periodic reports on Populandia, its problems and progress, as the world's newest nation continues inexorably to grow.

POPULANDIA CLIMBS TO 22ND LARGEST OF WORLD'S COUNTRIES

The last time we visited Populandia, it was the world's 33rd largest country. But that was three months ago, and now, six full months after the first citizen landed on its shores, Populandia has become Number 22, and has nowhere to go but up. Its population as of June 30 stands at 36,322,537, which places the infant nation between Spain (the world's 21st largest nation) and Poland (bumped to the 23rd position). With 227 people per square mile, Populandia's population density is now about the level of Austria's.

Populandia has a flag (a cradle on a field of pink and blue), but no army, or money, and its citizens will not need an official language until later this year. What it does have is diapers. With each Populandian baby using 10 regular-sized cotton diapers every day of the week, including holidays, it means that over 52 square miles of diapers must be delivered, picked up and washed daily. A perpetual cloud of steam hangs over the valley site of Populandia's central laundry, which is about the size of two Boeing aircraft plants.

Even more impressive are the vast nurseries. Imagine being inside an immense, tinted-glass geodesic dome, with thousands of rows of playpens stretching into the dim distance. In every direction diapers are being changed, inoculations dispensed, and toys flying out of the cribs and being retrieved. The very audible sound of crying echoes around the dome as some one-fifth million new babies begin teething for the first time every day.

Meanwhile, the other 170-odd countries of the world have stopped growing. Babies are still being born at the same rate, but to keep the balance, a country like Sweden (with a birth rate of 12 and a death rate of 11) sends 12.5 percent of its newborns to Populandia. China (with rates of 22 and 8), sends more than 63 percent of its new arrivals, while Libya (with rates of 48 and 9) sends about 80 percent of all babies born there to the verdant minicontinent. The population crunch is seemingly solved; Populandia has become the cradle of the world. But for how long?

POPULANDIA: A POWER TO BE RECKONED WITH

Populandia is getting more crowded.

The world's newest nation, which has been absorbing the total natural increase of the world since January 1, is now a world power to be reckoned with—that is, if having a lot of (in this case, infant) population makes a country a power.

In fact, only nine months after starting from scratch, Populandia is now the 14th most populous country in the world. Its population of 54,784,821 (as of September 30) places it just below the United Kingdom (in 13th place) and just above France (bumped to 15th place).

The density of the California-sized country is now up to 342 people per square mile, somewhat higher than Denmark's 304 per square mile. Great tinted-glass nursery domes now cover most of the land area of Populandia, and last year's dreams of using Populandia to absorb indefinitely the future natural increase of the world would seem to have been a little premature.

The older Populandians are now nearing one year of age—crawling, standing, even some toddling a few steps. Syllables and an occasional word can occasionally be heard amidst the general caterwauling in the wards, and soon the first Populandian will be talking.

But in what language?

It's not a simple question. Language is something that infants acquire from their environment, in this case nurses. And the new nation's founders— the delegates at the august WLC—were on guard lest the infants from their own country be swallowed up by another cultural heritage and lose their own.

The French did not want the future natural increase of the world to be anglicized; the Americans were aghast at the thought of the younger generation speaking Russian, etc., etc. Chauvinism hit new heights.

To allay this fear, it was originally proposed that a national, neutral, nondiscriminatory "constructed" language be used. The most successful of these is Esperanto, invented in 1887 by a Russian, Lazarus Zamenhoi, who created it in a belief that the national and racial hatreds of history are exacerbated by language barriers. Esperanto today has 500,000 speakers around the world, making it the most successful of the constructed languages, far ahead of Ido, Volapuk, Novial, and Interlingua.

Nonetheless, the thought of living in a new world in which the world's elders would not be able to communicate with those born after January 1,

1977, proved a little too much for the bald-pated WLC delegates, and the idea of teaching Populandia's young a single "international" language was dropped.

Instead, in one of those maddening compromises that have marked historical conflicts, it was decided that the proportions of the infant Populandians speaking a given language should correspond to the proportion in which that language is spoken in the world. Nurses would be hired and instructed accordingly. (No attempt was made to organize things so that a Populandian infant of French parents would speak French—he would be just as likely to grow up speaking Bengali.)

The result—out of every 100 Populandians, 14 are being brought up speaking Mandarin (Chinese); 9 speak English; 5 each, Hindustani and Spanish; 4 each, Arabic and Russian; 3 each, Portuguese, Japanese, and German; and 2 each, Bengali, French, Cantonese, and Italian.

Other languages that would be spoken by at least 1 percent apiece would be Javanese, Wu (Chinese), Telugi (Indian), Korean, Punjab (Indian), Ukranian, Tamil (Indian), Marathi (Indian), and Vietnamese. And the rest of the Populandians—about 40 percent of the total—would be subdivided among about 3,000 other languages.

So starting next year Populandia is likely to sound like a replica of the larger world outside—that is, like Babel. But one language will probably end up dominating. When Populandia was organized, the founders had the problem of picking a common administrative language, for bulletin board notices, paychecks, laundry lists, and the like. Such a language would have to be widely known, or easily learned, and usable for communication to the outside world.

It would be difficult to choose three more difficult, recalcitrant, and grammatically gnarled languages than the world's three most popular ones: Mandarin, English, and Hindustani; in fact, it's a miracle that anyone ever communicates anything using them. But the world's fourth most popular language is grammatically simple, logically pronounced, and phonetically spelled. This language, already spoken by one-fifth billion people (and growing) is Spanish. So Spanish was chosen as Populandia's administrative language. PA announcements begin: "Buenos dias, trabajadores de Populandia." And despite attempts to inculcate 3,000 other languages, it is likely that Populandia will ultimately have a Latin flavor.

HAPPY BIRTHDAY, POPULANDIA!

Populandia has joined the giants. On January 1, 1978, for about 4/10ths of one second, Populandia had a population of 1; namely, little Beverly Ming, of the Tonga Islands, the first child to arrive on the verdant Pacific minicontinent.

But that was a year ago, right after Populandia was designated by the WLC as the repository of the world's natural increase. At 200,677 new arrivals a day, the Populandian population has mushroomed to 73,247,105 (as of January 1, 1979) and the infant nation has stormed up through the ranks to become the 10th largest country in the world.

The roll of world population heavyweights now reads as follows: China, India, the Soviet Union, the U.S., Indonesia, Brazil, Japan, Bangladesh, Pakistan, and Populandia. And because all the nations of the world now have stable populations (the result of exporting their natural increase), Populandia can only rise.

Populandia is now growing by 199,177 new arrivals per day, instead of 200,677, an adjustment that takes into account the latest 1978 world figures for natural increase.

There are now about 457 Populandians per square mile—near the density of India—and now that the oldest citizens are beginning to toddle and move about, the island is not quite as spacious as it used to be. The vast nursery domes of tinted glass have sprouted all over the island like mushrooms, and presently, each Populandian (exclusive of support staff) has about 6100 square feet of land area (an area about 78 $\times$ 78 feet) to call his or her own.

Of the approximately 122 million children born each year in the world, Populandia receives about 60 percent. Consequently, the International Year of the Child has promoted world interest in the newly created "Pied Piper" country of the Pacific. Besider regular visitors, tourists now flock to Populandia to observe the world's fertility in action and to gasp at the island's unique age structure. And on January 1, the tourists could also marvel at the tinted-glass domes, all aglow with birthday cake candles as the nurses helped little Beverly Ming and some 200,000 other Populandians celebrate their first birthday.

POPULANDIA POWER ISLAND NOW NO. 8

Fifteen months after the first babe landed on its shores, Populandia is now the 8th largest country in the world.

Designated as the repository of the world's natural increase, the verdant super island's population has burgeoned at the rate of 200,677 new arrivals per day. (In January 1979 this figure became 199,177 per day to reflect the latest 1978 figures for world natural increase).

As a result, the world roll call of population Mega-powers now reads: China, India, the Soviet Union, the U.S., Indonesia, Brazil, Japan, Populandia, Bangladesh, and Pakistan.

Populandia's population now stands at 90,717,493 (as of April 1, 1979) and growing. This latest figure takes into account a new factor in Populandia's growth: infant mortality. Although Populandia has the world's most comprehensive child care staff, consisting of several million doctors, nurses, pediatricians, cooks, and orderlies, infant deaths continue to occur—albeit at the world's lowest rate, 7 per 1,000 arrivals per year. This works out to about 256,000 infant deaths during Populandia's first year of existence.

Outside of Populandia, the world's lowest infant mortality rate is Sweden's—8 infant deaths per 1,000 live births (see PRB's new 1979 **World Population Data Sheet**). The African continent has the highest continental rate—143—and Afghanistan currently shows the world's highest infant mortality rate—226—which means that nearly 1 out of every 4 infants there never reaches age 1.

With good fortune and hard work, Populandia's rate may drop. But for all infants, the first year is perilous. In the U.S., the death rate for infants under 1 is 15.36 per 1,000 population at that age as of 1976. But from age 1 to age 2 the death rate drops dramatically down to 0.94 per 1,000—less than one-sixteenth the risk of the crucial first year of life. Thereafter, as the infants grow up and pass through adulthood, mortality rates remain low, and then rise up in the middle ages. But in the U.S., only at age 60 and beyond does the death rate (15.42 at age 60) exceed the death rate (15.36) of those under age 1. In other words, being an infant under age 1 in the U.S. is as perilous (from the standpoint of survival probability) as being 60 years old.

The statistics in other developed countries follow a similar pattern. And even in Populandia, it's clear that when babies attain their first birthday, they have passed a great hurdle on their road of life.

POPULATION GROWTH IN POPULANDIA:
121 MILLION PEOPLE IN 20 MONTHS

Populandia, PRB's incredible population island, erupted out of the Pacific in late 1977. Soon after, its verdant and unpopulated land area was designated by the World League of Countries (WLC) as the repository of all the world's population increase starting January 1, 1978. From that time on, all babies born who represented a surplus of births over deaths would be flown to Populandia. Thus, all the nations of the world would cease to grow, and the much discussed World Population Problem would be solved at last.

(Parenthetically, it might be noted that some 40 percent of the world's births serve to replace those who have died in the same time period; the remaining 60 percent contribute to population increase.)

Since the first baby, little Beverly Ming, landed on its shores that fateful New Year's Day, Populandia has grown at a steady clip—with 1.4 million new arrivals every week (199,177 every day; 8,351 every *hour*). In the interval since our last report (in April 1979 INTERCOM), Populandia has barged to the forefront of the world's nations, and has now passed Japan and then Brazil to become the sixth most populous country in the world. Its population (as of September 1, 1979) stands at 121,191,574 people, all no older than 20 months of age.

Populandia's fame has spread far and wide. An excerpt from these articles appeared in the *Congressional Record*. Julian Bond based a "Today" show commentary upon it. And recently, the mighty mini-continent was used as the basis of a class project at the New Lincoln School in New York City, where teacher Irma S. Jarcho asked her "Science and Society" class to write their own continuations of the Populandia saga.

Jarcho's students contributed some surprising alternate futures for the burgeoning land of children. Among them:

(a) World Domination: In this scenario by Ted Williams, the immigration gates shut after one year (leaving the population at 91 million). Eighteen years then pass, before Populandia plays its trump card: oil. (Well, why wouldn't a verdant mini-continent of 16,000 square miles have the world's last untouched oil?) In 1995 Beverly Ming flies to New York and "with a cute smile" delivers Populandia's terms for its petroleum: disarmament; world cooperation (insuring that "the world works as a whole to help the world, not each country trying to be better than another country"); and a two-child limit for families ("Populandia is a good reason why").

(b) Social Disintegration: A Populandia wracked by severe emotional problems is imagined by Tovan Beiser, all due to "the lack of family unit. The children must share adoptive mothers, the WLC nurses. But the nurses haven't enough time to give to each child to qualify as a parent, and the genetic parents haven't enough time to visit their children, either." The result: "Children (who) are at best insecure and mistrustful and have great difficulty in getting along with others and making friends." Whether the situation can be corrected in time or gets out of control, Beiser warns darkly, only time will tell.

(c) Old Age Home: Due to money problems and the energy crisis, the world begins to realize that Populandia is too expensive to maintain over the long haul. So the children of Populandia are returned to their countries and families, and the world grows on much as before.

Instead, speculates Michael Fineman, Populandia is used to alleviate population growth in a different fashion. Rather than ship newborn babies to the mini-continent, people are transported there as they reach their 70th birthday.

Populandia as the ultimate retirement home? It would work—at least for a while. According to the U.S. Census Bureau projections, in 1980 the world may have 146,344,000 people 70 years old and over—about 3.3 percent of the world. As near as can be guessed, however, people over 70 and over account for (*very* roughly speaking) about 20 percent of the world's deaths. If they exited for Populandia, the world's natural increase would jump up to perhaps 83 million per year; which means the world (not counting Populandia) would increase by some 228,000 per day. Consequently, if those 70 years and over were to emigrate to Populandia, they would have to emigrate at a rate of 228,000 per day.

However, only (again roughly speaking) about 38,000 people per day celebrate their 70th birthdays. This means that the ranks of the over-70s might be exhausted within two years. And once all the elderly were dispatched to Populandia, the island's WLC administrators would soon have to reach down into younger and younger ages in order to keep the flow at 73 million per year. Ultimately, everyone would be shipped off as they passed their 18th birthday, if not before, and the world would become a haven of young people, while Populandia contained everyone else, elbow to elbow.

But all this is simply speculation. In fact, the "real" Populandia is getting along swimmingly these days down in the South Pacific, doing what it does best. What ultimate destiny awaits it is still shrouded in mystery, but in the meantime its youthful population is happy, healthy, and just a little bigger every day.

8

Food from Plants

As population increases, pressure on available land to produce food will grow. Suitable land itself is already in short-supply and these remain the only two major areas in the world which scientists believe to be capable of sustained food production. These are the Sudan in Africa, and the Amazon basin in South America. In other parts of the world, land is either too cold, too dry or too mountainous. Some of this land could be brought into production but the economic costs are prohibitive.

With the increase in population, pressure will grow to provide more calories for humans from plant sources and less from animal sources. At present, food from animals presents a kind of food insurance since in times of poor harvests, the animals could be eaten as well as the cereals normally fed to animals. A reduction in the safety factor will inevitably lead to a destabilization of the food supply system and wider swings in the feast-famine syndrome.

Modern agriculture is an incredibly complex and finely tuned system, both in the agriculturally sophisticated countries and in the developing countries. The following four papers are isolated examples of concern and progress.

Can We Broaden Our Food Base?

by George Sollenberger

The plant world is remarkably varied. Scientists speculate that there may be as many as 350,000 different plant species growing on earth. These range from the giant sequoia trees of California to single-cell plants so small that 500 of them will fit in a drop of water.

Thousands of these species have parts that are edible by humans. Yet, modern man has come to rely on only a few to provide his food. Plant species that are significant food sources number barely 100. Of these, no more than two dozen could be considered major food-crop plants. And most human nourishment comes from just seven species: corn, barley, rice, wheat, the potato, the soybean, and the common bean.

This reliance on a few species also extends to animal food sources. The animals that humanity now uses for food represent only a minute fraction of the world's diverse animal kingdom.

In terms of man's long history, dependence on such a narrow food base is relatively new. Early man was a food opportunist. As a hunter-gatherer, he exploited a wide range of wild food sources. His food base narrowed when he began to cultivate crops and domesticate livestock.

The food base has narrowed even more in modern times. Commercialization of agriculture has led to specialization, and many plants that once provided food are no longer harvested.

Continuing. This process is still taking place. For instance, in the high plateau country of Bolivia and Peru, Indians have traditionally grown grain-bearing crops called quinoa and canihua. Their small, high-protein seeds are used to make soups and beverages. Other traditional crops, well adapted to the harsh environment, include a vegetable-bearing vine, a lupine, broad beans, and a few other legumes. Recently, however, the Indians have begun to replace this local food with wheat and other less-nutritious imports from the lowlands.

Some scientists would like to reverse this trend and return more diversity to food production. They say that for many of the world's peoples, especially those in developing countries, this could increase nutritional status and reduce the vulnerability and insecurity that come from depending on a few crops.

From *The Furrow,* 82 (5) May–June 1977, 8. Reprinted by permission of John Deere & Company.

A good place to start might be in arid and semiarid regions, which cover about a third of the earth's land mass. For the most part, the native food crops of these regions are now ignored in favor of food crops transplanted from temperate or tropical regions. These have thrived, but only when irrigated.

Now, however, production of these transplants is becoming uneconomic in some areas because of water shortages and high energy costs. Given these circumstances, some experts are suggesting that we look into the agronomic potential of native desert plants, which are well adapted to arid conditions.

Desert bounty. There is certainly no shortage of possibilities to check, for the desert is not as barren as it seems. According to two scientists with the Arizona-Sonora Desert Museum, the Sonoran Desert of southwestern North America is home to more than 375 species of wild food plants. The natives of the region used about 40 of these as food staples.

The Arizona scientists say a number of these native plants produce protein-rich seeds, which are smaller but more nutritious than those of currently cultivated grains. Some other native plants produce carbohydrate-rich fruit or pods.

So far, little research has been done on these plants, but scientists say they believe some of them would lend themselves especially well to cultivation. One example is the tepary bean, which is high in protein, quite productive, and drought resistant. It can outproduce many presently grown crops under dryland farming conditions. Another example is buffalo gourd, now considered a desert weed. The entire buffalo gourd plant is high in protein and fat.

No one is suggesting that we plant the Plains to buffalo gourds or turn the Corn Belt into the tepary-bean belt. However, if we could broaden our food base by bringing some wild food plants under cultivation, we might be able to make better use of land that is now marginally tillable or impractical to irrigate. And that would be good news for a hungry world.

The Plight of the Humble Crops

by Noel D. Vietmeyer

A friend recently told me that he had discussed the winged bean with an influential Filipino family: "They were incredulous that such a miraculous plant could exist," he said. "So, on a hunch, I took them out back to the servants' quarters. There, climbing along a fence, was a winged bean plant laden with pods."

" 'But that's just seguidillas,' " one of them said, " 'it's only a poor man's crop.' "

It is a universal phenomenon that certain plants are illogically stigmatized because of their humble associations. Scores of highly promising crop-plants around the world receive no research funding, no recognition from the agricultural community—they are ostracized as "poor man's crops."

For information on a poor man's crop one has to turn, more often than not, to botanists and anthropologists; only they have taken an interest in the plant. Often there has been no agricultural research expended on it at all—no varieties have been collected or compared, no germination or spacing trials have been conducted, no yield determinations or even nutritional analyses have been made. And yet such a crop may be crucial to the life style—even the survival—of millions of people.

Botanists and ethnobotanists can reel off long lists of poor man's plants that seem to warrant recognition. In recent questionnaires sent out by the National Academy of Sciences for its studies of underexploited tropical plants, neglected tropical legumes and trees for energy (firewood) plantations, respondents named over 2000 species that deserve much greater recognition. Few have been given agronomic attention.

Just 50 years ago, the soybean was a poor man's crop, too. In the United States, it was spurned by researchers for more than a century after Benjamin Franklin first introduced seeds from the Jardin des Plantes in Paris. To be a soybean advocate then was to risk being considered a crackpot. Even early in this century, Americans considered the soybean a third-rate crop fit only for

From *Ceres*, 11 (2) March–April 1978, 23–27. Reprinted with permission of the Food and Agriculture Organization of the United Nations.

Dr. Vietmeyer, *citizen of New Zealand, is a Professional Associate of the U.S. National Academy of Sciences. Trained as an organic chemist he now works on neglected areas of science that could be important for the future well-being of developing countries.*

export to the Far East. But, in the 1920s, University of Illinois researchers established a comprehensive soybean research programme, which helped sweep aside this discrimination. The soybean acquired new status as a "legitimate" research target, and its development gained so much momentum that it now perhaps provides the world with more protein than any other plant species.

Nowhere is the neglect of poor man's crops greater than in the tropics—the very area where food is most desperately needed. The wealth and variety of tropical plant species are staggering, but most agricultural scientists are unaware of the scope and potential offered by them. Tropical botany and tropical agriculture are neglected largely because the major scientific research centres are located in temperate zones.

AN UNCUT GEM

Some of the best crops in the developing world may already be in the farmer's gardens, ignored by science. Merely to have survived, these plants have to be superior. They are already suited to the peasant's small plots, to his mixed farming, his poor soils, to his diet, and to the way of life of his family or village.

To illustrate the inherent promise of some of these crops, I have selected the following five examples, which were brought to my attention by the National Academy of Sciences studies mentioned above. Each of these plants appears to be an "uncut gem," a crop that awaits the polish of research to bring out its full quality.

Known only in the Kalahari and neighbouring sandy regions of southern Africa, the marama bean[1] rivals the soybean and groundnut in nutritional value. It feeds some of the poorest of the earth's people: the Bushmen and isolated Bantu tribes in Botswana and in Namibia who still subsist solely on wild fruits and plants, game and birds. To the Kung Bushmen, it is the second most important food.

Yet, the marama bean has been so neglected by agronomists that it is still a wild plant. Its cultivation has never been formally attempted.

The plant is native to droughty, semidesert areas of the Kalahari. It is a creeper, which sends several long viny stems out as far as 6 m over the sandy soil. In the early autumn, the plants are clad in golden yellow blossoms, which give rise to large, flat, woody pods containing chestnut brown spherical beans. The beans have a hard woody shell but the seeds inside are cream coloured with firm, oily flesh. When roasted, these seeds have a rich nutty flavour, which has been likened to that of roasted cashews or almonds. Africans often pound and boil them to make porridge or soup.

The seeds appear to be exceptionally nutritious, with a protein content essentially the same as that of soybean (37 percent). In addition, marama seeds contain 33 percent of a light-coloured, pleasantly flavoured oil (soybeans contain only about 20 percent oil). In nutritional energy, the marama bean rivals the groundnut (560 *vs.* 587 calories per g), one of the best food energy sources in the plant kingdom. The seeds also provide nutritionally important minerals.

Thus, the nutritional value of the marama bean ranks with soybeans and groundnuts, two of the world's most important crops.

In addition to its seeds, the marama bean provides another rather astonishing food. Below ground it produces a tuber that can weigh as much as 40 kg and be 1 m in diameter. Africans in the Kalahari region dig up the young tubers when they weigh about 1 kg. Boiled or roasted they have a sweet, pleasant flavour and make a good vegetable dish. The tuber is succulent, sometimes containing as much as 90 percent moisture; in arid and semiarid regions, it is an important emergency source of water for humans and animals.

With all of these basic attributes, the large-scale cultivation of the marama bean should have been investigated long ago. Given research, particularly plant breeding, it could become a valuable new crop for semiarid lands everywhere.

Perhaps no other crop offers such a variety of foods as the winged bean.[2] Yet is is a little-known crop, used extensively only in New Guinea and southeast Asia. Taken together, the winged bean's products make up an impressively palatable and nutritious diet, one that appears to meet many dietary needs of the tropics, especially of the wet tropics where protein deficiency is not only great but difficult to remedy. Every bit of the winged bean plant is eaten—leaves, pods, shoots and flowers all go into the cooking pot, and when the season is over, the villagers dig up the fleshy, tuberous roots and roast them. Any stems that remain are fed to livestock.

A BUSHY PILLAR OF GREENERY

The winged bean grows easily and quickly in tropical climates and yields profusely. Bacteria in its masses of root nodules (many hundreds have been counted on a single plant) convert nitrogen from the air into nitrogenous compounds, which the plant uses to build protein. Indeed, protein pervades virtually every part of a winged bean plant.

A bushy pillar of greenery with viny tendrils, blue or purple flowers and heart-shaped leaves, the winged beans resemble a runner bean plant. It forms succulent green pods—as long as a man's forearm in some varieties. The pods, oblong in cross-section, are green, purple or red and have four flanges or "wings" along the edges. When picked young, the green pods are a chewy and slightly sweet vegetable. Raw or boiled briefly, they make a crisp, snappy delicacy. Pods are produced over several months and a crop can be collected every two days, thus providing a continuous supply of fresh green vegetables.

If left on the vine the pods harden, but the pea-like seeds inside swell and ripen. When mature, the seeds are brown, black or mottled. In composition, they are essentially identical to soybeans, containing 34 to 39 percent protein and 17 to 20 percent polyunsaturated fat. The protein is high in the nutritionally critical amino acid, lysine.

In addition to the pods and seeds, the winged bean's leaves and tendrils make good spinach-like potherbs. Its flowers, when cooked, make a delicacy with a texture and taste reminiscent of mushrooms.

Perhaps the most startling feature of the plant is that, in addition to the foods it produces above ground, it also can grow fleshy, edible tuberous roots below ground whose firm fibreless flesh has a delicious nutty flavour. The winged bean is like a combination of soybean and potato plants. Not all types produce tubers big enough to eat, but those that do are potentially important as root vegetables in the humid tropics where sweet potatoes, yams, cassava (manioc) and other roots are already staples. This is because winged bean tubers are uniquely rich in protein—they can contain more than ten times the protein of cassava, for example.

A TROPICAL SOYBEAN

The winged bean is so popular in the diet of highlanders in Papua New Guinea that tribes often hold winged bean sing-sings (festivals). The plant is also well known to villagers in Indonesia, Malaysia, Thailand, the Philippines and Burma. Yet, it was not until 1973 that the first concerted efforts to investigate the crop's agronomy were begun. In 1975, the plant was given worldwide recognition in a National Academy of Sciences booklet, and so many researchers and landowners have introduced it in so many countries that a special newsletter, *The Winged Bean Flyer,* is published just to keep up with their findings.

So far this crop is withstanding the scrutiny of modern science. Most research results are positive. The winged bean seems to be well on its way to becoming a "tropical soybean," a highly nutritious vegetable specially suited to the small plots, kitchen gardens and backyards of the poor majority in some of the world's most malnourished zones.

Practically unknown outside South America's Andean region, tarwi[3] is a common crop of the Indians of Peru, Bolivia and Ecuador. Indeed, maize, potato, quinua (another grossly neglected poor man's crop) and tarwi together form the basis of the highland Indian's diet. Pre-Inca people domesticated this lupin at least 1500 years ago, and today tourists visiting Cuzco, the ancient Incan capital, find baskets of tarwi seeds a common sight in the markets.

To the Indians, meat is a luxury, but tarwi is extremely rich in protein, richer in fact than peas, beans, soybeans and groundnuts. It, therefore, makes a very important contribution to the nutritional well-being of the Andean regions.

For all its importance and potential, tarwi remains grossly neglected by science although about a dozen researchers scattered as far abroad as Peru, Chile, the United Kingdom, the U.S.S.R. and Australia have, in the last few years, initiated tarwi investigations.

Like other poor man's crops, tarwi is hardy and adaptable. It is easily planted and tolerates frost, drought, a range of soils and many pests. It grows vigorously, sometimes reaching almost 2 m in height, and produces masses of foliage and showy blue-purple flowers. High above the leaves are many tiers of seed pods, each containing bean-like seeds that are white, speckled, mottled or black.

The seeds are exceptionally nutritious. Protein and oil make up more than half their weight. Individual seeds containing up to 49 percent protein are known, though an average seed contains about 46 percent. Oil content varies from 5 to over 20 percent, averaging about 14 percent. This combination of oil and protein makes tarwi seed roughly comparable to soybean in composition.

Tarwi protein is digestible, and has a nutritional value equivalent to that of soy protein. Tarwi oil is light coloured and acceptable for kitchen use. In fact, tarwi appears to be a ready source of protein and vegetable oil not only for humans but also for animals, as well as for the manufacture of textured protein products, high-protein meal for food and feed, and cooking oil and margarine.

But tarwi desperately needs research attention for it has one fundamental drawback: the unprocessed seeds are bitter due to the presence of toxic alkaloids. To overcome this, the Indians soak the seeds in running water for a day or two until the water-soluble alkaloids are washed out.

From the fragmentary research already completed, it seems clear that tarwi strains with almost no alkaloids are available in nature; they can also be induced artificially by using radiation. Much follow-up research yet remains to be done to confirm and consolidate these initial findings. But, with low-alkaloid tarwi varieties and breeding for specific locations and needs, this now little-known plant could become a major crop for the Andes as well as for cool, tropical highlands and temperate regions all over the world.

A NUTRITIONALLY COMPLETE FOOD

Bambara groundnut[4] plants look and grow like groundnuts. But whereas the groundnut is one of the most intensively developed crops in the world, the bambara groundnut has received little research attention. Yet, along with groundnut, cowpeas, pigeon peas and haricot beans, it is among rural Africa's most popular grain legumes (pulses). It is among the top five most important protein sources for much of Africa. A staple from Senegal to Kenya and from the Sahara to Madasgascar, the bambara groundnut remains one of the most scientifically neglected of all crops.

The crop is cultivated like groundnuts. As the plant matures, its flower stalks bend downward and push the flower head slightly into the soil. The round, wrinkled pods—each containing two seeds—then form underground.

The seeds make a nutritionally complete food. They have less oil and protein than groundnuts, but they are richer in carbohydrates, thus providing as much food energy as a good cereal grain. Unripe seeds are eaten fresh, but the ripe seeds are hard and must be roasted, boiled or ground to flour to be edible. They then become sweet and pleasant to eat: Africans often prefer them to groundnuts. Sometimes the roasted seeds are ground into a nutritious flour that can be incorporated into many dishes. The protein has a high lysine content, which makes the bambara groundnut a good supplement to cereal diets.

Bambara groundnut grows best where groundnuts or sorghum thrive, but it is one of the most adaptable of all crops and tolerates exceptionally harsh conditions. This adaptability and hardiness allow it to survive and yield food under conditions too arid for groundnuts or sorghum. It needs bright sunshine and high temperatures, and it appears particularly valuable for hot, dry regions where diseases, poor soils or the threat of droughts make growing other pulses too risky.

Although when the plants are scattered in an African farmer's small plot, per-hectare yields are low, there is much evidence suggested that, with good management and dense stands, the bambara groundnut can match yields with better known grain legumes.

A chief preoccupation of agronomists and nutritionists has been the improvement of protein in the diet of rural Africans. The bambara groundnut deserves more of their attention. One particular research challenge is to improve the digestibility of its protein, which would bring a sweeping and immediate benefit to rural areas over most of the continent.

At least five amaranths[5] are poor man's crops. All are half-wild, multipurpose, New World plants, a rich source of vegetable protein, food energy and fibre. So far they have been largely neglected by research organizations.

Major grain crops in the tropical highlands of the Americas at the time of the Spanish Conquest, amaranths reached Asia, New Guinea and Africa in Spanish colonial times and then were spread and assimilated by local farmers. Today they are important to rural farmers in Central and South America and to hill tribes in Asia, New Guinea and parts of Africa.

EXCEPTIONALLY EFFICIENT

Vigorous and tough, amaranths have been termed "self-reliant plants requiring very little of the gardener." They germinate and grow well under adverse conditions. They are easily cultivated and they adapt well to the rural farmer's small plots and mixed cropping. Furthermore, they are relatively easy to harvest by hand and to cook and use in foods.

Amaranths belong to a small group of plants, termed C_4 whose photosynthesis is exceptionally efficient. The sunlight they capture is utilized more effectively than in most plants, and amaranths grow fast.

Amaranths are annuals, reaching 2 m in height, and have large magenta-tinged leaves. They produce full, fat, sorghum-like seed heads up to 30 cm long and 12 cm wide. (A related ornamental amaranth is called Prince of Wales' Feathers because of its brilliant crimson seedhead.) The seeds are small but occur in prodigious quantities. Their carbohydrate content is comparable to that of the true cereals. But amaranths are superior to cereals in protein and fat.

When heated, amaranth grains burst, and a popcorn-like confection—called *alegrias* in Mexico, *laddoos* in India and Pakistan—is made from them. However, in many areas, the grains are more usually parched and milled into flour. The starch in the flour is glutinous and has excellent baking qualities. Bread made from it has a delicate nutty flavour. Pancake-like *chapatis* made from it are a staple in the Himalayan foothills.

Recently, W.J.S. Downton, an Australian researcher, has found that the grain of at least one amaranth (*Amaranthus caudatus*) is rich in protein and exceptionally rich in lysine, one of the critical amino acids usually deficient in plant protein. Indeed, the amount of lysine present exceeds that found in milk or in the high-lysine maize now under development.

Grain amaranths worth much greater attention from researchers are *Amaranthus caudatus* (a native of the Andean regions of Argentina, Peru and Bolivia), *Amaranthus hypochondriacus* (highlands of Mexico, Himalaya foothills), and *Amaranthus cruentus* (Guatemala).

In addition to their seeds, these species also have edible and nutritious leaves that are widely consumed as a boiled vegetable. Two other species, *Amaranthus lividus* and *Amaranthus tricolor,* are common potherbs in Asia and are grown and eaten in the Western world under the names of Chinese or Malabar spinach.

In a far-sighted research venture in 1977, Rodale Press, a private U.S. corporation, distributed 14 000 lots of *Amaranthus hypochondriacus* seeds to gardeners across North America. From the response, it seems clear that this Central American poor man's crop has important potential in some of the most highly developed pockets of civilization anywhere. There is no doubt that science has been wrong to neglect the amaranths.

PIONEERING WORK

The species discussed are just a handful of examples of worthy plants, still largely overlooked by researchers. To develop such crops could be an exciting task, one that should be the responsibility of agricultural research stations in developing countries. It is pioneering, world-class work in a field where the wealthy laboratories in industrialized countries are at a disadvantage simply because they do not have the plants. It is, however, very hard to get grants for research on these plants. Funding agencies resist. The plants are unknown to most of them, and the literature to support any claims may be sparse.

Nonetheless, it is now time for agricultural research facilities to incorporate poor man's crops into their ongoing research efforts. Third World agricultural development needs this balance, for only when his own crops are improved will the subsistence farmer be able to feed his family adequately. In future decades it may, as in the case of the soybean, be today's neglected plants that are feeding the world.

NOTES

1. Tylosema esculentum (*Burchell*) A. Schreiber. Also known as Bauhinia esculenta *Burchell. Family Leguminosae. Commonly called tsi or tsin bean (Kung Bushman names), braaiboontje (Afrikaans), gemsbok bean, tamani berry, marama or morama (Tswana), ombanui or ozombanui (Herero), or gami (Hottentot).*
2. Psophocarpus tetragonolobus (*L.*) *DC. Family Leguminosae. Also known as goa bean, manila bean, seguidillas (Philippines) hap-bin (Papua New Guinea), Tu-a-pu (Thailand).*
3. Lupinus mutabilis *Sweet. Family Leguminosae. Tarwi is its Peruvian name (also spelled tarwhi, tarhui, tagui). Ecuadorians call it chocho. Also known as altramuz or pearl lupin.*
4. Voandzeia subterranea (*L.*) *Thouars var. subterranea. Also known as Congo goober, earth pea, baffin pea, Madagascar groundnut, voandzou (Madagascar), epi roui (Yoruba), okboli, ede (Ibo), guijiya (Hausa), nzama (Malawi). Sometimes spelled bambarra groundnut.*
5. Amaranthus *species. Family Amaranthaceae.*

Building a Better Corn Plant

by John J. Reagan

During the past 30 years, plant breeders have increased the genetic yield potential of corn by more than a bushel per acre per year.

Is there room for further improvement? Plenty, according to most breeders. Their goal now is a corn plant adapted to ultra-high plant populations and capable of consistent yields of 200 to 300 bushels per acre. They say such a goal is practical, but reaching it may call for considerable redesign of the corn plant itself.

More leaf area. One thing that may change is the leaf area of corn plants. Scientists have long known that adapted hybrids with large leaf areas tend to produce more than those with smaller leaf areas.

Dick Johnson, DeKalb AgResearch corn breeder at Thomasboro, Ill., is among those working on leaf-area selection indexes to help develop better inbreds. Johnson measures leaves after tasseling, when plants are mature. Selecting several plants per row, he measures each leaf on them for length and width (he plants 24,000 kernels per acre in 30-inch rows). A computer converts these measurements into estimates of average leaf area for all plants in the plot.

"Leaf area looks like an excellent supplement to plant height as a guideline for speeding up inbred selection," Johnson says. "Crossing inbreds that have large upper leaves may produce higher-yielding hybrids."

Changes in leaf position may be in the offing, too. Early results indicate that corn yields may increase 10 to 20 percent when leaves are oriented to soak up more sun. Iowa State University researchers are comparing upright and horizontal leaf arrangements in 20-inch rows at populations of 16,000, 32,000, and 64,000 plants per acre. In one test, they tied upper leaves to the stalk to check the effect of vertical leaf placement.

"Erect-leaf varieties showed up best at high plant populations," says J.J. Mock, an Iowa State breeder. "We're trying to get an erect leaf above the ear and a flat leaf below the ear to get the most good from solar energy."

More ears. Tomorrow's corn plant may also be a prolific type. Bill Russell, another Iowa State breeder, has been working with prolific hybrids for 15 years. Early lines produced a second ear only at low plant populations, but

From *The Furrow*, 80 (5) September–October 1975, 26–27. Reprinted by permission of John Deere & Company.

Russell says recent crosses are capable of much more. These new multi-ear types may be the key to eliminating a major corn yield barrier: barrenness at very high populations. Commercial breeders are now using some of this promising parent stock.

Pioneer Seed Company researchers are crossing prolific lines with their elite inbreds. One experimental cross outyielded all other varieties planted by 40 bushels per acre in tests at Pioneer's Wilmar, Minn., station.

"We select plants that have three ears when they're planted at moderate densities," says Forrest Troyer, research coordinator at Pioneer's Mankato, Minn., station. "We're trying to develop a prolific that provides more than a hedge against drought or population stress. A commercial prolific has to outyield normals by producing more grain per acre. These new hybrids will be capable of doing this by setting two ears per stalk at normal populations and one ear per stalk at extremely high populations."

Tassels and stalks. Some corn hybrids of the future may even produce grain on the tassel rather than on the ear. So-called tassel corn could offer several advantages. For instance, it could be harvested with a grain platform. Also, its kernels dry as much as two weeks sooner. Tassels come out earlier and develop faster than ears; more air exposure and absence of cobs allow faster drying. In one DeKalb study, tassel grain tested 13 percent moisture on September 23; normal corn tested 26 percent moisture the same day.

Yields of tassel corn are inconsistent, but a typical tassel does have perhaps three times as many florets (seed-bearing sites) as an average ear.

"Some tassels weigh more than half a pound and have 3,000 kernels," says Robert Rosenbrook, a Pioneer plant breeder. "We're selecting lines with sturdy roots and stalks to hang those heavier yields on."

Pioneer researchers are also working with an exotic "hard rind" stalk that gives some inbreds bamboo-like strength. Troyer says these tough stalks reduce lodging dramatically.

Faster Breeding. The whole process of developing new hybrids may soon be speeded up by a technique called single-cell hybridization. This involves fusing the components of two cells from widely different plants to form a new hybrid. It would bypass traditional, time-consuming breeding procedures, and it would permit breeders to make wider crosses.

Scientists attempting to perfect the technique say it holds great potential for improving crops. Uniting cells from grain sorghum and corn, for instance, might produce better rootworm resistance. So far, the main problem has been to raise a mature plant from the union of two unrelated cells.

Whatever the breeding technique used, researchers will be trying to develop corn plants that do well in adverse as well as favorable conditions. Ideally, tomorrow's corn will perform well on poorer soils, will tolerate more cold, will have more disease resistance, and will stand up better to hail and other physical damage.

So what will this super corn look like? It may well be 5 feet tall and have a Christmas-tree silhouette, according to I.C. Anderson, an Iowa State plant physiologist. "Two or three ears may be placed toward the top," he says. "Higher ear placement, plus upright leaves, will allow the plant to use light more efficiently and allow air movement in the plant canopy."

Better Wheats Are on the Way

by John J. Reagan

Deciding which wheat varieties to grow isn't as cut and dried as it used to be. More good varieties are available now, and scientists say the choice will be even wider in the years ahead.

An example of these new varieties is Key, which was released recently by a team of Purdue University and USDA plant breeders.

Key is 2 to 3 percentage points higher in protein than similar varieties, according to Fred Patterson, leader of the Purdue small-grain breeding team. He says Key will likely be used for special purposes, such as making high-protein breakfast foods and snacks. It's one of the first eastern varieties bred for improved nutritional qualities. Limited amounts of seed will be available soon for contract growing.

Beau, another new Purdue variety, will be available to commercial growers this fall. General resistance to Septoria leaf blotch, high Hessian fly resistance, and excellent straw strength are among its advantages.

Beating bugs. Pest resistance in wheat has a tremendous economic impact, according to Patterson. He explains: "For example, farmers now save a potential loss of about 10 million bushels of wheat each year by planting varieties that resist Hessian fly. Our task is to continue developing varieties with resistance to new races of diseases and insects."

Fuzz, Downy, and Vel are names of promising Purdue releases that feature built-in obstacles to the cereal leaf beetle, which has now spread into 14 eastern states and Ontario. Tiny leaf hairs interfere with egg-laying by adult beetles and feeding by larvae. The fine hairs also keep Hessian fly larvae from migrating to the plant crown in the soil, where pupae develop.

Last fall, 100 farmers seeded Fuzz in a 16-square-mile area straddling the Indiana-Michigan border. "This experiment will determine whether a resistant variety will reduce cereal leaf beetle populations," says Robert Gallun, project coordinator and a USDA entomologist at Purdue. "We also hope to find out whether resistant wheat maintains its resistance to other pests, such as leaf rust, stem rust, and powdery mildew."

Dodging disease. Ruler, a new midseason soft red variety especially suited for Ohio and surrounding areas, is resistant to loose smut and scab, and very resistant to the soil-borne virus known as wheat spindle streak mosaic. It is

From *The Furrow*, 80 (4) July–August 1975, 34–35. Reprinted by permission of John Deere & Company.

moderately susceptible to powdery mildew and most races of leaf rust and stem rust. But it hasn't shown any significant yield reduction from these diseases, according to Howard Lafever, a plant breeder at the Ohio Agricultural Research and Development Center, Wooster.

"I think it's important for growers to realize some disease and insect problems are magnified by untimely seeding, failure to follow crop rotations, or use of improper fertility levels," Lafever says.

Antler, a soft red winter variety released last year by Pennsylvania State University and the University of Missouri, is a deer-resistant wheat developed for growers near wooded areas. It is also very resistant to wheat spindle streak mosaic and fairly resistant to Hessian fly.

Henry Shands, DeKalb AgResearch, Inc. agronomist at Lafayette, Ind., says few varieties now grown have satisfactory resistance to barley yellow dwarf virus (BYDV). "Until now, few people have considered the disease important," he explains. "But 60-percent yield reduction has become rather standard in susceptible-type wheat varieties during severe BYDV attacks, such as we had in 1972, '74, and '76. However, we have been breeding lines with this problem in mind and we now have very resistant germplasm in our advanced generations."

Coming up. DeKalb is putting major emphasis on development of a hybrid soft red winter wheat. Shands says some of the crosses he has made have excellent tillering ability and good straw quality. With new hybrids, he's aiming for a 7-bushel-per-acre yield advantage over adapted varieties.

Howard Lafever says future varieties will produce higher yields more because of greater vigor than because of greater disease and insect resistance. But future varieties may also have better straw strength, more tolerance to micronutrient imbalances, and daylight insensitivity (in spring wheats).

Lafever is developing acid-tolerant varieties for soils with high native acidity. He's also investigating the possibility of incorporating flood tolerance into varieties for seeding on chronic overflow or poorly drained areas.

New white winter wheats, such as the Michigan-developed variety Tecumseh, are a step toward earliness and better yield. And Ticonderoga, a New York white wheat, is shorter strawed than many standard varieties.

Quality remains the big test for pastry wheats. At the USDA Soft Wheat Quality Laboratory at Wooster, Ohio, chemists test 2,500 soft red and white winter lines annually. "A new line may have great potential for high yield, good straw, and disease and insect resistance, but if it won't turn out good pastry, the breeder usually abandons it," says William Yamazaki, laboratory director. "Fortunately, many lines in the tests show excellent potential."

Wheat specialists say that as world markets grow and change, so will the need for new wheat varieties. And plant scientists are determined to have those new varieties ready ahead of demand.

9

Food from Animals

Man is considered to be an omnivorous animal and has been encouraged to eat a variety of foods for optimum nutrition. Meats have played an important part in mans food intake both from a nutritional and a gustatory point of view. In most cultures, meat is considered to be a highly desirable food and probably will continue to be highly regarded. The inclusion of a proportion of meat in the normal diet is also a form of food insurance as pointed out in the previous chapter.

Beef and milk, or milk products, are two of the major sources of animal protein in the human diet. The following two papers discuss the situation with the dairy cow and beef production. The third paper presents an interesting view of possible things to come.

The Role of the Dairy Cow in Meeting World Food Needs

by K.E. Harshbarger, Ph.D.,

The anticipated increase in population during the last 25 years of this century can be expected to place critical demands on the food production resources of the world. With earth's limited land resources, a time must come when the production of additional food on a given land area will be very difficult, if not impossible.

LAND RESOURCES

Based on FAO estimates, only about 11 percent of the world land area is utilized as permanent crop land. Another 22 percent is used for permanent pasture and meadows, and about 30 percent is covered with forests. About 27 percent is not available for agricultural production. Some of the land now classified as grassland or permanent pasture may be shifted to crop land by making major investments in reclamation and irrigation projects. The high costs involved and climatic limitations restrict the potential conversion of grassland to crop use.

PLANT RESOURCES

Plants utilize soil nutrients, water, carbon dioxide, and solar energy to produce food for humans and animals. The seeds of wheat and rice are primary sources of food energy for people. By-products of wheat and rice, and the forage parts of food crops, are available for animal feeding to produce additional food.

The need to balance the food supply on a world-wide basis by shipping cereal grains to the food-deficit areas has received much attention during the last few years. In 1971 approximately 43 percent of the wheat and 15 percent of the corn produced in the United States were exported. It has been estimated that 85 percent of exported feed grains is actually used for livestock produc-

From *Nutrition News,* 38 (3) October 1975, 1–4. Reprinted by permission of the National Dairy Council.

Head, Department of Dairy Science University of Illinois at Urbana-Champaign, Urbana

tion. In effect then, land in the U.S. is supporting livestock production in other countries to upgrade their diets with animal products. As the cost of energy increases, higher shipping costs should tend to encourage the export of livestock products rather than bulky feed grains.

ANIMAL RESOURCES

Animal products have been a part of man's food supply for thousands of years. Cattle were domesticated about 5000 years ago for a more reliable food supply, animal power, and other purposes. Now, with a critical food shortage facing the world, the competition between man and food-producing animals for the available crop foods needs to be critically evaluated. Animals must be utilized which are able to convert materials non-edible to humans to high-quality, essential nutrients in order to reach maximum world food production.

Ruminant animals, such as the cow, possess a unique digestive system which is able to convert inedible plant materials to human food in the form of milk and meat.

Efficiency of the dairy cow in relation to other animals in the utilization of land and feed resources for the production of more food is presented in Figure 1.

About 60 to 65 percent of the feed nutrients used for milk production comes from forages or fibrous feeds. By-products from the processing and refining of food crops for human consumption can be utilized to supplement forage and reduce the need for feed grains. For example, dried beet pulp from the manufacture of sugar can be fed to dairy cows. After milling wheat seed, only about 40 percent of the original energy and 36 percent of the original protein produced by the plant remain for human consumption. Thus, the nutritive values in the by-products from the milling process and, to a limited degree, in the wheat straw can be recovered by the cow.

Basically, the proportion of a specific plant nutrient recovered in the animal product has been used to express the biological efficiency of conversion of crop nutrients to human foods. Estimates of the efficiency of protein and energy conversion by various classes of livestock are presented in Table 1.

Food-producing animals which can efficiently convert roughage and food crop by-products to high-quality human food must be used for the benefit of mankind.

MILK PRODUCTION IN THE U.S.

In the United States and other temperate zone countries, milk has been an important part of the national diets, providing a large amount of high-quality protein, calcium, phosphorus, and riboflavin, and a moderate amount of vitamin A, and energy or calories.

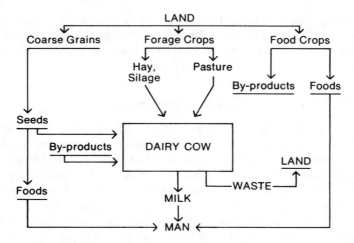

Figure 1. Utilization of land resources for milk production.

TABLE 1. Efficiency of Livestock in Converting Feed Nutrients to Edible Products.[2]

Class	Efficiency of Conversion, %[a]	
	Protein	Energy
Nonruminants		
Broilers	23	11
Turkeys	22	9
Hens (eggs)	26	18
Swine	14	14
Ruminants		
Dairy Cattle	25	17
Beef Cattle	4	3
Lambs	4	—

[a]Based on lifetime production and feed consumption.

The amount of milk produced has increased slightly in recent years on a world-wide basis and has remained relatively stable in the U.S.

However, in the last 30 years, as new knowledge in genetics and inheritance; and of feeding and management of dairy cows was applied, feed efficiency in U.S. milk production increased about 54 percent.(1) This increased efficiency of milk production saved about 50 billion pounds of total digestible nutritents, or the equivalent of 1.1 billion bushels of corn per year. Even though more grain was used per cow, each cow produced a greater quantity of milk; therefore, the total feed resources used for milk production were reduced.

PRODUCTION IN DEVELOPING COUNTRIES

Under adverse conditions in animal production, these efficiencies of conversion of feed by animals are not obtained. For instance, less than optimum biological efficiency is obtained from livestock production in the developing countries where these animals are scavengers. Developing countries maintain about 60 percent of the world's livestock, but produce only 20 to 30 percent of the world's livestock products.(3) In these countries where the milk supply is very limited, the average diet tends to be low in calcium, protein, and riboflavin. Thus, major changes in upgrading livestock management systems in developing countries are needed to improve efficiency of food production.

In some developing countries special dairy production projects have been established to increase milk production. The increased milk is used to nourish recently weaned children and to improve the protein quality in the diets of their people. With greater economic development and full utilization of feed resources, milk production can be expected to increase substantially in many developing countries.

FUTURE ROLE OF DAIRYING

The future role of the dairy cow in world food production appears favorable because:

1. The dairy cow efficiently converts roughage, food crop by-products, non-protein nitrogen, and feed grains to a high-quality human food.
2. High-quality milk protein effectively balances the amino acid patterns present in plant proteins.
3. Milk is a critical source of nutrients for most infants and children as well as adults.
4. Mechanization in the dairy industry can increase productivity.
5. Dairying favorably effects conservation of land resources by using forage crops, preventing soil erosion, and returning animal manure to the land to maintain fertility.

Only by managing our land resources to assure ourselves of a continuing food supply can we protect the current and future generations. Individually, and on a world basis, man must accept the responsibility for planning his future to utilize world resources and establish stable systems of agriculture.

REFERENCES

1. Salisbury, G.W., Harshbarger, K.E., Lodge, I.R., Fryman, L.R., and Marcoot, R.E. Returns from the public investment in research on milk production. Dairy Marketing Facts, April, 1973. AE–4314.
2. Ruminants as food producers. Council for Agricultural Science and Technology, Special Publication No. 4, March, 1975.
3. A hungry world: the challenge to agriculture. Summary Report, University of California Food Task Force, July, 1974.

Beef Production Efficiency

by Allen Trenkle and R.L. Willham

Summary

In the production of high quality protein, feed grains will continue to be used to finish cattle for market as long as economics dictates. Production systems could be developed that would make ruminant animals less competitive with humans for feed grains, but the costs of instituting such programs would be prohibitive. Sufficient genetic variation exists either between or within breeds for the cattle population to be adapted to new management programs and for current methods of beef production to be significantly improved.

Today in the United States, questions are being asked about the role of animals in food production because they consume feed grains that could otherwise be used directly for human consumption. However, livestock, especially cattle, have been an integral part of grain production agriculture for thousands of years. They have served as power; refuse scavengers; a means of transportation of the grain after consumption; producers of fertilizer; a highly flexible food reserve; sources of fiber, leather, and biochemicals; harvesters of forage from adjacent nontillable land areas; as well as a source of high quality protein that nutritionally complements basic grain diets.

Because ruminants utilize many materials not digestible by simple-stomached animals, including man, they have attracted attention in several recent reviews[1]. Ruminants are not as efficient as some other species in converting feed grains and oil seed meals to meat. Whether agriculture becomes limited to crop production in the future depends on the ability of the livestock industry, especially that part of the industry utilizing ruminants, to integrate efficient production systems into total agriculture output, and on the potential for improvement in animal production through the application of research. In this article we discuss research developments in nutrition and genetics which may improve the efficiency of meat production from beef cattle, currently the most conspicuous consumers of feed grains.

From *Science,* Vol. 198, pp. 1009–1015, December 9, 1977. Copyright 1977 by the American Association for the Advancement of Science.

The authors are professors of animal science, Iowa State University, Ames 50011.

EFFICIENCY OF PROTEIN PRODUCTION

Efficiency is the production of a desired effect with a minimum of input, or it can be considered as the ratio of output to input. There is no single expression that describes the overall efficiency of the beef industry, much less that of animal agriculture. The inputs and desired outputs for a breeding herd are quite different from those for animals used for slaughter. The desired output for breeding animals is reproduction, whereas that for market animals is production of high quality beef. Economically, inputs of labor, capital, land, and population size are most important. Around four animals exist in the breeding herd per market animal produced(2). To assess the outputs or inputs of animal agriculture in the same units is impossible. For feedlot cattle, the efficiency of protein production may be expressed as protein produced over protein consumed, but there is no efficiency ratio that can be used to include the value of insulin extracted from the pancreas. To simplify the discussion, biological efficiency will be considered as product nutrients per feed nutrient.

Changes in body composition can have a marked effect on efficiency. Fatty tissue contains more energy per gram than muscle tissue, so that a given quantity of feed will produce less fat than lean muscle. On a caloric basis the accumulation of fat is more efficient than protein gain because there is less heat loss from lipid synthesis. When protein utilization is the basis for comparison, young lean animals are more efficient in converting feed protein to product protein than animals which mature early and accumulate fat. Already in the United States there is a trend toward the consumption of greater proportions of lean beef. This trend alone will have a great influence on the efficiency of beef production in terms of converting feed supplies to lean meat, and will bring about changes in feeding and breeding systems used by the beef industry.

The singular advantage of the ruminant animal is its ability to use large quantities of low quality roughages and proteins in the production of a high quality protein. Cellulose, being a basic structural carbohydrate in all plants, is one of the most abundant organic compounds in the world. It makes up about 10 percent of the dry weight of leaves and about 50 percent of the structure of plants and is widely distributed in all parts of the world. Modern harvesting methods collect the grain and leave the fodders and straws in the field. Much of the land, because of topography, soil type, and climatic conditions, is not suited for extensive crop production and must be left in native vegetation or used to produce forage crops (for example, grass or legumes). Only about 10 percent of the earth's surface can be tilled for intensive crop production. Forage plants are often sparce and not easily harvested. Most roughages lack density and are not easily packaged for transport over long distances. Consequently, much of the roughage is not utilized in any food-producing system. It could be used effectively, however, by grazing animals or by harvesting it and feeding it to nearby cattle or sheep.

Cellulose is a polymer of glucose molecules joined by β-1,4 linkages. Many bacteria and fungi produce enzymes capable of hydrolyzing this bond, and the digestive tract of all herbivorous animals has developed to provide an environment in which microorganisms that digest cellulose can grow and multiply. The stomach of ruminants is divided into the rumen, reticulum, omasum, and abomasum. The ruminoreticulum provides the environment for the microbial fermentation of feeds before they are subjected to the gastric secretions and digestion in the abomasum. Ruminants are better adapted to use low quality roughages than other herbivores because the end products of the fermentation, as well as the microbes, are made available to the host animal. In ruminants, the microorganisms utilize part of the food consumed by the host animal for their own growth and metabolism before any nutrients become available to the host. Cellulose and starch are broken down to glucose which then is rapidly fermented by anaerobic glycolysis to short-chain fatty acids of which acetate, propionate, and butyrate are the most abundant. These acids are absorbed from the rumen and serve as a source of energy for the host. Most proteins are also extensively degraded to amino acids which are deaminated and decarboxylated to produce fatty acids, carbon dioxide, and ammonia. The ammonia is utilized by the microbes to synthesize proteins or is absorbed from the rumen and converted to urea in the liver. Part of the lower efficiency of ruminants in comparison with other species is attributable to the energy and nitrogen losses from the fermentation.

NUTRIENT METABOLISM AND
THE REFINEMENT OF FEEDING STANDARDS

Historically, the greatest improvements in efficiency related to food production from animals have come from a better understanding of the metabolism of nutrients and of the nutrient requirements of the animals themselves. Animals will be most productive when all the nutrients required to satisfy their needs are supplied by the diet or, in the case of ruminants, by the diet and fermentation, no nutrient being given in excess of these requirements. The proper balance of nutrients will vary for animals from different genetic sources, for animals in different stages of their life cycle, and for animals with different levels of production. In addition to having knowledge of their nutrient requirements, we need to have knowledge of the biological availability and concentration of nutrients in feedstuffs. Data on the chemical composition of feeds has been accumulating over many years. Laboratory methods to measure the biological availability of nutrients in feeds are not available for every nutrient. Some techniques have been developed, and the refinement of these methods continues to attract the interest of scientists. When more data become available on the nutrient requirements of the animals, the nutrient composition of the feed resources, and the biological availability of the nutrients in feeds it will be possible to formulate diets which best supply the nutrient needs of the animals. In many modern cattle feed yards, computers are used to formulate these diets. In the developing areas of the world, however, increased supplies of feeds will have the greatest influence on improvements in animal production rather than the use of complex technology to refine the feeding standards.

REGULATION OF FEED INTAKE

In the life cycle of cattle production, most of the feed is needed for maintenance (vital body functions, movement, and body temperature). Basal metabolism is related to body surface and often is expressed as a function of body weight according to the equation: basal metabolism (kilocalories) $= 70 \times$ (body weight)$^{0.75}$. It is unlikely that significant improvements in the efficiency of animal production will be brought about by decreasing basal metabolism. Because larger animals require more feed for maintenance, they have to be more productive (more pounds of calf, meat, or milk) to be as efficient as the smaller animals. The relation of size of cattle to efficiency of production is being investigated(2, 3). The ideal size will probably vary with several factors such as intensity of production, level of feed supplies, and input of management. Improvements in efficiency will be realized with a better understanding of these interrelationships.

As illustrated in Fig. 1, for a given size of animal a greater proportion of the feed consumed is used for productive purposes as level of feed intake is increased. This is because the maintenance requirements are related to body weight and remain constant at a given weight. The physiological regulation of feed intake of ruminants is complex and not completely understood(4). It is thought that a full digestive tract physically limits the consumption of bulky feeds such as forages. The consumption of diets composed largely of grain are thought to be regulated by sensitivity to chemical factors which serve as signals in the regulation of caloric homeostasis. Several studies, which have not been published, have been conducted at various experiment stations to evaluate a feed intake stimulant given the common name Elfazepam. The use of this compound shows some evidence of increasing feed consumption, especially of diets composed of roughages.

Because the energy is more concentrated in grains than roughages, cattle can obtain more metabolizable energy from diets containing grain than from those containing roughage. Also, the starches of grain are fermented differently in the rumen so a greater proportion of the gross energy of the grain is available to the animal for productive purposes than that from roughages. These two factors make grain a more efficient feed than roughages for fattening cattle. Therefore, when there are surpluses of grain and prices are low,

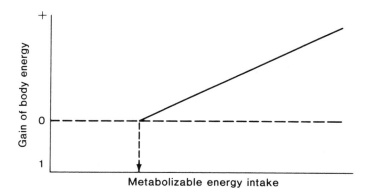

Figure 1. The relation between intake of metabolizable energy and level of production. If animals are fed less than the level required for maintenance, there will be a loss of body weight. Metabolizable energy is gross energy of the feed corrected for losses of energy in feces, urine, and digestive gases.

high concentrations of grain are used in cattle feeds. Only as grain prices increase relative to the cost of roughage, will roughages be substituted in large quantities for grain fed to cattle to be slaughtered. For maintenance, the useful energy available from roughages and grains is more nearly equal, so that the prices of grain usually favor the use of more roughages for maintaining breeding animals. As demand for grain in the world trade increases it will be necessary, in those parts of the world where large quantities of grain are fed to cattle, to feed less grain and more roughage. A large part of the increased amounts of roughages fed will probably come from the by-products of crops and crop residues.

INCREASING THE AVAILABILITY OF NUTRIENTS

Efficiency of beef cattle production could be increased if more of the nutrients in a given quantity of feed were available to the animal during digestion and absorption. Lignin, which is present in the woody parts of plants, occurs in close association with cellulose and prevents attack of the cellulose by microbial enzymes. Partial breakdown of the lignin by treatment of roughages with strong alkali increases the availability of the cellulose. The treatment of large quantities of roughage with alkali is cumbersome, however, and not widely practiced, but other methods may be more applicable. For example, the partial predigestion of roughages with enzymes or selected microorganisms may greatly improve the nutritional value of roughages. The processing of feeds by grinding, steaming, flaking, pelleting, and ensiling is being widely practiced in the cattle feeding industry(5).

The energy losses from the fermentation in the rumen are less if propionate is produced instead of acetate and butyrate. The production of propionate from glucose results in the utilization of hydrogen, whereas conversion of glucose to acetate or butyrate produces hydrogen and carbon dioxide, which results in the formation of methane. Methane is lost from the rumen as a gas and represents a significant loss of energy. Attempts are being made to reduce the generation of methane in the fermentation, but to date no method has been found that has practical applications. Changing the fermentation in favor of propionate has been used as the basis for the development of monensin, which is used as a feed additive for the improvement of feed utilization of feedlot cattle(6). The formation of greater quantities of propionate results in more metabolizable energy being available to the animal from a given quantity of feed. Cattle feed monensin require 10 percent less feed per pound of gain. This compound is effective in cattle fed grain or roughage. It has been cleared for use in feedlot cattle and in the near future may be available for use in grazing cattle.

Because the loss of nutrients during the fermentation can be excessive with certain feeds, attention has been given to protecting nutrients as they pass through the rumen. The protection of proteins has been studied the most(7), the object being to protect those of high nutritional quality so that more of their amino acids are made available to the animal, and to allow the poorer quality proteins or urea to serve as a source of nitrogen for the microorganisms. Some protection has been achieved by careful heating of the proteins or by treating them with chemicals, such as formaldehyde, with which they form complexes. Much remains to be learned in this area but some recent studies at Iowa State University indicate that cattle require only one-third as much supplemental protein when soybean meal is treated with formaldehyde as they require when this protein source is fed unprotected. Protection of proteins will be more important when low-quality roughages are used as cattle feeds because they contain only small amounts of protein and therefore require more supplemental protein than other feeds. Protection of other nutrients may also be possible to improve efficiency of their utilization. Protection of lipids to increase the bypass of unsaturated fatty acids is being researched as a means to reduce the concentration of saturated fatty acids in meat and milk from cattle.

IMPROVING EFFICIENCY OF FEED UTILIZATION BY THE ANIMAL

It has been known for many years that younger animals are most efficient in the conversion of feed to meat, and that bulls are more efficient than steers in this conversion(8). These differences are partly related to the composition of the gain, the gain of the young animal containing more lean and less fat, but other factors related to the endocrine system are also involved. It was discovered over 20 years ago that estrogens increase the growth of cattle and sheep(9), the increased weight being made up of more muscle and bone and less fat (Table 1). Estrogens increase the efficiency of utilization of dietary protein or energy for growth by more than 30 percent. Because diethylstilbestrol, the synthetic estrogen used extensively in beef cattle, is a carcinogen, its use may not be continued in the future. There are other products, however, which contain naturally occurring estrogenic compounds and bring about responses similar to diethylstilbestrol in cattle. Estrogens are thought to stimulate growth of cattle by increasing the secretion of growth hormones from the anterior pituitary gland(10).

It has recently been observed that the effects of monensin, which acts in the gastrointestinal tract, and the effects of hormones that change endogenous growth hormone levels are additive. The increase in gain brought about by combined monensin and hormone treatment has been over 20 percent and the improvement in conversion of feed to gain has been about 29 percent (Table 2). As our knowledge of the endocrine system involved in the regulation of growth of cattle increases, other methods for the administration of hormones may be developed that will produce even more dramatic improvements in the conversion of dietary nutrients to beef. It may also become possible to prolong the high conversion efficiency of the young calf up to the time of slaughter.

ALTERNATIVE FEED SUPPLIES

If cattle were fed sources of nutrients which could be digested by ruminants but not utilized by humans, then beef production would become less competitive with human food supplies. The use of by-products and crop residues has already been referred to. With greater knowledge of the nutrition of cattle and increased availability of nutrients from roughages it will be possible to produce acceptable finished beef entirely with noncompetitive feeds, such as by-products and crop residues. A group of cattle fed a ration containing 77 percent noncompetitive feeds (60 percent corncobs, 15 percent cane molasses, 2 percent urea, 15 percent corn, 7 percent soybean meal, and 2 percent vitamins and minerals) in an experiment in progress at Iowa State University are gaining 1 kilogram per animal per day.

One nutrient source that has received much attention is urea, which can be used to replace a portion or all of the supplemental protein in cattle feeds(11). Nutritionists generally agree that protein is a major limiting nutrient for animal production, especially ruminants fed forages and roughages. The use of urea in the United States has increased from no use of practical significance in the early 1940's to 180×10^6 kg in 1976. The present annual usage is equivalent to the nitrogen in 1050×10^6 kg of soybean meal.

TABLE 1. The influence of diethylstilbestrol on the utilization of dietary energy and protein for body weight gain of feedlot cattle. Data calculated from Fowler et al. (28).

Diethyl-stilbestrol (mg/day)	Animals (No.)	Empty body weight gain (kg)	Composition of Gain (%)			EG/EC*	Efficiency of Gain*	
			Moisture	Protein	Fat		PG/EC†	PG/PC‡
Cattle fed on corn grain								
0	9	158	24.7	9.5	63.4	33.5	3.2	11.3
20	9	181	30.9	11.7	54.4	29.6	4.2	15.0
Cattle fed on corn silage								
0	10	144	20.9	8.2	68.7	34.7	2.0	7.7
20	10	177	31.6	12.1	53.3	30.0	3.5	13.3

*Ratios of energy gained to energy consumed.
†Ratios of protein gained to energy consumed.
‡Ratios of protein gained to protein consumed.

TABLE 2. Influence of hormone implants and monensin on weight gain and efficiency of feed utilization by feedlot cattle. Summary of eight experiments conducted in Indiana, Iowa, and Minnesota.

Treatment	Gain (kg/day)	Ratio of Gain to Feed (kg)
None	1.08	0.119
Implant	1.23	0.129
Monensin	1.13	0.136
Implant + monensin	1.30	0.153

The combined use of urea and protected proteins could result in beef production becoming even more efficient.

Animal and poultry wastes are also an alternative source of nutrients for animal production. These materials contain nitrogen, minerals, and energy which can be utilized by cattle. These wastes contain the end products of protein metabolism which can be degraded in the rumen and utilized in a way similar to the way urea is used by rumen microorganisms. Some of the undigested energy components of the feed are further modified by the microorganisms in the large intestine of ruminants and nonruminants, before excretion; and if the wastes are properly processed (ensiled, heated, dried, or chemically treated) they can be fed to cattle.

BREEDING

The efficiency of beef production could be increased by genetic manipulation of the cattle population. Such increases would be brought about primarily through the impact of size, rate of maturity, and milk differences on economics rather than by biological efficiency. Exploitation of existing genetic differences and the creation of capital improvement through selection are both viable means to achieve increased efficiency. For a historic account of the development of existing genetic differences in cattle, see(12).

Before the Charolais breed of cattle gained importance in the early 1960s, only the three British beef breeds (Hereford, Angus, and Shorthorn) were available to beef producers in the United States. In 1967 the Canadian government provided the means to import frozen semen into the United States from numerous continental European breeds. These imports included semen and then breeding stock from a variety of types from dairy, dual-purpose, to beef breeds. This introduction of new germ plasm, although sought by the scientific community(13), was accomplished by the beef industry. Only recently(14) has there been a large-scale comparative evaluation of these introductions. These diverse genetic groups or breeds are important to the beef industry because breed formation is a slow process with the low reproduction rate of cattle (0.86 calf per cow per year on the average).

Commercial producers of beef now have a choice among at least 30 breeds and their cross combinations. After this initial selection of breeds or breed crosses, the producer has a choice among the breeding herds and the animals within these herds of the chosen breeds or he can use frozen semen. This is the current population structure or hierarchy existing in the breeding herd that supplies the germ plasm to the roughly 97 percent of the beef industry engaged in market production. Beef breeding is still done primarily by small breeders rather than by large breeding companies.

The design of sound breeding programs by breeders and producers requires a knowledge of the kind and amount of genetic variation available to make genetic change(15). For breeders and producers to use new and relatively sophisticated technology in the conduct of their breeding programs requires economic incentive and creative extension programs. Table 3 shows a synthesis of beef breeding research that has been accomplished to describe the kind and amount of genetic variation available in the beef population. The synthesis is derived from many research papers on beef breeding that have appeared primarily in the *Journal of Animal Science*, from reviews on beef breeding(16, 17), and from knowledge of the genetic characteristics of the species studied. The table has been used extensively to disseminate breeding technology(18–20). Coupled with the genetic values are relative economic values that are just now receiving attention from economists and geneticists.

To simplify the table, the numerous traits measured in beef research are placed in three classes: reproduction, production, and product. In broad biological terms, the classes can be defined as reproductive, physiological, and morphological. The reproductive traits, such as calf crop percentage weaned, are complex traits dealing with the interaction of the sire, dam, and the resulting calf. The production traits in the breeding herd, such as cow weights and weaning weights of the calves, deal with mature size and milk production differences. These traits influence the costs of calf production. The production traits in market animals, such as rate and efficiency of gain in the feedlot, deal with growth and maturity rate differences. The product traits, such as yield of edible product and meat quality grade, deal with lean-to-bone ratio and fat deposition rate differences in the product, beef.

TABLE 3. Current beef industry values: a synthesis of research information on genetic values and some relative economic values. The reproduction class of traits includes calf crop percentage, calving interval, calving ease, and survival percentage, for example. The production class of traits includes mature size and milk production in the breeding herd and rate of gain and efficiency in the feedlot for market animals. The product traits include measures of the amount of product and its eating quality.

	Genetic Values			Economic Values (relation)	
Class of Traits	Breed Types Differences* (%)	Heterosis† (percentage increase)	Heritability‡ (percentage of variation)	Breeding herds§	Market Feedlots‖
Reproduction	20	10	10	5	0
Production	50	5	40	1	2
Product	10	0	50	0	1

*These are average differences among breed types when given comparable treatment expressed as a percentage of the mean performance. The relative values are the issue rather than the absolutes. Large differences among breed types exist for production traits while relatively small differences in product traits exist when types are taken to a similar composition.

†Heterosis is defined as the difference between the cross and the average of the parental breeds. This difference is expressed as a percentage of the mean performance.

‡Heritability is defined as the fraction of the variation, among individuals of the same breed that are treated alike, that is genetic. Selection advance is predictable by the product of heritability and the superiority of the selected parents.

§The relative economic value of the trait class in the breeding herd under commercial production.

‖The relative economic value of the trait class in the market animals under commercial production.

The headings under genetic values in Table 3 refer to differences, expressed as a percentage of the mean performance for the particular class of traits, among broad types such as dairy, dual-purpose, or beef breeds; to the amount of heterosis, expressed as a percentage of the mean performance for the particular class of traits, expected from crossing breeds either between or within the types; and to the fraction or percentage of the differences among individuals of the same breed that are treated alike, which is genetic or is available for selection. All the figures under genetic values are an expression of genetic differences that are given either as percentages of the mean or as percentages of the variation found for the traits in a particular class. These figures give a general description of the kind and amount of genetic variation available in the beef cattle population.

Large differences exist among types and even among breeds within types, especially for the production class of traits, because of differences in growth rate and milk production among the breeds. Heterosis can be obtained from crossing breeds, especially for the reproductive complex. The heterosis potential is large enough to be commercially important. The amount of genetic variation available for selection within breeds is high enough for the production and product traits to suggest commercial improvement. Note that the amount of heterosis to expect and the amount of genetic variation within breeds is negatively correlated. This relationship is true for most species and does create problems in breeding program design.

The columns under economic values refer to the commercial herds that produce the market calves and to the market product, calves which are not expected to reproduce. This division, which emphasizes the segmentation of the beef industry into calf producers and feeders, clouds the economic incentives for the breeders producing germ plasm for the beef industry. Reproduction, or the creation of new wealth, is at least five times as important in commercial operations as growth and milk production, as indicated by calf weaning weight. Production traits, such as gain in the feedlot, are about twice as important as the quantity or quality of the product currently, but this relation could change quickly depending on market demands.

Table 3 summarizes the genetic potential for change and the relative importance of such change and clearly suggests some opportunities for improving the efficiency of beef production. The importance of reproduction to commercial producers coupled with the heterosis potential for improving the reproductive complex indicates that cross-breeding could effectively increase overall efficiency of beef production. The large differences among breed types, especially for the production traits, suggests that complementarity or the selection of breeds to use in a program that complement each other could affect big changes in the industry. The column labeled heritability indicates that the breeders producing germ plasm for the commercial industry can improve the production and product traits by selection and pass this increase directly to the producer through the use of superior stock. No one breed or type appears to be best for all classes of traits or economic situations, so crossbreeding for both heterosis and complementarity, together with selective improvement of the breeds, appears to offer opportunities for improving efficiency by optimizing growth rate, mature size, milk production, and rate of maturity (important because of the age at which rapid fat deposition occurs) and to a limited extent by improving biological efficiency.

The basic problem encountered in applying the genetic potentials commercially is the extremely low reproductive rate of cattle. Heterosis has been exploited in species such as corn, poultry, and swine, which all have a much higher reproductive rate than cattle. That is, the extent to which an optimum breeding structure can be attained rests on whether it can be practiced economically, given the reproductive potential. When this is coupled with small herd size (less than 50 head on the average), a secondary enterprise except for ranches, and the increasing value of grazing land, the probability of research information being fully utilized is remote. However, the beef industry completely replaced the Longhorn and other cattle with British beef breeds and has introduced new germ plasm since 1967 which has definitely expanded the genetic potentials of the beef population. The key is to have the research information available when the economic incentives arise.

Improving the reproductive potential of cattle can reduce the cost of production (by spreading breeding-herd expenses over more animal units), increase the potential that can be realized from crossbreeding, and increase the response to selection (by having larger numbers from which to choose). Improving calf crop 1 percent from 86 percent with 30 million cows gives 200 thousand more calves or 340 thousand fewer cows for the same number of calves. Artificial insemination provided the means for introducing new germ plasm and now is recognized as a tool for breed improvement when used in conjunction with sire evaluation. The dairy industry has obtained a greater than 1 percent improvement in milk production per year by using superior sires evaluated through their early progeny test for milk(21). The use of artificial insemination to spread the daughters of a sire over many herds, and the Dairy Herd Improvement Association's record program coupled with the sire summaries published by the U.S. Department of Agriculture, has made such improvement possible. The general use of artificial insemination in the beef industry could produce similar results in seed-stock production and enhance the use of systematic crossbreeding programs. Breakthroughs that would make artificial insemination as easy as using a bull in commercial production are being researched.

Research in the field of reproductive physiology includes work on twinning. Investigators are using hormone manipulation in attempts to exploit this in herd situations where twinning would be desirable. Breeding by artificial insemination at ovulation is nearly ready for application in the field. With newly introduced breeds, "super-ovulation" of purebred females and techniques for ova transfer to donor cows are being used to produce several offspring per valuable cow per year. It is more difficult to evaluate cows accurately than it is to evaluate bulls that can have large numbers of progeny in many herds in a short time. General increases in calf crop percentages hold a high potential for increasing efficiency.

Directional genetic change in the cattle population can benefit the beef industry. The exploitation of heterosis and complementarity by selection of breeds and breed crosses in a systematic crossbreeding program can improve efficiency as well as the selection of superior individuals within the breeds. Current research is directed primarily toward the evaluation of the germ plasm introduced into the United States(17). Matching genetic potential to available management resources (such as feed available) has presented new problems of evaluation(20, 22). Just how best to exploit this new resource of breed differences is also receiving attention(23). Systematic rotational crossbreeding (with sires from two or more breeds being used in rotation); specific three-breed crosses (that can better utilize the complementarity of a small, crossbred cow for maternal heterosis and a large sire breed for growth and carcass merit); and synthetics (which are cross-combinations of several breeds used to circumvent the difficulty of systematic crossbreeding in small herds) are all options to be researched(24). Improvement in biological efficiency through the use of breed differences is not the primary issue, because Smith et al.(25) showed that there are small differences among breeds when all are slaughtered at a constant carcass composition.

Large improvements in the efficiency of beef production can be obtained by reducing the costs of the breeding herds, reducing the costs of time and in feed for maintenance by increasing growth rate, and reducing the amount of fat produced in the carcass from the optimum utilization of breed differences. Utilization of crossbreeding in the breeding herd alone can improve output from 20 to 50 percent. By simply taking feedlot cattle of a given breed combination to their optimum slaughter weight can improve the efficiency of production. As research information makes it possible to evaluate and define the potentials for the newly introduced germ plasm, the industry will better utilize the potentials that are available to improve efficiency.

Genetic improvements within breeds are being made. Most beef research in this area has been to describe the amount of genetic variation available and the genetic correlations among the traits within breeds, but a few long-term selection studies are under way(26). Eleven breeds have established sire evaluation programs on a national scale. Through these programs, the genetic structure of the breeds (which are subdivided into small partially isolated genetic groups, herds within breeds) can be clarified such that sires can be accurately evaluated and the superior one used extensively through artificial insemination for breed improvement. This opportunity came through the Beef Improvement Federation which is a federation of all performance organizations in the industry. The federation has codified the record systems and through participation of beef researchers has acted as the innovator for genetic technology use in the industry(12). Genetic improvement by selection within a herd is slow. For a single trait with 40 percent of the observable differences heritable, around a 1 percent improvement in the mean per year is expected. Current changes in the performance of particular breeds have come about by exploitation of existing herd differences through the widespread use of the germ plasm from these herds over the breed. Breed changes in skeletal size, and the resulting changes in rates of maturity and growth, can be made because of the high heritability of general size. The big problem, as always, is in the choice of goal or direction of selection by the many individual breeders producing the germ plasm for the industry.

Improvements in the efficiency of beef production within the immediate future are most likely to come from the matching of breed and breed-cross potentials with management systems. Such matching and use of crossbreeding could improve beef efficiency by 15 to 20 percent on a national basis where the improvements within the breeds might result in a 1 percent advantage per year at best, but they would be capital gains.

SYSTEMS

The beef industry is highly segmented, as is the research work of the various disciplines of animal science that contribute information to the efficiency of beef production. Efforts are under way to integrate the disciplines of genetics, nutrition, and physiology with economics to define production functions and develop optimum beef production systems. Such analyses are useful to point out areas where basic knowledge is imperative but lacking, to examine possible interactions among discipline inputs, and to formulate sound, demonstrable recommendations for extension. Examples of systems research in beef production have been discussed(2, 27). Systems research is a new area of opportunity in the beef industry.

CONCLUSION

The primary justification for animal production today is society's desire and need for high quality protein. In the production of such protein, domestic animals are consumers of, as well as producers of, protein and energy. Beef production in the United States will continue on a large scale, especially in operations in which the cow-calf pair is used as a harvester of low quality roughage. Feed grains will continue to be used to finish cattle for market as long as economics dictates because of the maintenance savings and the more palatable product that can be obtained from cattle at a younger age. The challenge is to develop production systems that will make ruminant animals less competitive with humans for grains and high quality protein feeds. Current knowledge of ruminant nutrition would be adequate to accomplish much of this, but the costs are prohibitive. Sufficient genetic variation exists either between or within breeds for the cattle population to be adapted to new management systems and for current methods of beef production to be significantly improved.

In European nations, beef production will continue to be a by-product of the dairy industries. For the developing nations with the potential to produce cattle, the development of a beef industry will depend on the economic climate and world trade. History is replete with cattle populations with no markets.

REFERENCES AND NOTES

1. T.C. Byerly, *Science* **195**, 450 (1977); J. Janick, C.H. Noller, C.L. Rhykerd, *Sci. Am.* **235** (No. 3), 75 (1976); G. VanVleck, *Prof. Nutritionist* **7**, 1 (1975); H.J. Hodgson, *BioScience* **26**, 625 (1976).
2. G.R. Long, T.C. Cartwright, H.A. Fitzhugh, *J. Anim. Sci.* **40**, 409 (1975).
3. C.A. Morris and J.W. Wilton, *Can. J. Anim. Sci.* **56**, 613 (1976).
4. C.A. Baile and J.M. Forbes, *Physiol. Rev.* **54**, 160 (1974).
5. National Research Council, *Effect of Processing on the Nutritional Value of Feeds* (National Academy of Sciences-National Research Council, Washington, D.C. 1973).
6. A.P. Raun, C.O. Cooley, E.L. Potter, R.P. Rathmacher, L.F. Richardson, *J. Anim. Sci.* **43**, 670 (1976); E.L. Potter, C.O. Cooley, L.F. Richardson, A.P. Raun, R.P. Rathmacher, *ibid.*, p. 665.
7. W. Chalupa, J. *Dairy Sci.* **58**, 1198 (1974).
8. T.R. Preston and M.B. Wills, *Intensive Beef Production* (Pergamon, Oxford, 1974), pp. 286–288.
9. W.E. Dinusson, F.N. Andrews, W.M. Beeson, *J. Anim. Sci.* **9**, 321 (1950); W. Burroughs, C.C. Culbertson, E. Cheng, W.W. Hale, P. Homeyer, *ibid.* **14**, 1015 (1955).
10. A. Trenkle, *Environ. Qual. Saf.* **5**, 79 (1976).
11. National Research Council, *Urea and Other Nonprotein Nitrogen Compounds in Animal Nutrition* (National Academy of Sciences-National Research Council, Washington, D.C., 1976).
12. R.L. Willham, *World Rev. Anim. Prod.* **10**, 20 (1974).
13. R.W. Phillips, in *Germ Plasm Resources*, R.E. Hodgson, Ed. (AAAS, Washington, D.C., 1961).
14. U.S. Meat Animal Research Center, *Beef Cattle Research at the U.S. Meat Animal Research Center* (North-Central Region, Agricultural Research Service, U.S. Department of Agriculture, 1976).
15. G.E. Dickerson, *Techniques and Procedures in Animal Production Research* (American Society of Animal Science, Champaign, Ill., 1969), pp. 36–79.
16. E.J. Warwick, *J. Anim. Sci.* **17**, 922 (1958); L.V. Cundiff, *ibid.* **30**, 694, (1970).

17. L.V. Cundiff, *ibid.* **44**, 311 (1977).
18. R.L. Willham, *Genetics of Fat Content in Animal Products* (National Academy of Sciences, Washington, D.C., 1974), pp. 85–100.
19. ———, *Principles of Cattle Production* (Butterworth, London, 1975), pp. 387–404.
20. ———, *Breed and Breed Cross Evaluation for Beef Production in the U.S.* (European Economic Community, Verden, 1976).
21. P.D. Miller, W.E. Lentz, C.R. Henderson, *Comparison of Contemporary Daughters of Young and Progeny Tested Dairy Sires* (Cornell Univ. Press, Ithaca, N.Y., 1969).
22. K.E. Gregory, *J. Anim. Sci.* **34**, 881 (1972); R.L. Willham, in *Proceedings of a Working Symposium on Breed Evaluation and Crossing Experiments with Farm Animals* (Research Institute for Animal Husbandry, Zeist, Netherlands, 1974), pp. 245–259.
23. W.G. Hill, *Anim. Prod.* **13**, 37 (1971); in *Proceedings of a Working Symposium on Breed Evaluation and Crossing Experiments with Farm Animals* (Research Institute for Animal Husbandry, Zeist, Netherlands, 1974), pp. 43–54; M. Koger, *Crossbreeding Beef Cattle: Series 2* (Univ. of Florida Press, Gainesville, 1973), pp. 448–453; G.M. Smith and V.L. Harrison, *J. Anim. Sci.*, in press.
24. G.E. Dickerson, *Proceedings of the Animal Breeding and Genetics Symposium in Honor of Dr. Jay L. Lush* (American Society of Animal Science, Champaign, Ill., 1973), pp. 54–77.
25. G.M. Smith, D.B. Laster, L.V. Cundiff, K. Gregory, *J. Anim. Sci.* **43**, 37 (1976).
26. R.M. Koch, K.E. Gregory, L.V. Cundiff, *ibid.* **39**, 459 (1974).
27. H.A. Fitzhugh, Jr., C.R. Long, T.C. Cartwright, *ibid.* **40**, 421 (1975); G.E. Joandet and T.C. Cartwright, *ibid.* **41**, 1238 (1975).
28. M.A. Fowler, S.A. Adeyanju, W. Burroughs, E.A. Kline, *ibid.* **30**, 291 (1970).
29. Contribution J–8825 of the University of Iowa, Ames.

2074 and All That

by Professor J.L. Gnileerb

The many food products formulated from soybeans have been a staple of the American diet for generations. Increased use of soybeans in plastics for electromobile bodies and spaceship A-frames has created a serious potential for shortage. The purpose of this investigation, therefore, was to locate alternate sources of protein if the need should arise.

Animal tissue and, in particular, beef provided a large portion of the protein in the American diet at one time. A few very old Americans may actually have tasted beef, and they may remember that some of the first soybean products on the American market were beef analogues.

The raising of beef cattle is not the most efficient way in which to produce protein since each animal requires an enormous input of plant tissue to produce one pound of edible animal tissue. This productive inefficiency is a major reason cited in 20th century history texts for the decline of the meat industry. Recent advances in tissue culture, however, make it possible to produce almost unlimited amounts of nearly any kind of animal tissue.

TO BE VIEWED, NOT EATEN

It seemed that this potential source of protein, although foreign to American taste, should not be overlooked in our search for new foods.

An animal of the type known as a "prime beef heifer" was located in a Buenos Aires zoo. With the permission of the zoo director, one gram of muscle tissue was extracted from the hind quarter of the animal by needle biopsy and transferred immediately to the organ preservation bottle. In our laboratory, the tissue sample was placed in standard growth solution for quick reproduction.

At the end of two weeks, 100 kilograms of beef muscle tissue was harvested from the growth tanks. One kilogram was flash dried by laser light and pounded in a sonic chamber to the consistency of soy flour. Standard chemical score tests indicated that protein value had been retained through this treatment after which the remaining 99 kilos of tissue were similarly prepared.

Beef tissue flour replaced soy flour in a standard rat ration; after two generations, growth and reproductive capacity of the animals was unharmed.

Meanwhile, technologists at the Cumulo Nimbus Soy Company kindly consented to compound 50 kilos of beef protein flour into an edible human food closely resembling the soyburgers served in outlets of a popular franchise chain. Treatment of the product with 0.5 gram per kilogram extracted soy essence produced the most satisfactory odor and flavor although a somewhat meaty off-flavor persisted in the opinion of some members of the taste panel.

The imitation soyburgers were fed as the major source of protein for one month to 20 volunteer human subjects randomly selected by an IBM Series 8,000,000 computer from appropriate age, sex, socio-culturo-economic, geographic, and biochemical profile groups.

Fifteen of the 20 test subjects experienced varying degrees of difficulty in consuming the first few meals due to off-flavor and lingering fears of possible anti-nutritional agents in the meat. Diarrhea was minimal. After one week, however, all subjects were eating the imitation soyburgers as the major source of protein.

All criteria indicate the beef muscle protein is apparently as effective as soy protein in maintaining growth, reproduction, and other aspects of human metabolism for one month. An experimental commercial product will go into limited clinical marketing when Food Documentation Agency (FDA) laboratories complete analyses of the 37 essential nutrients for nutrient labeling.

Several groups demand that such experimentation be halted as wasteful and dangerous. Environmentalists contend that proliferation of the nearly extinct species will harm the atmosphere, causing sulphurous inversion layers over our cities. Conservationists express fears over the trampling under of soya lands by wandering herds of those mammoths, quaintly called range cattle in ancient times. Lastly, food activists, with the eminently indisputable claim that you can't be sure of anything, warn of possible dangers to man of a diet of body-foreign protein.

10

Food from Fish

From time inmemorial, the sea has attracted man as a source of food. For centuries the food potential of the sea seemed limitless and, in the 1950s and 1960s, it formed the basis of the greatly expanded marine operations of many nations. However, the past decade has shown that the potential of the sea is not infinite and very definitely has man-made limitations. Actually, fish landings in the past ten years have stabilized at approximately 70 million tons and there is good evidence that nearly all the major fish species have been overfished. This obvious overexploitation has led to demands for a 200 mile limit around nearly all coastal countries and attempts to implement catch quotas, which can be sustained in future years, are well underway.

There is considerable optimism that conservation measures for ocean fishing will lead to sustainable yields in the foreseeable future, but little grounds for optimism that the total catch can be significantly increased. Any increases in total catch will probably have to come from fish farming in the sea or in ponds on land. The following three papers discuss the possibilities of fish farming.

Farming the Sea: Fact and Fancy

by Clarence P. Idyll

Man still gets most of his food from the sea by hunting. He catches fish by dangling hooks and floating nets beneath the surface. On land, hunting as an important method of producing food was abandoned at least a thousand years ago, it being far more expensive and less efficient than farming. This transition is considered to be a major step in man's rise to civilization.

With regard to the sea, one of the brightest and most widely held hopes is that we are about to emerge from the primitive hunting phase. The idea of farming the seas, or "aquaculture," has quickened the imagination of the public, though relatively few sea farms exist, and difficult biological, engineering, social and political problems must be solved before substantial marine fish cultivation industries can develop. But there is good reason to be hopeful that these problems will be solved, and that aquaculture will play an important role in supplying food and wealth in many parts of the world.

Because of the marked upsurge of interest in aquaculture in recent years many people have assumed that it is a new idea. Yet aquatic culture goes back at least 4 000 years in China, Japan and Egypt, well over 3 000 in Java and India, and a least 2 500 in Europe. Despite this ancient history, fish farming has had very little scientific help. Most of its methods are traditional, developed by trial and error.

Fresh-water animals seem easier to manipulate than marine animals and their environment easier to control; consequently far more fish are raised in fresh water than in the sea. But many successful brackish water farms are in operation, especially in the Indo-Pacific. In that region about 20 species of fish (the most important of which are milkfish and mullet), 25 species of crustaceans (principally shrimp), and 20 molluscs (mostly oysters and mussels) are being raised—about a third of them on an extensive scale. Worldwide, oysters are the estuarine species most commonly farmed, while mussels are

From *Ceres*, 5 (4) July–August 1972, 43–46. Reprinted with permission of the Food and Agriculture Organization of the United Nations.

Clarence P. Idyll *is Professor and Chairman of the Division of Fisheries and Applied Estuarine Ecology at the Institute of Marine Science, University of Miami, Florida. He is the author of* Abyss: The Deep Sea and the Creatures that Live in it, *and* The Sea Against Hunger.

cultivated in large quantities in Spain. Yellowtails (fish similar to jacks) are raised in Japan in mesh cages, and in 1968 more than 31 000 tons were produced for the market. Other animals cultured in Japan include shrimp, crabs, clams, abalone, scallops, pufferfish and plaice. None of these can be said to be in substantial commerical production, and most of them are being studied at the laboratory or early pilot stage.

Aquaculture is characterized by four general types of activity. The first is the hatchery, where large numbers of young are raised and then released into coastal waters with the expectation that they will increase the size of the natural population and the commercial catch. This expectation has almost never been fulfilled. An exception is the cultivation of some species of salmon. In the western United States coho and chinook salmon are raised in hatcheries on the Columbia River, and released to be caught by sport and commercial fishermen. The value of the fish caught is three times the cost of production. In the Baltic Sea release of Atlantic salmon by Swedish hatcheries is credited with returning at least US$1.60 for each $1.00 of cost of raising the fish. Not only the salmon fisheries of Sweden but those of both political divisions of Germany, Poland and other countries operating in the area are materially helped by this kind of fish culture.

Salmon may be a special case, however, having characteristics favourable to this technique not shared by the great majority of other animals of commercial interest: high natural survival from the egg stage, and the homing instinct which brings the fish back to a restricted area, thereby making harvesting more efficient. Nonetheless, the success with salmon hatching in recent years, and with sturgeon in the U.S.S.R., encourages research for other species on this release technique.

The second kind of acquaculture involves the capture and impoundment of the young. In enclosures, they may be left to fend for themselves, the water may be fertilized so that natural food is increased, or supplemental food may be added. Most successful aquaculture operations are variations of this second type.

Third is production of young from eggs and their retention until they reach marketable size. Japanese shrimp culture is an example of this.

The last and most sophisticated method involves the full control of the life cycle of the animal. Eggs are hatched, the young are raised in ponds or other enclosures and the juvenile and older stages are fed until marketing. Brood stock is maintained by the farmer. This is the only method that is comparable to land farming. Trout and catfish culture are fresh-water examples, but no marine culture seems to have reached this level except for oysters on a very small scale.

MISTAKEN ACCOMPLISHMENTS

The proposition that we should farm the sea rather than gather its animals by hunting seems so obvious to many people that they are impatient with having been so long in coming to it, particularly in the light of recent reports that sea farming has succeeded spectacularly in Japan and other places. This has sometimes led to a general over-optimism about the present and potential roles of marine and aquaculture in providing food, jobs and wealth. The fact is that aquaculture is of considerable importance in the production of animal protein in many parts of the world, and the improvement in technology in recent years promises far more in the future. But sometimes, as is the case with many new enthusiasms, too much has been made of early progress and what are really only plans or hopes have been mistaken for accomplishment.

A common misunderstanding has been that success achieved in raising fish, shrimp and other animals through the critical young stages means that the key to successful commercial operations has been found. These successes are biological triumphs and have put the art of aquaculture significantly forward, but in most countries and for most species critical problems still remain before we can develop systems of handling animals from the post-larval and juvenile stages to adult size at costs which would enable substantial quantities to be marketed profitably.

Aquaculture has been most successful in areas of low living standards, where operations are at a simple level of technology. Culture methods have been developed, sometimes with the backing of centuries of experience, to rasie milkfish, mullet and prawns, either singly or in combination. These traditional kinds of aquatic farming are being improved through research, but the greatest promise of aquaculture seems to lie in the development of more complex systems, where full control of the life cycles of the animals is obtained. Yet sea farming will probably never replace fishing as the major source of seafood. There are limits to the amounts and kinds of fish and shellfish that can be produced in farms, and to the areas where this will be possible.

Acre for acre the sea is probably about as productive as the land, and there are some very rich areas—mostly close to shore. By proper management water areas can be made more productive than they are in nature. For example, in the United States during a recent year 185,000 acres of cultivated beds produced the same amount of oysters as four million acres of uncultivated areas. Milkfish ponds in some Asian countries average about 350 kg per hectare per year of production by traditional methods of culture, while the average is one ton per hectare using more sophisticated methods. High density, intensely managed shrimp ponds in Japan can yield two tons per hectare, and some ponds produce 2.5 tons. The most spectacular figures are for Spanish mussel culture: in one region yields of 560 tons of meat per hectare have been reported. These figures compare with about 0.9 ton per hectare as maximum production of beef on a well-managed pasture.

In contemplating the prospect of sea farming some people are dazzled by the immensity of the ocean, multiplying production figures like those quoted above by the area of the sea surface. But the greatest part of the ocean is unsuitable for aquaculture. The open sea is relatively unproductive. Moreover, it is an unmanageable environment and is beset with knotty problems of ownership. Thus it is unlikely that aquaculture can be conducted beyond the continental shelves, which constitute only about three percent of the ocean's surface. And usually it will be possible to farm only the shallower areas, probably less than 100 feet deep, where the shorelines are not too rocky or the water too cold. Perhaps only one or two percent of the ocean is suitable for cultivation.

Nonetheless the sea is so large that vast areas are potentially usable for aquaculture. In some Asian countries about 425,000 hectares of coastal waters are now under culture and an additional 1.5 million hectares are believed suitable (see Table 1). And this calculation does not include Japan, China,

TABLE 1. Area Under Coastal Aquaculture in Some Countries of the Indo-Pacific and Additional Area Which Could be Used

	Area (in hectares)	
	Developed	**Additional potential**
Australia (oyster farming alone)		
N.S. Wales	6,400	600–1,200
S. Queensland	4,000	over 4,000
Tasmania	20	8,000
Indonesia	165,000	over 400,000
Khmer Republic	—	over 50,000
Korea (Rep. of)	27,549	10,000
Malaysia	3,200	over 50,000
Phillippines	166,000	500,000
Singapore	600	1,000
Sri Lanka	10	41,000
Taiwan	27,549	10,000
Thailand	over 20,000	500,000
Viet-Nam (Rep. of)	2,600	150,000

Source: FAO

or India, three of the biggest countries and those most active in this field. In Africa a single country, Nigeria, has at least one million hectares of mangrove area that could be made into sea farms, and it is not inconceivable that half of this could be used more profitably for aquaculture than for other uses. There are additional millions of hectares along the edges of other countries of Africa, while South America and many other regions also have enormous areas of coastline suitable for aquatic farms.

The number of marine animals which can be cultured successfully is very small—milkfish, mullet, yellowtails, eels, oysters and mussels are among those of greatest importance. For culture purposes an animal must be abundantly available in young stages, or must be capable of being raised easily from the egg. It should be fast growing, on cheap and abundant food, preferably of plant origin; it should be resistant to disease, parasites, and unfavourable environmental conditions; and it should have a high market value. Unfortunately, very few marine animals exhibit all or most of these characteristics. Most of the open ocean fishes—such as tuna, mackerel, and herring—require large quantities of food and a great deal of ocean for maneuvering. They probably could not be raised in aquatic farms, no matter how big.

Since any animal which is to be raised profitably on a commercial basis must bring in a high unit return, for the time being—and perhaps for many years in the future—aquaculture will be limited to production of high-priced foods.

The actual amount of food produced in sea farms can only be guessed since production statistics are scanty and unreliable. Any calculation is further complicated by the fact that for most countries records of brackish and fresh-water production cannot be separated. Perhaps the best estimate of the present production by aquatic farms was made in 1970 by the Fish Culture Section of FAO on the basis of answers to questionnaires and other data (see Table 2). For 36 countries the production of finfish by fresh-water and brackish culture was estimated at over three million tons. Since this total did not include figures from many countries active in fish culture (e.g., the Republic of Korea, Ceylon, Spain, France) the total is certainly low. About another million tons of shellfish are produced each year, for a total of four million tons. Some experts believe that present production could be increased five times, putting the potential at not less than 20 million tons. My own veiw is that a ten times factor is reasonable, taking into account yields which can result from improved techniques, and new areas that can be put into production. This raises the potential to 40 million tons for fresh and brackish waters combined—equal to almost 65 percent of the 1970 world fish production from the sea.

Table 2. Production by Brackish Water and Fresh-water Culture for 36 Countries for Various Years in the Late 1960s

	Metric Tons
China	1,190,000
Japan	487,000
India	480,000
U.S.S.R.	190,000
Indonesia	141,000
Thailand	136,413
Philippines	86,711
Taiwan	50,511
United States	40,200
Pakistan	37,540
Malaysia	25,048
Hungary	22,137
Viet-Nam (Rep. of)	12,650
Romania	12,000
Poland	10,909
Czechoslovakia	10,641
Israel	10,408
Yugoslavia	10,000
Brazil	9,967
Denmark	9,065
Mexico	9,026
Madagascar	8,500
Italy	6,000
Khmer Republic	5,000
Germany (Dem. Rep.)	3,669
Germany (Fed. Rep.)	2,627
Burma	1,494
Zaire	1,406
Bolivia	1,400
Austria	780
Hong Kong	690
Zambia	689
Uganda	670
Norway	600
Singapore	400
Kenya	122
Total	3,024,073

Source: FAO

MANY LIMITATIONS

But whether this or some other figure represents the true theoretical limit, the full amount will not be realized. The limitation is not only a biological one but also a combination of social, political and economic factors. Edge-of-the-sea areas are highly prized, and the aquatic farmer finds himself competing with commercial and sport fisherman, pleasure boaters, swimmers, water skiers, oil and other mineral explorers, housing developers and those who seek a place to dump wastes. The fierce competition for water areas, the lack of ownership of these areas, and the high cost of coastal land in many countries pose even greater deterrents to the development of aquaculture industries than do the biological problems.

Perhaps the greatest threat to new aquaculture industries struggling to emerge is pollution. Fouling the waters with sewage, industrial wastes, fertilizers, DDT and other pesticides, silt, heated water, trash, oil, and radioactive substances may cancel the hope that a new era in harvest of the sea is possible. Pollution of the water is increasing at a cancerous rate: while the human population doubles about every 35 years, pollution in many parts of the world multiplies six times in the same period. Estuaries are under the greatest threat since over half the world's population lives within 100 miles of the sea, and most industry is concentrated close to the water. Unfortunately it is almost entirely in these very estuarine areas where aquaculture can be carried out.

Sewage uses up the oxygen in the water, thus killing fish and shellfish or driving them away. Moreover, sewage carries pathogenic microorganisms which make the seafood in the area unfit to eat. In the United States about 1.2 million acres of grounds have been closed to the harvest of shellfish since pollution has made them dangerous to eat. This is eight percent of the potential shellfish grounds of the U.S. coastline; in Canada the situation is even worse: 25 percent of their potential grounds are closed to harvesting.

Industries produce an enormous variety of poisonous substances which contaminate the waters, including heavy metals such as mercury. This has been in the public eye lately since mercury has been found in some kinds of fish. Oil is another pollutant whose effects on shallow-water animals are increasing alarmingly.

Hard pesticides, especially DDT, may be the greatest threat of all to estuarine animals, and thus to aquaculture, DDT kills some creatures in amazingly small concentrations: six parts per thousand million for commercial shrimp. In 1969, some 41 million fish were destroyed by hard pesticides in the United States. The sea is accumulating DDT in damaging amounts, and despite the unquestioned usefulness of hard pesticides in agriculture, some countries have already decided that on balance the enormous harm they do outweighs their value.

But whatever decision is made in this particular case, it is clear that the world must quickly stem the tide of pollution. One interesting partial solution is to turn polluting substances like sewage and water heated by power plants to useful purposes, such as fertilizing and heating aquaculture enclosures.

CONFLICTING DEMANDS

Legal obstacles are set in the path of aquaculture development. Since in many countries it is impossible to establish ownership over a water region, it is not worth while for a individual or a company to spend money improving and cultivating a sea area as a farm. In some states a system of leases has been established, but this commonly applies only to certain very restricted shallow water regions, and it often runs up against the necessity to provide for the free passage of ships.

Further, in many countries the protection of fish stocks by conservation regulations sometimes prevents the development of aquaculture by prohibiting the capture of young animals or of mature females. This makes it impossible to gather seed for culture operations. Few states have yet attempted to unravel the many conflicting demands by establishing a code of laws that protect and stimulate aquaculture.

Thus aquaculture remains many centuries behind land farming, and some of the rosiest expectations held about sea farming are unlikely to be fulfilled. Nevertheless, it is still possible that aquaculture can produce animal protein of high quality and value in amounts equivalent to substantially more than half the present total harvest from the sea—ample reason to encourage earnest attacks on the technical, social and legal problems for which solutions are necessary to make the promise come true.

Fish Culture: Problems and Prospects

by A.H. Weatherley and B.M.G. Cogger

Fish culture—the rearing of fish for food—is at least 2000 years old, but only a small fraction of the fish that man consumes is derived from this source. Nevertheless, it is important to certain communities for food and livelihood. Recently, interest in the potential of fish culture has increased, not only in such traditional strongholds as China and the Far East, but also in India, Africa, Europe, North America, and the Pacific rim countries. Fish culture is thus rapidly assuming the appearance of an idea whose time has come. It can certainly be expected to expand among those nations most affected by the recent introduction of the 200-mile fishing zone. The forms of such activity will range from hatchery-based restocking and sea-ranching programs to various types of intensive pond culture.

Some of the reasons for the new interest in fish culture are: (i) Fears that global overfishing and marine pollution will destroy fish harvests. (ii) Realization that coastal, estuarine, and inland waters constitute the only areas over which a country can be relatively certain of exercising control of fishing intensity, water quality, and labor deployment. (iii) Realization that, as in agriculture, man should view edible aquatic products as fruits of a system that not only can be exploited, but whose management can be planned and controlled at every level of the production pyramid.

PROBLEMS

Unfortunately, fish culturists lack an organized overview of their field of knowledge and of its operational scope. Reference works exist which contain prolific information on regional skills and practices but not many broad conceptualizations of the subject or penetrating interregional comparisons (1–3). There has been general failure to exploit such techniques as systems analysis and cost-benefit analysis, while, with a few notable exceptions (4), the influence of geography and sociocultural factors has been treated superficially or ignored. This is unfortunate in view of the ample evidence of the effectiveness

From *Science*, Vol. 197, pp. 427–430, July 29, 1977. Copyright 1977 by the American Association for the Advancement of Science.

Dr. Weatherley is a professor in Life Sciences, Scarborough College, University of Toronto, Ontario, Canada M1C 1AA.

of such techniques in exposing the essential organization and patterns of energy use in other complex human activities, such as the U.S. food system (5), or in examining modern marine commercial fisheries (6).

It is important to examine details of various fish-culture practices and also to derive some general principles to guide the progress of this activity and limit the further spread of needless and costly mistakes of a type that have become not uncommon. The various versions of fish culture in different parts of the world cannot now be viewed in a common frame for valid comparisons of origins and rates of use of food energy, efficiencies of fish energetics, and dynamics of fish growth in different pond systems. For example, the common assumption that the polyculture of fish species practiced in Chinese ponds is an effective way of exploiting the total food energy of the pond ecosystem has not been initially tested (1). There has been no investigation of whether the development of European fish culture from long-practiced methods of agricultural stock-rearing (2) has been appropriately adapted to the biology of fish growth, which is different in kind from that of terrestrial vertebrates (7–9). The famous milkfish (*Chanos chanos*) culture practiced in Indonesian brackish water ponds (a method recently adopted in the Phillippines) is another system for the evaluation of which there are no adequate analytical techniques; yet, when the complex procedures of this fish culture are considered carefully, there emerges a distinct impression that they have evolved through unconscious application of optimality principles over an extended time (1,3,4,10,11). If this is correct, this method of fish culture may provide important lessons for the entire industry.

HIGH OPERATING COSTS

Numerous developing countries are showing interest in utilizing new forms of fish culture. It will be regrettable if such countries are encouraged to emulate certain costly, technically sophisticated, but otherwise not particularly satisfactory, systems of fish culture recently developed in the West. For example, the culture of salmonid fishes in the United States, the United Kingdom, Canada, Scandinavia, and Japan (1), of channel catfish in the United States (1), and of yellowtail in Japan (1, 12) are all distinguished by the use of remarkably expensive high-protein foods comprising so-called "trash" fish caught in the sea. Salmon, for example, are fed 60 to 70 percent of fish meal (from trash fish) by wet weight—a wasteful use of food energy from the ecological standpoint. If one adds to this the high operating costs, capital outlay for plant, depreciation, and loan repayment, then economic success can result only through a very high fish sale price—that is, such fish culture must tend to lead to a luxury food industry.

In Japanese yellowtail (*Seriola quinqueradiata*) culture, food (trash fish) accounts for half the production costs. In 1972, the production of 74,000 tons (metric) of yellowtail required 570,000 tons of trash fish, the approximate conversion ratio being 1:8. In the production of a 1-kilogram fish, food costs 320 yen [300 yen are equivalent to $1 (U.S.)]; the fish as a fingerling, 105 yen; depreciation, 70 yen; labor, 50 yen. Production costs totaled 652 yen. At the wholesale price of 951 yen, producers could make a considerable net profit, but such wholesale prices are naturally reflected in a very high consumer price. However, a preoccupation with profitability has not always led yellowtail producers to financial success. Early yellowtail culture was on too large a scale, and lack of research on site selection, design, and suitable materials for enclosures caused costly errors. This form of culture remains expensive. Nets in sea enclosures become fouled and must be replaced almost weekly. As the production of yellowtail expands, trash fish to feed them are becoming scarcer and dearer.

Various other examples of high operating costs and hazards are encountered in the production of salmonids and channel catfish (1). "Failures" are not necessarily due merely to unsound application of economic principles, but also to haste and inexpertness on the part of entrepreneurs who expect too much without adequate knowledge of plant operation or of fish diseases, for example (13). For instance, since 1960 the area of channel catfish ponds in the United States has increased from zero to some 50,000 acres (1 acre = 0.4047 hectare), but the industry has had numerous problems related to production costs and product diversification, and for any secure future may have to aim at reduction of unit production cost, shifting the industry "from a luxury-food industry to a staple food source" (1).

THE ENERGY ASPECT

While we are not opposed to profits being made, we do think that more attention should be directed toward efficient energy use in the production of human food, including maximum efficiency of energy transfer between food and fish. When salmonids, channel catfish, and yellowtail are fed wholly or partly on trash fish, an energy pyramid is being tapped that is at least two trophic levels above that utilized by herbivorous fish (for example, mullet), or by sheep and cattle in terrestrial farming. Trash fish may be highly edible, even if they now happen to lack a market. If they are edible, their use as food for cultured fish must, in energy transfer terms, be regarded as absurd. If for reasons of present economic expediency, their use in a luxury-food industry can be tolerated, this should not lead to complacency, especially because fish culture based on this method cannot produce more than about 1 kg of cultured fish for every 5 to 10 kg of trash fish fed (13). Wherever possible, attempts should be made to use trash fish more directly for human nutrition. Much research is already being conducted on the preparation of optimal artificial diets, replete with correct quantities of vitamins, minerals, proteins, and fats (1). However, for application in fish culture, it is important that such studies should have as their major aim the more efficient use of food for growth.

Production costs that increase will cause corresponding increases in the market price of fish. Fish sales tend to relate inversely to price—although, admittedly, demand is involved, and this can sometimes be influenced by promotion. However, lower prices would bring luxury fish more within the reach of mass markets. Net profits could then be as great or greater than present ones even at reduced prices per kilogram. Much recent fish-culture research has, unfortunately, been subservient to the demands of entrepreneurs whose sole aim has been to make profit. To the eventual disadvantage of all concerned, such research has frequently failed to test the assumptions and practices of the industry, and may also have opposed long-term national or regional interests.

IMPROVING THE OUTLOOK

A fish culture based on an integrated body of knowledge and well-formulated concepts would view regional aspects as particular instances of a problem set, to be investigatad by the application of established principles and experience. This is how better-based applied sciences such as engineering and agriculture approach problem-solving. Prediction and management guidelines in new ventures would be simplified and improved, and major failures would be less likely. A multimillion-dollar salmonid culture operation begun in Nova Scotia in 1969 had failed by 1972. Full-scale research and planning of this operation might have led to its success—at least in commercial terms. In Puget Sound, salmon-rearing has been a relative commercial success because of better planning and closer cooperation of research and government agencies with commercial interests (14).

There should be congruence between type of fish cultured, the environment, and consumers' needs. Not only should the species be acceptable as food, but its life cycle should be readily manipulable (13). An ideal species might complete its life cycle within the pond system and be physiologically robust. Some of the most popular species reared, however, require hatcheries (salmonids, channel catfish) or the sea (milkfish, mullets) for completion of their life cycles, though such species may, of course, have compensations such as good growth and flavor. It has been said that hatcheries frequently constitute one of the more expensive aspects of fish culture and that their cost may be prohibitive in some underdeveloped countries. This leads us to suggest three areas in which research should be conducted.

(1) The culture of potentially valuable fish species is frequently prevented through ignorance of their life histories, including breeding habits, their survival, food requirements, and the growth rate of the young stages. The carp, *Cyprinus carpio,* several tilapias (mainly *Tilapia mossambica*), a few salmonids, and several dozen other species constitute the basis of world fish culture. Since there is no general routine for testing the culture potential of new species, the prospects of discovering fish with superior characteristics of growth, productivity, robustness, and flavor remain largely a matter of chance. This situation should not be allowed to continue. In situations where many young fish are required to stock ponds, research could lead to the design of hatcheries capable of more economical and efficient operation, thereby helping to reduce the high costs of this aspect of fish culture.

(2) Figure 1 shows a scheme of possible food sources for cultured fish. The simplest trophic route to fish flesh is from the carbohydrate and protein of plants growing in the fish pond (for example, *Tilapia* spp., *Chanos,* and mullet). Many fish can eat terrestrial plant material (for example, *Ctenopharyngodon,* the Chinese grass carp), which is bioenergetically advantageous in pond culture, since fish may be held at high densities in very small ponds while their food is conveniently produced on agricultural land. Far more tropical fish are herbivorous than their temperate counterparts, which is why, aside from the more favorable temperature conditions, the tropics offer greater potential for fish culture. However, genetic research might lead to fish being bred with changed food habits. If salmonids could be bred as even partly herbivorous, actually digesting plant carbohydrate as well as protein, major increases in their productivity could be effected.

(3) The role of genetics in growth remains an enigma. Fish somatic growth is more flexibly responsive to environmental factors (such as temperature) and biotic factors (competition for food) than growth in higher vertebrates (8), but there has been little obvious understanding of this in attempts to breed faster-growing fish. Most present claims that stocks with superior growth have been produced by genetic selection are suspect (15), though some recent work seems much more soundly based (16), and the basic genetic principles involved in the selection of individuals of superior somatic growth rate can be simply stated (9). If geneticists became more aware of the peculiar properties of fish growth, they would almost certainly be able to select for physiologically superior growth. Certain physiological factors are particularly involved in influencing growth. For example, levels of such hormones as somatotropin and thyroxine have been shown to be significant (17). There are numerous data on the importance of temperature (8). The pattern of partitioning of the net energy, derived from the food, among the "competing" demands of the standard metabolic rate, specific dynamic action, nitrogen excretion, and spontaneous activity, must affect growth, that is, the elabora-

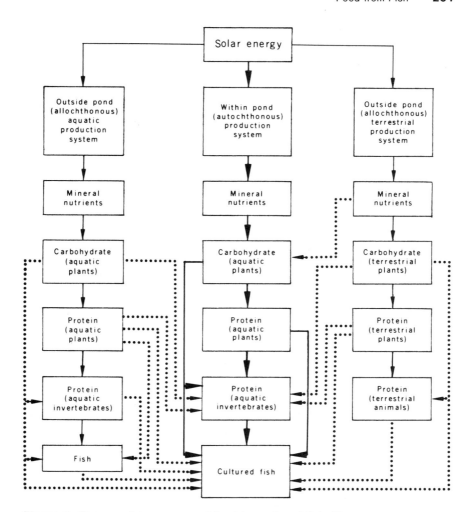

Figure 1. The possible sources of food for cultured fish. The
heavy solid arrows indicate a direct line of food production
wholly within the pond system (autochthonous); light arrows
indicate direct lines of food production leading to fish (aquatic
allochthonous) and terrestrial (allochthonous) animals,
respectively, both of which could also be the food support
systems of cultured fish. The broken arrows indicate the
various whole or partial contributions to the food production
of cultured fish which may be made by various components of
the allochthonous systems. The range of options is great and
the trophic potentialities indicated in the scheme have not
been realized by fish culturists.

tion of new tissue, especially muscle, liver, gonad, and fat (9, 18). Maximum growth should be sought in terms of the most useful edible product, protein. Also, the dynamics of protein and fat are linked in growing fish, but in ways that are not well understood (8, 9, 19, 20). Fish given plentiful food may show increases in both components, but in migratory fish, fat may be stored periodically in muscles and liver to be utilized in preference to protein. In *Oncorhynchus keta,* the ratios of glycine to alanine change from 1.3 in immature to 0.5 in mature fish (8, 19, 20). By studying the genetics and physiology of growth, methods for increasing the relative growth rate of muscle over that of liver, gonad, or adipose tissue might be found.

FUTURE POSSIBILITIES

The scope of fish culture is enormous. Any unpolluted area of water, fresh, brackish, or salt, is a potential space for fish-rearing. Countries of the most diverse climate and geography might turn to fish culture because it offers an economical, attractive use of "waste" water. Water simultaneously employed for other primary purposes such as irrigation, stock watering, or even for drinking can be used for fish culture. Wetlands, including swamps and mangroves which are of little value for agriculture, could be used for fish-rearing with little damage to their recreational value or appearance.

Fish-culture research in developed countries may eventually make major contributions to the management of exploited wild fish stocks. For example, the present exploitation of salmon is based partly on captures at sea and partly on captures during spawning runs in various parts of the Northern Hemisphere. It has been suggested that the strategic location of salmon hatcheries in the vicinities of the Aleutians, the Magallanes region of Chile, and Iceland could lead to the establishment of new major salmon runs and sea fisheries in suitable feeding areas (21, 22). In some instances, hatchery-rearing of young salmon might be followed by subsequent pen-rearing in streams where, it is claimed, rapid growth could be obtained economically by means of supplementary feeding (22). Eventual release of subadult salmon in the ocean would follow. However, the advantages of establishing new salmon stocks should be weighed against possible damage to already existing fisheries which may occupy the same areas in the oceans (22).

The role of fish culture in "enhancing" exploited fish stocks by permitting "massive planting programs [which] can produce spectacular results" has recently been noted (23). By means of such programs the yields of salmon in the U.S. Pacific Northwest and in Lake Michigan have already been improved.

With more attention being given to basic aims and production strategies (24), to improving the technology, and to developing fish with superior growth rate and superior food-conversion efficiency, fish culture could make a major contribution to world food needs. Much basic research will have to be done in developed countries because of inadequate facilities for research and development in many of the developing countries. People who are truly aware of the needs and problems of developing countries will have to participate in the planning of these studies, and there will have to be massive exchanges of scientists, technical experts and, in some instances, practicing fish culturists.

Money and scientific expertise from the West could power such programs. However, Western countries have made various mistakes about fish culture, and a misplaced positivism is even now underlying various false objectives. To develop sound policies and practices for its own fish culture, the West must put the subject into perspective with such questions as the intensifying pressures on marine fisheries, especially in view of the new opportunities introduced by the establishment of the 200-mile zone. If the West wants to increase production of cultured fish of high food value and palatability to satisfy mass domestic (and possibly export) markets, it must greatly reduce its production costs. Such reduction could be brought about by improving the food-conversion efficiency and the growth rate of fish and by finding more plentiful sources of food energy, or by selecting species of fish capable of feeding closer to the base of the trophic pyramid.

Perhaps the West should not involve itself at all in fish culture, given its already high production of foods of every kind. This option should at least be given careful consideration. However, there may be some opportunities for effective culture that have not been considered seriously enough. For example, an interesting form of fish culture is being practiced in Canada in the many small prairie ponds which can be readily stocked with small trout. It is reported that the fish grow from fry size to 200 g or more in a single 6-month growth season (1, 25). The main costs are those of distributing the fry and of catching the fish again, while the cash return is two and half times that of wheat farming on an areal basis (1). Recoveries as high as 86 percent of the number of fingerlings stocked are reported, and the major mortality is a "summerkill" produced by occasional severe oxygen depletions induced by decomposing algae (25). Winterkill removes all stock not fished out at the end of the growing season.

There are various forms of aid the West can provide to developing countries to help solve their food needs. Better than offers of food surpluses at low cost would be long-term investments of time, money, and scientific expertise in attempting to revamp food production enterprises, including fish culture.

REFERENCES AND NOTES

1. J.E. Bardach, J.H. Ryther, W.O. McLarney, *Aquaculture: The Farming and Husbandry of Freshwater and Marine Organisms* (Wiley, New York, 1972).
2. W. Schaeperclaus, *Textbook of Pond Culture* (Parey, Berlin, 1933, F. Hund, Transl., and issued as *Fish. Leafl. Fish Wildl. Serv. U.S. No. 311*); M. Huet, *Textbook of Fish Culture* (Fishing News, London, 1971).

3. C.F. Hickling, *Tropical Inland Fisheries* (Longmans, London, 1961); *Fish Culture* (Faber & Faber, London, 1962).
4. W.H. Schuster, *Indo-Pac. Fish. Counc. Spec. Publ. No. 1* (1952).
5. J.S. Steinhart and C.E. Steinhart, *Science* **184**, 307 (1974).
6. G. Borgstrom and A.J. Heighway, Eds., *Atlantic Ocean Fisheries* (Fishing News, London, 1961).
7. R.A. McCance and W.M. Widdowson, *Proc. R. Soc. London* **156**, 326 (1962).
8. A.H. Weatherley, *Growth and Ecology of Fish Populations* (Academic Press, London, 1972).
9. ————. *J. Fish. Res. Board Can.* **33**, 1046 (1976).
10. S.L. Hora, *Handbook on Fish Culture in the Indo-Pacific Region* (Food and Agriculture Organization of the United Nations, Rome, 1955).
11. T.V.R. Pillay, Ed., *Coastal Aquaculture in the Indo-Pacific Region* (Fishing News, London, 1972).
12. M. Fujiya, *ibid.,* p. 911; A. Furukawa, in *Coastal Aquaculture in the Indo-Pacific Region,* T.V.R. Pillay, Ed. (Fishing News, London, 1972).
13. J.H. Ryther, *Oceanus* **19**, 10 (1975).
14. J.R. Brett, in *Aquaculture in Canada, Bull. Fish. Res. Board Can. No. 188* (1974).
15. L.R. Donaldson, in *Marine Aquaculture,* W.J. McNeil, Ed. (Oregon State Univ. Press, Corvallis, 1970).
16. R. Moav and G.W. Wohlfarth, in *Agricultural Genetics. Selected Topics,* R. Moav, Ed. (Wiley, New York, 1973).
17. D.A. Higgs, E.M. Donaldson, H.M. Dye, J.R. McBride, *J. Fish. Res. Board Can.* **33**, 1585 (1976).
18. C.E. Warren and G.E. Davis, in *The Biological Basis of Freshwater Fish Production,* S.D. Gerking, Ed. (Blackwell, Oxford, 1967).
19. G.E. Shul'man, *Life Cycles of Fish: Physiology and Biochemistry* (Wiley, London, 1974).
20. R.M. Love, *The Chemical Biology of Fishes* (Academic Press, New York, 1970).
21. T. Joyner, *J. Fish. Res. Board Can.* **33**, 902 (1976).
22. J.R. Calaprice, *ibid.,* p. 1068.
23. K.H. Loftus, *ibid.,* p. 1822.
24. G.I. Pritchard, *ibid.,* p. 855.
25. G.H. Lawler, L.A. Sunde, J. Whitaker, *ibid.,* **31**, 929 (1974).

What's So Hard About Growing Lobsters?

by Elisabeth Keiffer

With all the regularity of hiccups, articles appear in the newspapers suggesting that the commercial enterprise of growing scarce and expensive American lobsters in captivity is just around the corner. Possibly it is, but the corner is a good deal longer than most reports acknowledge.

Although such accounts frequently point out how long it takes lobsters to reach market size (five years or more in the ocean, perhaps half that in the laboratory), how expensive it is to feed them in captivity and how difficult to keep them from injuring or killing each other when they're crowded together, they seldom make clear how extraordinarily complex an undertaking it is to duplicate this marine animal's normal environment. Scientists have had to start from square one for almost every aspect of it because so little is known about lobster behavior in the wild.

Recently, a group of lobster aquaculturists met in a two-day workshop at the University of Rhode Island to exchange information, and though their discussions were for the most part highly technical, even the most unscientific reporter could get a notion of the awesome variety of questions to be answered, problems to be mastered and details to be ironed out before these delicate creatures can be raised on a money-making, chicken-farming basis.

Even the water they are grown in presents problems. Its quality is critical to the lobster's survival. In the ocean, impurities—including the crustacean's own metabolic wastes—are diluted. In a tank they are concentrated. A successful lobster farmer will need to know what levels of chemical impurities his animals can tolerate, and whether the chemicals can slow growth or have other long-term effects. He will have to have a system for cleaning the water that not only suits the lobsters but the EPA's standards on discharging wastes—and his pocketbook. The scientists adressed themselves to all these biological and systems engineering questions.

Some years ago it was discovered that lobsters grow faster in water that is warm the year round than in the fluctuating temperatures of the ocean. But the exact effects of heated water on their molting and egglaying patterns is

From *NEMRIP Information*, July 1975, 1–4. Reprinted by permission of the University of Rhode Island.

still a question mark. Meanwhile, the possibility of using the heated discharge from power plants is being investigated. A group of California scientists reported on their experiments in cooperation with a power company to learn, among other things, whether the water's chemistry is as suitable as its temperature.

Besides being free of toxic wastes and the right temperature, the water must also be continuously oxygenated. This can be accomplished fairly simply, unless the lobsters are being raised in high densities. Then it is found that "dead spots"—unoxygenated areas—can occur which are fatal to any lobster that stays in them long enough.

Water is only a part of the lobster's surroundings that must be finely tailored to its exacting requirements. Scientists have found that the size of the container affects the rate of growth. It also has an important bearing on cannibalism. From the research that has been done, it appears that individual containers, at least for some growth stages, are the answer for best growth and survival. But can they be designed to also be the answer economically for a lobster farmer? A number of scientific groups are working on this puzzler.

With optimum container size established, there's another fine point to consider. In the ocean, lobsters habitually live solitarily, in natural shelters. What happens if there are no shelters in their rearing tanks? And if there are, does placement affect their behavior? And does their behavior affect their growth? Because it is assumed that a low level of activity would promote faster growth, one group of researchers carried out a year-long experiment to answer these questions. From hours of observation they found that the amount of activity and of aggressive behavior varied depending upon whether or not shelters were placed in the tanks. They also found that the positioning of the shelters—how close together they were and which way their entrances faced— had a definite effect on aggression. They determined too that artificial conditions affect activity patterns in another way. In nature, lobsters normally move around at night. If they are held in groups without shelter, they become active both day and night. Next question: what effect, if any, does the substrate have on behavior? That is being investigated.

But none of these questions are as critical or as difficult to answer as those concerning nutrition and disease. Feeding is still by far the most costly aspect of raising lobster artificially. After close to a hundred years of study no one knows for sure everything lobsters-at-large eat during their entire lives, or even just how their feeding patterns may change in different growth stages. How then do you arrive at the optimum food to produce healthy, fast-growing animals? So far, partially by trial and error.

The most satisfactory food used to date is live brine shrimp, followed by frozen brine shrimp. However, live brine shrimp currently costs $1 a pound so, with the lobster's roughly estimated conversion ration of 4:1, $4 worth of food goes into producing a one-pound lobster. Added to his other costs, this means the lobster farmer would have to charge a pretty steep price for his product to show a profit.

A number of artificial foods have been developed, some costing as little as 19¢ a pound. Although lobsters find them palatable (and there is another problem: these crustaceans are picky eaters) they grow much more slowly on cheaper foods. Using a computer model, scientists on the West Coast are projecting the costs and trade-offs involved in various diets. One possibility for the future is discovering what the brine shrimp has that makes it so satisfactory, in order to try to duplicate it less expensively. Another is to use a different method of rearing lobsters—in a polyculture system with other marine animals where they could feed on a natural diet of the tiny invertebrates in the water.

Besides the pressing problem of how to lower feeding costs more satisfactorily, a number of other questions to do with nutrition have come up. Some have been answered, others not. How much food does a lobster need? It has been established that it will eat more than it can assimilate, a costly waste when the feed is expensive. How do you make it attractive? How do you keep it from disintegrating quickly in the tank? How does it affect the taste of the lobster's flesh? Can it affect its color? Does it contain everything the animal needs or may it produce deficiency diseases over the long term?

Disease is the dread specter of the aquaculturist and very little is known about it yet. Keeping animals in elevated water temperatures with minimum space and maximum feeding rates, all of which appears necessary for commercial operations, makes them more susceptible to disease, especially in the early stages of life. It should be remembered that juvenile lobsters are tiny delicate replicas—weighing perhaps only a few grams—of the tough looking specimens one sees in fish market tanks. It would take extraordinarily careful watching to spot one out of many who was sick, and when disease strikes in a lobster population, it may well wipe it out. Althougth an increasing number of researchers are working to identify the diseases that are appearing in aquaculture populations and to find ways to control them, lobster medicine still has a long way to go. So far, the best remedy that has been found is to keep the water quality high.

If commercial lobster farming does indeed become a reality within the next few years, as many predict, it will certainly be a major accomplishment.

As one of the participants in the conference pointed out, "To grow these animals successfully, we must control every aspect of their life cycle and environment." It would appear that the answer to the often-heard question, "What's so complicated about growing lobsters?" is "Just about everything."

Participants in the URI conference, "Recent Advances in Lobster Aquaculture" held last April came from San Diego State University, Environment Canada, University of California at Davis, Woods Hole Oceanographic Institution, University of Rhode Island, University of Delaware and Boston University Marine Program.

11

Energy

Production of food requires energy in many forms. The dramatic price increases and possible future shortages in supply have caused considerable rethinking in the practice of producing food. The higher cost of fertilizer, pesticides, irrigation, cultivation, harvesting, drying and preservation will all reflect in various proportions in the ultimate cost, quality and quantity of food. The impact of oil costs will be greatest in the developed countries with so-called sophisticated agriculture with a high dependence on energy in oil. Countries with more emphasis on human labor will also feel the impact due to the higher costs of fertilizer and pesticides.

This chapter relates primarily to the impact of higher energy costs for food production, but obviously this is only a portion of the energy supply problem. One of the obvious suggestions for alternative fuel is alcohol from agricultural sources and there are a number of possibilities. Two possibilities are corn and cane sugar. Several studies have shown that production of ethanol in a form suitable for fuel requires more energy for production than one gains from burning the alcohol. Obviously if the energy input is mainly fossil fuel, this process is self-defeating. However, if the energy can be obtained to a large degree from plant refuse, the processes may become economically desirable. On the other hand, methanol from coal or garbage or any other source may be a more desirable way to go. Methanol production may not conflict to any significant degree with materials suitable for food, but ethanol production certainly will compete. It may well be desirable to keep materials suitable for food for use as food and restrict energy production to other products. The future of the Brazilian experiment which is designed to use surplus sugar and other products as discussed in Paper No. 4, may shed some light on this important consideration.

There are many potential ways of using renewable biomass as a source of energy, and one of the more novel ones is described in the fifth paper. However, apart from biomass as a source of energy, it is likely that significant progress in the coming decade in energy conservation will have to come from agricultural practices which use less energy. One of the more exciting of these is the "no-tillage" concept as discussed in the last paper.

Energy and Agriculture

by Donald R. Price

A stable supply of quality food is a matter of paramount importance in every country throughout the world. The availability of energy to produce and process food, maintain other industrial productivity, and to power transportation systems, as well as to heat and cool buildings, is also a matter of concern to much of the world. In the United States, the production of food is related to energy in two important ways. First, it takes energy to produce the food—nearly 20 percent of this nation's energy use is related to agriculture—and second, we produce such an abundance of food and fiber products that exports of the surplus offset the cost of imported oil.

In the past two decades, the United States has been able to double its agricultural output while reducing farm labor requirements by about half. Public approval as expressed through purchases has encouraged the development of high quality, conveniently packaged preserved foods that are available at all times from coast to coast. The penalty for this progress has been that we now rely on much greater quantities of fossil fuels.

In former times, research, design, and development of food production equipment did not include dependence on energy as one of the primary restraints. But in recent years, modern equipment and new technologies have vastly increased the use of fossil fuel. It will be difficult and costly to reverse the trend; however, it is going to be essential.

Nearly every facet of the food-production system is being scrutinized to determine where and to what extent energy can be saved. To recover and use the heat that has customarily been discarded in food processing plants is now of considerable interest. Investigations are under way to examine the processing, packaging, and preservation of food products to determine new methods that will conserve energy.

Technology is being developed to extract the energy from animal and crop residues before putting the organic material back on the land. If we learn to practice the proper management of these wastes, some day it will be possible to produce a dependable source of energy right on the farm. The New York State College of Agriculture and Life Sciences is recognized as a leader in this area of research.

From *New York's Food and Life Sciences*, 11 (1) 1978, 3. New York State Agricultural Experiment Station.

Plants have been collecting and converting solar energy into useful, transportable, and storable energy for eons. By improving plant varieties and agronomic practices, researchers at Cornell University have made major contributions toward increasing the energy produced from crops. Because environmental restrictions have put added restraints on the use of chemicals for agriculture and because the amount of energy necessary to produce them is high, we must stimulate interest in, and stress the importance of, even greater efficiencies in the photosynthesis process.

Since many of the power requirements on the farm are small and scattered over large areas, the use of wind and solar energy may become feasible in agriculture sooner than in most other industries. Wind energy was once widely used for pumping water for livestock pastured in remote areas. But not all of these wind-powered water pumps have disappeared—many can still be seen in operation throughout the western plains states. Interest has been revived, and researchers at the College are investigating new concepts for putting the wind to work to heat water for the dairy farm. How quickly these new technologies are adapted depends on the availability of the equipment at a reasonable cost.

The use of solar energy has been an essential part of agriculture from the beginning of time as plants have "done their thing." Plants grown in greenhouses use the sun's energy for continuous production. In fact, the greenhouse is a solar collector, albeit not a very efficient one. The improvement of the greenhouse as a solar collector and as a place to store excess heat for later use is the subject of a research program in the College. Other applications, which involve capturing and storing solar energy for space heating, crop drying, and food processing, are being researched at other institutions throughout the United States.

In the future, perhaps as soon as 1990, we will begin to shift from heavy reliance on oil and natural gas to other forms of energy. Agriculture and the food-processing industries will need to change many of their methods in order to maintain production while reducing dependence on scarce fuels. The transition will not be easy because it will be forced upon us and will probably cause some major disruptions. Scientists, designers, farmers, industrialists, and others will share a vital role in the tremendous challenge during the next several years. It is essential that they be successful—for an adequate food supply depends on it.

The Energy Crisis

by Yong H. Kim

Someday, American farmers will be using the sun, wind, and other alternative sources of energy on the farm to produce food and fiber. That "someday" may not be very far off, because oil and gas are running out fast. Before this happens, the United States must shift to other energy sources, and there may be little time left to get the job done.

The world is now burning oil at an astonishingly fast rate, consuming 60 million barrels a day. At this rate, most experts warn that the supply will last only 30 to 40 years. Even the most optimistic observers see the end no later than the mid-twenty-first century.

Donald R. Price, Director of the Energy Program for the New York State College of Agriculture and Life Sciences and for the New York State College of Human Ecology, sizes up the situation this way:

"Within a few decades—the exact date really doesn't matter—we are going to run out of oil and gas, and we will have to switch to other fuels. We have done that before in our history, but at that time it was a *desirable* switch. This time, however, it is going to be more painful because it will be a *mandatory* switch."

What the world now faces is a transition from the era of oil and gas to an age of different energy sources. One way to smooth the transition is to stretch out the existing fossil-fuel supplies so that science and technology can have a reasonably long "lead time" to work out solutions. Thus, conservation at this stage is crucial. In his energy program, President Carter emphasizes that conservation is "the quickest, cheapest, most practical source of energy."

Every day the United States uses 18 million barrels of oil, or 30 percent of the world's daily oil consumption. During 1977, we imported nearly half of our oil at a cost of $45 billion, reaching a peak that has been spiralling since the end of World War II, when oil became our primary source of energy. In 1950, we imported 900,000 barrels of oil, and by 1970 that figure had become 3.4 million, at a cost of $3 billion. The price has quadrupled since the 1973 oil crisis, yet oil imports have continued to rise. Experts predict that this country's demand for oil, if unabated, will probably reach 25 million barrels a day by 1985, of which, 16 million will be imported.

From *New York's Food and Life Sciences,* 11 (1) 1978, 4. New York State Agricultural Experiment Station.

The production, processing, distribution, and preparation of food use 16.5 percent of the total energy consumed in the United States. Another 5.5 percent goes into the production of natural fibers and forestry products. On-farm production itself uses 3 percent, which includes the energy needed to manufacture fertilizers, pesticides, and other agricultural chemicals and to power farm implements.

Thus, farm production takes only a small portion of the total energy consumed, but its importance should not be underestimated. Any disruption in the fuel supply at critical times could adversely affect production for much longer than the interruption lasts. A continuous and dependable flow of food for an expanding world population is essential.

Aware of the worsening problem of the energy situation, scientists at the New York State College of Agriculture and Life Sciences are taking a hard look at practically every step in the food system, from the farm to the dinner table, to determine where and how much energy can be saved. The goal is to develop a combination of conservation techniques and alternative energy sources to make the food system more energy-efficient.

Research. Solutions are being sought in numerous areas. Recent studies have determined the best possible estimates of the energy required for the production phases of agriculture in New York State. Indirect energy needs in the production and distribution of fertilizers, pesticides, and other agricultural chemicals also have been documented. These studies provide vital information for establishing more precise fuel allocation programs, when necessary, and also for developing new technologies for an energy-efficient food system.

Looking into alternative energy sources, researchers are developing a system for turning the wind's power into usable energy. Water becomes hot if agitated in an insulated container, and the wind's power can be used to drive such an energy-conversion device. A wind turbine to demonstrate the feasibility of this concept, tested successfully with laboratory-scale models is not under construction at Cornell's Animal Science Teaching and Research Center. Traditional windmills and virtually all modern turbines are used to pump water or generate electrical power. Researchers estimate that a wind speed of 10 miles an hour can produce about 120 gallons of hot water a day—an adequate supply for a 60-cow dairy farm. If the wind blows harder, production increases dramatically—up to nearly 1000 gallons with a 20-m.p.h. wind, for example.

Cow manure and other farm wastes are becoming an important source of energy because they produce methane, a clean-burning fuel with many uses, which is the major component of natural gas. Two full-scale demonstration units—a Cornell design and a conventional sewage-sludge digester—have been constructed to compare their performance. The Cornell digester is simple in design, consisting of a trench in the ground with a cover, and is easy to operate. It is capable of producing about 6000 cubic feet of methane every 24 hours. The object of this project is to develop a low-cost methane production system for small dairy farms.

In another project concerned with animal wastes, chemical engineers, poultry scientists, and microbiologists are developing a way to convert poultry manure into protein-rich feedstuffs. Using the manure as a growing medium under controlled conditions, microorganisms such as bacteria or yeasts are produced and harvested. The result is a microbial product called "single-cell protein," with a protein content of nearly 50 percent. Such a product can be fed to chickens as a substitute for much of the conventional high-protein feed supplements such as soybean and fish meals. The system may not significantly conserve direct energy, but it would offer farmers the advantages of a feed-production method that is largely independent of weather and fluctuations in grain prices.

Chemical engineers have recently developed improved fermentation processes for producing ethyl alcohol from agricultural materials rather than from petroleum. More than 90 percent of the 2 billion pounds of industrial alcohol used annually in the United States is produced from petroleum. As oil becomes more expensive and scarce, production of ethanol by fermentation is being more seriously considered as one way to conserve fossil fuel.

Solar energy is being tapped to reduce heating costs of greenhouse operations. Agricultural engineers and horticulturists have developed an experimental solar greenhouse shaped like an inverted "V." Designed to collect a maximum of energy from the sun, the greenhouse itself acts as the solar collector. The north wall and part of the north roof are merged into one solid structure at a steep angle, thus insulating that entire area. During the day, excess heat that builds up along the ridgeline of the structure is collected and piped down to storage boxes, arranged to serve as plant benches, that are packed with crushed limestone—an excellent medium for holding heat. This stored heat warms the greenhouse at night. Even under New York conditions, researchers hope to achieve 65 percent savings in fuel during the heating season. Meanwhile, a number of effective conservation techniques have been developed for conventional greenhouses.

Agriculture has always used solar energy, but contemporary science has a new approach. We are now beginning to understand the basic photosynthetic process by which green plants capture light energy and turn it into food energy. One day, this knowledge may help meet energy needs. A scientist involved in the studies of this life-supporting system suggests that hydrogen could be produced on a large scale by modifying the natural process of photosynthesis. If this could be done economically, hydrogen could replace most fuels now in use. Or a solar battery modeled after the photosynthetic machinery of the living plant—a device that could convert sunlight directly into electricity — is another possibility. Although realization of these ideas is many years away, they do illustrate the importance of basic or fundamental research.

A tremendous amount of fertilizer is needed to grow food, but its production requires energy. One exciting area of research is concerned with the ability of legume plants such as peas and beans, aided by certain types of microorganisms, to capture nitrogen from the air. Cornell researchers are hoping to find ways to make nonlegume crops such as rice and other cereals acquire the same ability. A breakthrough in this research would have worldwide impact.

Agricultural engineers and food scientists have developed new equipment designed to save electricity, water, and the detergents needed for cleaning and sanitizing milk-handling equipment on the dairy farm. Results show savings as high as 50 percent for electricity and 75 percent for detergents.

Analyses of canning and freezing plants indicate that substantial savings can be accomplished by insulating buildings, equipment, and steam pipes, and also by recovery of heat from discarded hot water. At 29 percent, food processing takes the biggest portion of the energy used in the food system.

Looking to future energy sources, scientists in other units of the University are working to harness the awesome power of thermonuclear fusion under controlled conditions. Still other recent research accomplishments outside the College of Agriculture and Life Sciences include a new type of solar cell and an experimental electric car.

Numerous studies also are under way to assess the long-term effect of the energy crisis on agriculture as it relates to the availability of arable land and the expanding world population; the relation between employment, income, and energy conservation; public policies affecting future energy demand; problems of coal production; and strategies for leasing offshore oil development rights.

Which Energy Crisis?

by Keith Abercrombie

The sudden raising of oil prices in October 1973 belatedly awakened the world to the realization that it is facing an energy crisis because of the rapid depletion of the non-renewable resources of fossil fuel on which it depends so heavily. This has stimulated a number of studies on the use of energy in agriculture. However, the main emphasis so far has generally been on only a few of the more obvious aspects of the energy crisis as it relates to agriculture. In reality, there are no less than six separate but interrelated problem areas in the agricultural sector.

The first of these to be given attention, starting with a famous article by Pimentel and his associates,[1] concerns the energy (mostly fossil fuel) required for the production and use of chemical fertilizers, farm machinery and other "energy-intensive" inputs that are mainly relied upon for raising agricultural production in the developed countries and increasingly in the developing countries as well. It is this area that has continued to receive the main emphasis. Some scientific attention has been paid to a second area, that of the efficiency of crops and livestock in converting solar energy (the ultimate source of all energy) into dietary energy that can be used by man. There have also been several studies, particularly in the United States, of a third area: the much larger quantities of energy (again mainly fossil fuel) used by the developed countries for the processing and distribution of food and agricultural products that for farm production.

Some of the more recent studies, including a general survey made by FAO,[2] have also looked at a fourth subject, namely the energy deriving from the agricultural sector itself, in the form of fuelwood and agricultural residues, which provides a large part of the total energy used for all purposes in the developing countries. A fifth facet, energy in the form of human and animal power—an important input for agricultural production in the developing countries—has been very little studied.

From *Ceres,* 11 (5) 1978, 13–13. Reprinted with permission of the Food and Agriculture Organization of the United Nations.

Keith Abercrombie is Deputy Director of the Policy Analysis Division of FAO, but is writing here in a personal capacity. He wishes to acknowledge the help of a number of colleagues in preparing this article, especially J.E.M. Arnold, J.M. Couston, L. Faidley, J. Hrabovszky, L. Naiken, J. Périssé and H. Quaix

There is another area that serves to link up the other five. It is well known that the available supplies of dietary energy are extremely badly distributed in relation to nutritional needs. It is seldom realized, however, that the very people who are the worst nourished include many of those who are obliged to use a large part of the dietary energy they can obtain as an input for its further production, both for themselves and for the non-agricultural population of their own and other countries.

Agricultural production takes only a small fraction of the total world use of "commercial" energy.[3] FAO estimates that its share was 3.5 percent in 1972–73, and that (despite a big increase in absolute terms) it will rise only slightly to 4.1 percent by 1985–86. As with the consumption of so many other things, developed countries, containing about one third of the population, are responsible for four fifths of the total. They use more than 30 times as much commercial energy per head of their agricultural labour force as the developing countries.

But the small share of agriculture in total energy use gives no grounds for complacency. The increase in production could well come to a halt without a continued expansion in the supply of the energy-intensive inputs on which present technology is so largely based. Farm machinery takes about half the commercial energy used in agriculture, its operation accounting for around twice as much as its manufacture. Chemical fertilizers take about 45 percent, but they already account for more than two thirds in the developing countries, and their share at the world level is rising rapidly. A special problem is that the production of nitrogen fertilizer is not very energy intensive but uses fossil fuels (natural gas and naphtha) as its main raw material.

Economies in the use of these inputs are clearly essential. Chemical fertilizer use declined temporarily in 1974–75 in the developed countries, where it is already so high that additional applications bring small returns. There is much scope for the more efficient use of chemical fertilizers in both developed and developing countries. There is even more scope (although many difficulties are involved) for expanding the use of organic fertilizers and other practices for maintaining soil fertility, particularly in the labour-surplus developing countries.

Until early in the nineteenth century, even the most advanced agricultures relied mainly on such practices as fallowing, crop rotation, catch-cropping (especially with nitrogen-fixing legumes), and the recycling of crop and animal residues for the maintenance of soil fertility. Fallowing has had to be reduced because of population pressure. With abundant and cheap supplies of easily portable and adaptable chemical fertilizers, emphasis has been put on the other practices with a few major exceptions, such as China, Japan and the Republic of Korea.

ONE GOOD RESULT

It has been estimated that the plant, animal and human wastes in the developing market economies, which could potentially be used for organic manuring, contain almost eight times the plant nutrients in the chemical fertilizers used today.[4] Difficulties involved in mobilizing even a small part of this vast potential include the need for radical changes in farming systems and in the orientation of extension services, transport problems, and the fact that much of the more accessible material is at present used for fuel. Although it is most unlikely that yields could be increased fast enough by the use of organic fertilizers alone, there is considerable scope for their greater use in suitable combinations with chemical fertilizers, and this must obviously be given high priority, both in applied research and in the planning of the necessary organizational measures.

The question of farm machinery is more complex, but perhaps less crucial—at least for the developing countries. Mechanization is unavoidable in the developed countries because of the high cost of labour. In developing countries, carefully selected mechanization is in many cases essential to increase agricultural production, especially where multiple cropping is possible. But one good result would accrue from the fossil fuel crisis if it were to discourage the somewhat indiscriminate mechanization that has so far occurred in some of the countries where labour is the only abundant resource.

Some studies have dealt with the whole question of the efficiency of the conversion of solar energy in agricultural production, both that captured in photosynthesis and that added by man (mainly fossil fuel energy) in the process of production. Only a minute proportion of the solar energy that reaches a plant is converted into plant tissue, and even less into grain or other edible parts. Different crops and cropping systems vary widely in the efficiency of their use of fossil fuel energy to produce dietary energy. Research has hitherto aimed mainly at improving the efficiency of photosynthesis by the use of inputs based on fossil fuels; it should now be directed to the same goal but for the purpose of economizing on these inputs.[5]

WHEN THE PRICES ARE HIGH

The question of livestock production looms large in this context. Livestock is a rather inefficient converter of the energy captured by plants. While in some parts of the world, ruminant livestock production on grassland neither competes with people for food nor uses much fossil fuel, livestock (particularly non-ruminants) produced in intensive modern systems does both. Almost a third of world cereal production is fed to livestock in developed countries. In the United States, the production, processing, transport, marketing and preparation of livestock products use about twice as much fossil fuel energy as that of the equivalent quantity of dietary energy from crop products.[6] However, the function of world food production is not solely to turn out dietary energy. There is an effective market demand for livestock products, which tends to be curtailed when the prices of cereals or of fossil fuels are high. Unfortunately, it has not yet been convincingly demonstrated how a reduction in the consumption of livestock products in the developed countries could (except in conditions of extreme shortage) help the poor undernourished people in developing countries.

It is perhaps not a very surprising feature of our industrial civilization that the richest countries use far more energy to get their food from the farm to the consumer than to produce it on the farm. In the United States, three times as much fossil fuel energy is used for the processing, transport, marketing and preparation of food as in its production on the farm, and the whole food system accounts for 13 percent of total energy use.[7] This is partly because of the transfer of many activities previously performed on the farm to off-farm industries. But it also involves many luxury activities: sophisticated processing, "convenience" preparation and packaging, the maintenance of the same consumption patterns throughout the year regardless of the seasons, and the disposal of prodigious quantities of waste. Since world energy use is so dominated by the developed countries, the use of commercial energy in the food system as a whole may well approach 10 percent of total world consumption.

To feed all the world with a United States type food system would take up to 60 percent of the present total consumption of commercial energy. This is obviously one of the main areas where economies are desirable in developed countries, and they seem likely to come as a result of rising costs. Whereas it will be difficult to avoid a continued rapid increase in the use of energy-intensive inputs for agricultural production in the developing countries, it should be easier to avoid the excesses of the developed countries in the rest of the food system. There is probably much scope for harnessing such sources as wind and direct solar energy for some aspects of food processing in the developing countries. However, one of the less noticed effects of the transnational corporations is to turn food consumption habits in developing countries increasingly toward those of the rich world.

In return for inputs of commercial and non-commercial energy, as well as the solar energy directly used in photosynthesis, the food and agricultural sector produces energy. By far its most important output is dietary energy. But it is seldom realized that crop and livestock residues, processing wastes and the wood used for fuel contain much more energy, even though it is perhaps of a less useful kind than dietary energy. In the United States, the energy in crop residues, manure and processing waste (i.e., excluding fuel-wood) is almost twelve times the production of dietary energy.[8]

IN IMMEDIATE HUMAN TERMS

Most of this is wasted in the developed countries, but in the developing countries (although it is wasted there, too) it is also a principal source of fuel: probably about 30 percent of the total (commercial plus non-commercial) energy supply in the developing countries as a whole, and perhaps as much as 40 percent in the developing market economies. In India, it was estimated as 56 percent of the total in 1970–71.[9] In the developing world as a whole, fuelwood is far more important than crop and livestock residues as a source of energy, representing some 88 percent of the total from these three sources. In Africa, the consumption of fuelwood may be almost one and a half times that of commercial energy. About 86 percent of the wood used in the developing countries is for fuel.

There is a fuelwood crisis in many developing countries that, in immediate human terms, is far worse than the world fossil fuel crisis.[10] Most of the half of the world's people who live in the rural areas of the developing countries depend mainly on fuelwood to cook their meagre food supplies and to keep warm in cold weather. In many places, the demand for fuelwood has so seriously depleted the available resources that families have to go farther and farther away to gather their requirements. It is urgently necessary to expand the production of fuelwood on a sustained basis, particularly in village community woodlots, including tree planting along roadsides. Self-help schemes for this purpose have been carried out in several countries, especially in China, India and the Republic of Korea. The planting of certain fast-growing leguminous shrubs on degraded land near villages would simultaneously improve soil productivity, produce more fuelwood, and greatly reduce the time and the human and animal power that have to be expended in gathering and hauling it. There are also many areas where much fuelwood is wasted in slash-and-burn agriculture. Moreover, it is somewhat irrational that so much wood is diverted from the deprived rural areas to provide fuel for urban people, who have greater access to alternative sources of energy, and for whom wood is expensive because of its low efficiency and high delivery costs.

MAINLY FOR COOKING

The demand for fuelwood in rural areas can be reduced by making greater use of crop and livestock (and human) residues as fuel. At present, no more than 3 or 6 percent of the potentially available energy in crop and livestock residues in the developing countries is used for fuel, mainly because of an understandable preference for fuelwood where it is available. However, the value of these residues as fertilizer (especially nitrogen) is destroyed if they are burned as fuel. There are many ways of converting them to conventional liquid and gaseous fuels, but their conversion to biogas (more successful with animal and human than with crop residues) is of particular importance, since this process not only produces methane as a very versatile fuel but also leaves a residue with a high content of plant nutrients. Household biogas plants, mainly for cooking, have been introduced in China, India and some other countries. Little work has yet been done on village community plants, but it is probably here that the main emphasis should be placed in the future, as biogas is somewhat expensive for cooking.[11] At the household level, there are many simple improvements that can be made with much more cheaply, especially in cooking stoves but also in utensils and methods, which would greatly reduce the work of the housewife as well as saving precious fuel.

RUNNING OUT

A crucial thread in the history of mankind has been his progressive mastering of different sources of energy.[12] In the earliest pre-agricultural societies, all the energy available to him came from his own muscle power and from the plant and animal converters of solar energy that he was able to obtain by hunting and gathering. The mastering of fire provided energy for warmth and cooking. The introduction of agriculture made it possible to control and increase the supply of dietary energy from plants and animals, as well as providing an additional supply of motive power through the use of the latter. However, except for some limited use of water and wind energy, the energy supply still consisted only of plants for food and fuel, animals for food and motive power, and men and women for motive power. The industrial revolution brought an enormous expansion in the available energy, making it possible to supplement and substitute these physiological sources by new sources of inanimate energy, very largely in the form of fossil fuel. The next step, now that fossil fuel is running out, must be a return, but this time with the help of modern technology, to the use of renewable sources of energy.

The industrial revolution also led eventually to big changes in the energy available for agricultural production. In the countries now described as developed, organic fertilizers have steadily been supplemented and even replaced by chemical ones, and human labour and animal draught power replaced by machines. The replacement of human labour has been particularly rapid in recent years, although the growth of unemployment in the rest of the economy, combined with rising fuel costs, has probably slowed it down in some countries. The agricultural labour force of the developed countries fell from 148 million in 1950 to 78 million in 1975, and from 38 to 15 percent of their total labour force. In developing countries, however, it is still increasing in absolute terms (from 559 million in 1950 to 709 million in 1975), although falling from 79 to 63 percent as a proportion of the total labour force. The agricultural labour force of the developed countries is thus only 11 percent of that in the developing countries, but it produces about one third more. This is to a great extent because, as mentioned earlier, it is supported by more than thirty times as much commercial energy per head as the agricultural labour force of the developing countries, which is in turn one of the reasons for the very serious prevalence of underemployment in this labour force.

In six prototypical composite villages in different parts of the developing world, human energy is estimated to supply from 6 to 20 percent of the total gross energy input, and animal draught from zero to 51 percent.[13] As regards the power (rather than the total energy) available for agricultural production, it has been estimated that, in the developing market economies of Asia, animal draught provides about half, and human and machine power about one fourth each; in Latin America the contribution of machine power is as high as 70 percent, with animals providing 20 percent and humans 10 percent; in Africa, where the power available per hectare is less than half that in the other two regions, machines provide almost 60 percent of the small total, humans just over one third, and animals as little as 7 percent.[14] Such comparisons of different types of energy input involve many problems, but it is significant that, in the developing world as a whole, the fuel used for the operation of farm machinery amounts, per head of the agricultural labour force, to less than 1 percent of that in the developed countries.

An important feature of the agricultural power supply in the developing countries is that it is generally less "efficient" than that in the developed world. It may be roughly estimated that the amount of "useful energy" obtained from the original energy input is generally less than half as much for humans and draught animals as for most farm machinery, although human labour in particular is probably more efficient for certain specific purposes. A substantial increase in both animal draught and machine power, as well as improvements in hand tools, are obviously needed if agricultural production in the developing countries is to be increased fast enough, and if the drudgery of so much agricultural work is to be reduced. But there are considerable difficulties concerning both animal and machine power.

LARGE AREAS OF LAND

There are many parts of the world where livestock production and the use of animals for draught power have been very little developed, especially in the immense areas of Africa in the thrall of trypanosomiasis. Because it is no longer of interest to the developed countries, little attention has been paid lately to the improvement of animal draught equipment, and many lines are going out of production. Animals require large areas of land to feed them, even when they are not working, so that they cannot be used to any great extent where land is short unless crop yields are very high. When there was an upsurge in the growth of the European population at the time of the industrial revolution, the replacement of fuelwood by coal and later of draught animals (and even more of those used for transport in the economy as a whole) by machines released large quantities of land for food production, to say nothing of the opening up of the huge land resources of the New World. No such easy solutions exist for the population explosion in the developing countries today.

The expansion of power mechanization poses even more difficult problems. It is undoubtedly essential in many cases in the developing countries, and in the long run, when their agricultural labour force finally begins to fall in absolute numbers, that a very big expansion will be required. In the meantime, however, apart from the problem of rising fuel costs, it has to be introduced on a highly selective basis if it is not to diminish still further the already insufficient employment opportunities for the rapidly growing labour force.

AT TOO LOW AN EBB

FAO's Fourth World Food Survey estimates the daily supply of dietary energy per head in the developing countries in 1972–74 as 2,200 kilo-calories, or 4 percent below the average nutritional requirement of 2,300 kcal. This would give a total annual supply of 2.18×10^{15} kcal for the whole population. The average nutritional requirement of the labour force is higher than that of the non-working population, and may be around 2,500 kcal per day. Assuming that the agricultural labour force received 5 percent less than this higher requirement, its annual dietary energy supply would be 0.60×10^{15} kcal, or almost 30 percent of the total.

It is unfortunately difficult to go further than this in trying to estimate how much of the total dietary energy supply of the developing countries, and in particular of their agricultural labour force, is used as an input for agricultural production, including especially the production of further dietary energy. The figure just suggested for the dietary energy supply of the agricultural labour force is already highly speculative. How much of this is used for body maintenance and for agricultural and non-agricultural activity is impossible to estimate without new surveys specifically carried out for this purpose.

What is clear, however, is that the members of the agricultural labour force of the developing countries are among the worst nourished people in the world. It is their own food supplies that must bear the main brunt of a bad harvest, but even in a good season they are undernourished for most of the year. Periods of intensive activity often result in temporary losses of body weight. They are often at too low an ebb of undernourishment and poor health to make the maximum imput of energy that is required at planting and harvest time to obtain the maximum dietary energy supply for the following year. Thus the cycle of hunger and malnutrition is self-perpetuating.

These people are supported in their task of agricultural production by only a tiny fraction of the commercial energy (especially that used for mechanical power) available per head of the much smaller agricultural labour force of the developed countries. They have to use up increasing amounts of dietary energy to gather the fuelwood required for cooking and other purposes. They are protected, if at all, by only the most rudimentary health services and sanitation. Pre- and post-harvest food losses are finally receiving increased emphasis, but the "post-eating" food loss caused by gastrointestinal diseases is still usually forgotten.

COULD JEOPARDIZE THE FUTURE

There is no doubt that, until cheap alternative sources of energy are developed (and this will inevitably take a long time), the fossil fuel crisis will continue to cause serious balance-of-payments problems for many countries, and could even jeopardize the future expansion of agricultural production. It is not intended to minimize the importance for agriculture of the fossil fuel crisis, but only to emphasize that there are other aspects, like the fuelwood crisis and the long-standing dietary energy crisis, which are even graver in immediate human terms.

Almost all countries are now attempting to devise energy policies for the future. There is a danger, however, that just because agriculture's energy needs are so small a proportion of the total, they may be neglected as unimportant. It is also essential that energy policy should take account of each of the six problem areas in agriculture that have been discussed here.

NOTES

1. D. Pimentel, L.E. Hurd, A.C. Bellotti, M.J. Forster, I.N. Oka, O.D. Sholes and R.J. Whitman, "Food Production and the Energy Crisis." *Science,* 182, November 1973.
2. *The State of Food and Agriculture 1976,* FAO, Rome, 1977. Unless otherwise stated, the statistics quoted here are derived from this survey of energy and agriculture.
3. Commercial energy either involves a technology of energy conversion or enters commercial channels. Non-commercial energy is consumed directly, without technological conversion and without being formally marketed.
4. J.J.C. van Voorhoeve, *Organic Fertilizer: Problems and Potential for Developing Countries.* World Bank Fertilizer Study, Background Paper No. 4, Washington, D.C., 1974.

5. Harold F. Breimyer, The Food-energy balance, in Douglas Ensminger (ed.), *Food Enough or Starvation for Millions*. Tata McGraw-Hill, New Delhi, 1977.
6. F.C. Stickler, W.C. Burrows and L.F. Nelson, *Energy from Sun, to Plant, to Man*. Deere and Company, Moline, Ill., 1975.
7. John S. Steinhart and Carol E. Steinhart, "Energy Use in the U.S. Food System." *Science*, 184 (4134), April 1974.
8. F.C. Stickler, et al., op. cit.
9. P.D. Henderson, *India, The Energy Sector*. World Bank, Washington, D.C., 1975.
10. For useful surveys of this aspect, see E.P. Eckholm, *The Other Crisis: Firewood*, Worldwatch Paper 1, Washington, D.C., Worldwatch Institute, 1975; J.E.M. Arnold and J.H. Jongman, "Fuelwood and Charcoal in Developing Countries: an Economic Survey," *Unasylva*, 118 (in press).
11. Arjun Makhijani, *Energy Policy for the Rural Third World*. International Institute for Environment and Development, London, 1976.
12. Carlo M. Cipolla, *The Economic History of World Population*. Penguin Books, Harmondsworth, 1970.
13. Arjun Makhijani and Alan Poole, *Energy and Agriculture in the Third World: a Report to the Energy Policy Project of the Ford Foundation*. Ballinger Publishing Company, Cambridge, Mass., 1975.
14. G.W. Giles, "The Reorientation of Agricultural Mechanization for the Developing Countries: Policies and Attitudes for Action Programmes." In *Effects of Farm Mechanization on Production and Employment*, Report of the Expert Panel Held in Rome, 4–7 February 1975, FAO, Rome, 1975.

Methanol Primed for Future Energy Role

by Stephen C. Stinson

Methanol At a Glance

Structure—CH_3OH
Weight vs. volume—0.7914 kg per liter, 6.604 lb per gal, 302.8 gal per ton
Energy content—66,700 Btu per gal
Price—46 cents per lb, $6.90 per million Btu
How made—Catalytic reaction of hydrogen and carbon monoxide from partial oxidation of methane from natural gas
Production—1.1 billion gal in 1979, worth $507 million
Capacity—1.25 billion gal per year
Producers—Air Products, Borden, Celanese, Du Pont, Georgia Pacific, Hercofina, Monsanto, Rohm & Haas, Tenneco, Valley Nitrogen

Planning the role of methanol in the U.S. energy future is like putting together a circus high-wire act. Successful articulation of raw materials, production, distribution, and use technologies would be a spectacular achievement. But the element that holds the act together is the delivered price of methanol.

To compete as fuel for electric power generation, methanol must cost no more than $3.80 to $4.30 per million Btu, delivered, according to Westinghouse Electric Corp. long-range planner Harry Jaeger. He presented this estimate to a symposium on methanol as a fuel, held at the American Chemical Society's Middle Atlantic Regional Meeting at Monmouth College, West Long Branch, N.J.

The Westinghouse estimate corresponds to 25 to 29 cents per gal of methanol. By contrast, current spot prices are 46 cents per gal, f.o.b. producers' plants. Jaeger says some California utilities evaluating methanol are paying 53 to 63 cents per gal, delivered, which comes to $8.00 to $9.60 per million Btu.

Technology now in existence for coal gasification and methanol synthesis can meet these maximum cost requirements, says Department of Energy technical adviser Neal P. Cochran. Relying on a study done for DOE in 1978 by Badger Plants, Cambridge, Mass., Cochran quotes prices of 24 to 30 cents per gal, f.o.b. producer plant, assuming a coal price of $25 per ton, or $1.00 per million Btu.

Methanol prices can be as low as 15 cents per gal, claims chemical engineering professor Donald F. Othmer of Polytechnic Institute of New York. He assumes such a gasification and synthesis plant would use lignite at 50 cents per million Btu.

Behind such estimates of methanol fuel price requirements and possibilities lies a complex interaction of technology, economics, and institutional relationships. The first ventures to test feasibility of methanol fuel on a commercial scale probably will be two 25,000 ton-per-day plants on the drawing board at Wentworth Brothers, Cincinnati.

One such plant will be located on the coast near Anchorage. Methanol made from Alaskan coal will be shipped by tanker to utilities plants near Los Angeles and San Francisco, according to Wentworth's David Garrett, who chaired the symposium. The other will make methanol from North Dakota lignite for midwestern utilities, he says.

The first methanol may leave Anchorage in 1983, with the plant fully on stream in 1985. The North Dakota facility may ship methanol beginning in 1984, Garrett says, coming up to full production in 1986.

As Othmer points out, such plants have important implications just because of their size. A 25,000 ton-per-day methanol plant using 50,000 tons per day of coal containing only 1% sulfur would produce 500 tons per day of elemental sulfur—more than 180,000 tons per year.

The air separation plant to provide needed oxygen would be the largest ever built. The 45 million to 90 million tons of air processed yearly has a potential yield of, for example, 750,000 to 1.5 million tons of argon. Othmer suggests that by-product nitrogen from air separation plus carbon dioxide from coal gasification may be injected into nearby oil fields to stimulate production.

Jaeger says advantages of methanol for electric power generation would show up best in a combined cycle plant. In a combined cycle, methanol would first be burned in a combustion turbine. Heat and steam from this step are recovered for further use in high-, intermediate-, and low-pressure steam turbines.

Methanol is superior to No. 2 distillate fuel oil in combined cycle plants partly because of the chemically combined water molecule of methanol. The modular construction of combined cycle plants also results in lower capital investment per kwh in comparison with other plant types, Jaeger says.

Increased amounts of water vapor from methanol combustion raise combustion turbine power output to 105,400 kw, compared with 95,700 kw from oil in the same plant. That water vapor goes on to give steam turbine outputs of 51,500 kw for methanol, as against only 49,200 kw with oil. The result, with today's technology, is a fuel cost of 7877 Btu per kwh for methanol and 7515 Btu per kwh for No. 2 oil.

Jaeger says that requirements can be lowered to only 7700 Btu per kwh for methanol by such measures as using combustion heat to vaporize methanol before entry to the combustion turbine, reforming methanol to carbon monoxide and hydrogen before burning, raising turbine inlet temperatures to 2300°F, lowering stack gas temperatures below 280°F, and preheating feedwater and combustion air.

These plant improvements set the stage for comparing required delivered prices of methanol fuel with performance of other fuels and systems with which methanol must compete. A conventional coal-fired steam plant with scrubbers would cost $838 per kw in capital investment and need 9928 Btu per kwh, resulting in power costs of 40.9 mills per kwh. To generate power for 40.9 mills per kwh, delivered prices of methanol would have to be $4.29 per million Btu, or 28.5 cents per gal.

A utility plant based on coal gasification would need $816 per kw of capital investment and 8813 Btu per kwh, resulting in power costs of 37.2 mills per kwh. A combined cycle plant would then compete if methanol cost $3.81 per million Btu, or 25.5 cents per gal delivered.

Cochran's estimates of prices for which methanol actually can be made show the importance of the type of financing used. The Badger Plants study assumed a capacity of 58,300 tons of methanol per day costing $3.1 billion. If the plant were financed 100% by equity with a 12% return on investment, the price of methanol at the plant gate would be 30 cents per gal. If the financing were 65% debt at 99% interest and 35% equity, the price would come down to 24.1 cents per gal.

A combination of debt and equity is just what Wentworth Brothers has in mind for the Alaska and North Dakota plants. Because methanol is a clean-burning fuel, some of the bonds could yield tax-free returns. Othmer points out that methanol created as a new fuel qualifies for DOE entitlements of 2.5 cents per gal.

But coal is not the only feedstock that can be used for methanol production. William H. Kumm, president of Arctic Enterprises, Annapolis, Md., proposed that the 2 billion cu ft per day of natural gas coproduced with 1.6 million bbl per day of oil from the Alaska North Slope be made into synthesis gas, converted to methanol, and piped through the existing unused capacity of the Alyeska pipeline. Alaska gas is currently being reinjected into the ground at a cost of 15 cents per 1000 cu ft, Kumm says.

Kumm sees the methanol approach as preferable to building a separate pipeline for gas. A methanol plant could be brought to Prudhoe Bay mounted on barges, just as Wentworth Brothers proposes to bring one to the Kenai Peninsula near Anchorage. Othmer says a 5000 ton-per-day methanol train can be transported on three to four barges. Water for a Prudhoe Bay methanol plant would come from desalination of Artic Ocean water, Kumm says.

Kumm thinks of conversion of Alaska gas to methanol as a first step toward comprehensive, long-term efforts to use all Alaska oil and gas resources most effectively. As oil and methanol transport increases to the full carrying capacity of the Alyeska pipeline, ocean routes to the U.S. East Coast—the opportunity market, according to Kumm—could be developed involving submarine tankers such as those now used in the Persian Gulf off Dubai.

Energy from Agriculture:

The Brazilian Experiment

by Leon G. Mears

Brazil's national alcohol program ("Alcohol is solar energy in liquid form") has evolved into a major government-industry effort aimed at replacing a large share of the country's petroleum imports with alcohol produced from sugarcane, manioc, and other plants. This comprehensive program has been given a boost by low world sugar prices that recently resulted in the Brazilian government's decision to allocate the sugarcane equivalent of 2.1 million metric tons of sugar to the manufacture of alcohol between June 1, 1978, and May 31, 1979.

Brazil is the world's largest producer of sugarcane and the current supply far exceeds the country's current sugar needs for the domestic and export markets. According to government estimates, direct conversion of sugarcane to alcohol in the 1978/79 sugar year will be adequate to produce about 2.4 billion liters of alcohol. This quantity, when combined with alcohol to be produced from residual molasses and manioc, would enable Brazil to pull ahead of schedule in the plan to produce sufficient alcohol to replace 20 percent of the gasoline projected to be consumed in 1980.

ADVANTAGES OF ALCOHOL

Extensive tests in Brazil have shown that with alcohol mixtures up to 20 percent no major adjustments in car motors would be required. Such a mixture would permit Brazil to reduce its petroleum imports by about 10 percent, thus generating foreign exchange savings in the early 1980s of roughly $450 to $500 million or more, depending on the import price of petroleum.

In addition to saving foreign exchange, the alcohol program is expected to provide a variety of other social and economic benefits to the nation. Included are higher employment (particularly in several low income, high unemployment regions); increased demand for selected capital goods such as agricultural machinery, transportation equipment, and distilleries; and greater utilization of the country's vast agricultural resources.

From the July 17, 1978 issue of *Foreign Agriculture,* a U.S. Department of Agriculture publication.

Brazil has long been dependent on imported petroleum as an energy source. In 1977 petroleum imports were valued at $3.8 billion, up $350 million from 1976 and eleven times the level of five years ago. In 1970, domestic petroleum production accounted for 35 percent of domestic consumption, but this share has been trending downward, and in 1977 local output accounted for only about 18 percent of domestic usage. Recognizing the adverse effects growing dependence on imported petroleum would have on the country's ambitious long-range economic development programs, the Brazilian government has launched a comprehensive program aimed at developing an alternative and renewable source of energy. The basic objective of the National Alcohol Program (PROALCOOL) is to harness solar energy indirectly by the utilization of plant materials formed through photo-synthesis to produce fuel.

FINANCING THE PROGRAM

The heart of PROALCOOL is concessional financing of expansion and modernization of current alcohol distilleries, new distilleries, and agricultural projects to supply them. Up to 80 percent (90 percent in north and northeast of Brazil) of the cost of establishing distilleries can be financed at an interest rate of 17 percent (15 percent in the north and northeast) for a maximum period of twelve years with three years of grace before repayments begin. One hundred percent of the cost of financing manioc production projects can be financed at rates as low as 13 percent per year with repayment over twelve years. The current commercial loan interest rates in Brazil range from 45 to 50 percent per year. According to government estimates, some $1.6 billion in government and private funds is expected to be invested in alcohol production between 1976 and 1982.

Brazil has long been a sizable producer and, in recent years, a significant exporter of alcohol. In the past, virtually all alcohol was manufactured from the residual molasses resulting from the sugar refining process. The residual molasses from the production of one bag (60kg) of crystal sugar is sufficient to produce on the average 7 liters of alcohol (the byproduct of one metric ton of sugar is 116.7 liters of alcohol). Most alcohol distilleries are currently linked to sugarmills, although there are some independent distilleries that purchase molasses from mills. Alcohol production is currently concentrated largely in the center-south area of Brazil, particularly in the State of São Paulo. Sugarmills in the northeast traditionally have not distilled their residual molasses into alcohol, but have elected to export molasses. However, a number of projects for building new distilleries in the northeast have been approved, and alcohol production is now beginning in some areas. Alcohol production for the 1978/79 crop year is expected to total about 2.7 billion liters, of which 2.2 billion liters will be used as fuel. As of December 1977, selected cities in eight States were utilizing alcohol-gasoline mixtures in ratios varying from 10 to 20 percent alcohol.

Little information regarding alcohol production costs under PROAL-COOL is available, as most of the approved projects are just being initiated. Available cost data are primarily for alcohol output by established sugarmills that have been producing alcohol by traditional methods for many years. According to recent studies, current alcohol production costs about $1.65 per gallon, about double gasoline production costs. Proponents of PROALCOOL say alcohol production costs will drop sharply when the modern distilleries now being approved begin operation and when research and experience lead to more efficient production techniques. They admit that current alcohol production costs are above gasoline costs but hold that the current high retail gasoline price, $1.60 per gallon, combined with the foreign exchange savings and other far-reaching economic benefits of the program, make use of alcohol as a fuel economically feasible for Brazil.

In addition to utilizing residual molasses from the sugar refining process, alcohol can also be manufactured directly from sugarcane. That is, the cane can be used to make only alcohol and no sugar. In this case, 67 liters of alcohol can be extracted from one ton of sugarcane. Most of the hoped for expansion in alcohol production during the next three to five years will probably come from direct conversion of sugarcane to alcohol. In the past the manufacture of alcohol served as an escape valve—the direct conversion of sugarcane to alcohol was used only when there was surplus sugarcane production. For the 1978/79 sugar marketing year, the government has authorized the sugarcane equivalent of 2.1 million tons of sugar for direct conversion to alcohol.

ALCOHOL FROM MANIOC

Alcohol can also be extracted from a variety of other plants, such as grains, sweet potatoes, babassu palm, and manioc. Perhaps the most apt for Brazil is manioc. Brazil is already the world's largest producer of this starchy root, with 1977 output estimated at 26.7 million tons. However, manufacturing alcohol from manioc is more complicated than using sugarcane, and there is no pool of experienced entrepreneurs in manioc processing as there is for sugarcane.

As a long-term raw material source for alcohol, manioc has a number of advantages over sugarcane, and some disadvantages, as well. This hardy root crop can be grown rather easily on practically all soils in Brazil with little use of fertilizers and other modern production inputs, although fertilizer usage increases yields sharply. In contrast, sugarcane requires good soil and abundant rainfall and most cane producers apply large quantities of fertilizer.

Manioc can be propagated and harvested throughout the year, whereas sugarcane is a seasonal crop with the harvest period between 150 and 160 days. Distilleries utilizing manioc could operate year-round, while distilleries based on sugarcane as the raw material source would stand idle more than half the year.

However, a major disadvantage of using manioc as an alcohol raw material is that the residue after crushing is too watery to burn to fuel the distillery. In contrast, the distilleries using sugarcane are largely fired by bagasse—the sugarcane stalk after the juice is removed by rollers. Proponents of manioc as an alcohol source say the manioc distillery plants can be fueled by the stalks and limbs of the manioc plant supplemented by wood from trees grown at low cost in the same area as the manioc. They also say the manioc residue can be sold for swine feed and the protein-rich manioc leaves can be utilized for cattle feed, thereby providing additional income for purchase of fuel for the distilleries. A number of experiments are underway to determine the commercial feasibility of using the manioc residue and leaves for animal feed.

Over the long term, solar energy may prove to be an efficient energy source for fueling the manioc distilleries. The high intensity of sunlight throughout the year in Brazil's tropical northeast is a favorable factor in considering the use of this energy source. The Solar Energy Laboratory at the Federal University of Paraiba currently is conducting a variety of experiments aimed at harnessing solar energy for industrial plants.

The world's first manioc-alcohol plant began commercial operation in January 1978. This plant, located at Curvelo in the State of Minas Gerais, was built by the government at a cost estimated at $6.5 million. Initial production capacity of this plant is estimated at 60,000 liters of alcohol per day. Results from this pilot plant will determine to a large degree whether or not alcohol production from manioc will continue to receive heavy government support. Technicians at the Curvelo plant say that a large share of the high construction cost should be charged to research and development and similar plants in the future will be much less expensive.

Per capita consumption of manioc for food in Brazil has been trending downward for several years, reflecting the migration from rural areas to the cities and changing food preferences and dietary patterns, particularly higher consumption of wheat, rice, and animal products as a result of increased consumer purchasing power.

Manioc production peaked around 1970, with output of about 30 million tons. Between 1970 and 1975, output trended downward, totaling 24.8 million tons in 1976. Favorable weather boosted production in 1977 to 26.7 million tons. Declining demand for manioc for food will tend to make available a larger supply for alcohol production in future years.

Over the long term, other plants may also be raw material sources for PROALCOOL. The babassu palm, which grows wild over vast areas of the Amazon Basin, is considered to be one of the most promising sources.

If Brazil reaches its 1980 goal of 3 billion liters of alcohol for mixing with gasoline, it appears likely that 500 million liters will be distilled from residual molasses from existing production capacity, 2.2 billion liters will be distilled directly from sugarcane, and 300 million liters will be distilled from manioc.

HOW MUCH LAND?

The agricultural land required to produce raw materials for this alcohol can be calculated as follows: For sugarcane, an alcohol extraction rate of 67 liters per ton would require 32.5 million tons of cane from about 550,000 hectares. And for manioc an alcohol extraction rate of 180 liters per ton would require 1.67 million tons of manioc from about 85,000 hectares of land. Current total area in sugarcane is 1.8 million hectares and area in manioc is 2.1 million hectares. Brazil currently has about 47 million hectares of land in crops. Sufficient raw material to meet the 1980 alcohol goal could be produced on 1.3 percent of the land now in production.

Proponents of PROALCOOL say the impact of the program on production of other crops for domestic consumption and export will be limited since Brazil has abundant agricultural land and manpower. A number of agricultural experts who have studied the program carefully, however, believe that an immediate sharp expansion of the area in sugarcane would result in some reduction of the area in several other crops, particularly in São Paulo, currently Brazil's leading agricultural State. São Paulo is the most important sugar- and alcohol-producing State and any short-term expansion is expected to take place there.

At the present time only about 5 percent of Brazil's vast land area is under cultivation, but land in crops is expected to jump sharply in the next decade as a significant part of the savannah area of central Brazil (15 percent of Brazil's total land area) and several frontier areas come under cultivation. Some Brazilian agricultural experts believe that the domestic and commercial markets abroad for Brazil's leading agricultural crops (coffee, soybeans, cocoa, sugar, and corn) will not be readily able to absorb the large production gains that are anticipated in the next decade. They believe expansion of the area devoted to sugarcane, manioc, and perhaps other crops for alcohol production will help prevent burdensome agricultural surpluses in addition to meeting the goals of the National Alcohol Program.

AN ATTAINABLE GOAL

It is becoming increasingly clear that the initial PROALCOOL target of 3 billion liters of alcohol mixed with gasoline will be reached, if not in 1980, almost certainly by the early 1980s. Alcohol usage as a motor fuel beyond that level will depend heavily on continued support of PROALCOOL, demonstrated through financing of additional production projects and purchase of alcohol output at remunerative prices.

Until now, the Brazilian government has been by far the largest supplier of capital and technology for PROALCOOL. In recent months a number of private firms—domestic and foreign—have demonstrated increased interest in investing in the program, and may become an important driving force behind Brazil's effort to harness solar energy indirectly through utilization of plant materials.

Algae Promoted as Power Plant Fuel

The potential of algae as a source of biomass for fuel is limited by such ideas as an assumption that a natural pond suitably fed by runoff and appropriate nutrients is the most economical system to use for algae cultivation. Judson G. Brown of Granger Filter Co., Andover, Mass., disputes that assumption and, at the 2nd Pacific Chemical Engineering Congress, hosted last week in Denver by the American Institute of Chemical Engineers, he suggested a novel way to increase the attractiveness of algae cultivation for biomass.

The principal stumbling block in most algae growing systems is low growth rate. To a municipality fighting eutrophication, the rates might not seem low, but to the potential algae farmer, they are.

To obtain maximum growth rates it is necessary to drastically exceed the natural rate of absorption of atmospheric carbon dioxide in natural ponds. Brown suggests that this be done by burning the algae on site to generate the carbon dioxide, scrubbing it, and absorbing it in mixed metal carbonates that would then be fed back into the pond as components of nutrient solutions. Methane from anerobic digestion of sewage would serve as a fuel, with none exported. Similarly there would be no algae export—via food fish for example—unless there is an equivalent return of carbon in some usable form.

Trace minerals needed to grow the algae are projected to come from the same scrubber that removes combustion particulates in the algae burner. That busy scrubber would do triple duty by also recovering nutrient nitrogen via a system such as the WARF regenerative air preheat system developed by the Wisconsin Alumni Research Foundation. Brown notes that this and similar systems already have been developed and should provide enough nitrogen to the algae.

Possible growth rates of algae usually have been assumed to be in the range of 30 to 50 tons per year per acre, but Brown believes that yields of up to 210 tons per year per acre are possible. Such high yields already have been achieved in some closely controlled experiments.

The wide variation in algae yields is attributed by Brown to the different methods of growing and collecting algae, most of which rely on natural ponds of some sort. He advocates a departure from this method by proposing a two-layer lake system. The bottom layer would be the natural lake. Above this would be an algae-growing layer, a nutrient-rich captive batch of water. The two layers would be separated by a plastic sheet that would be deep enough to avoid surface turbulence and biodegradation. Natural water flow would be in the bottom layer.

Algae from the top layer would fall to the plastic sheet and be collected through very large tubular plastic ducts placed in the film. The lower layer would act as a stabilizing heat sink and an anerobic digester of a conventional municipal sewage treatment plant, providing nutrients and methane fuel.

The biomass from such an installation would be dried and burned to provide heat and electricity as well as carbon dioxide and nutrients for recycle. However, for the system to make a significant contribution, Brown recognizes that some severe limitations must be overcome in the refuse collection systems now in use. Almost all municipal sanitary systems require pure water outfalls, and pure water provides little in the way of nutrients for algae ponds. The inference is that it might be well to examine the possibility of redesigning sanitary systems as nutrient sources for algae ponds, at least on a trial basis. The key element in Brown's system is on-site nutrient recycle. If all this were to come to pass, Brown suggests that as much as 10% of national power needs could be achieved with his algae ponds.

Agriculture without Tillage

by F.J. Francis

Summary

The age old practice of plowing, discing, harrowing, planting, and cultivating as used in agriculture for hundreds of years, is changing. It is being replaced by herbicide treatment to kill unwanted plants, followed by direct seeding through the plant residue. This results in very large reductions in energy use, good control of erosion, less soil compaction, greater yield and less pollution by fertilizer and pesticide run-off.

The time-honored practice of plowing the land prior to planting which has been practical for millenia is changing. The new concept of crop production without any tilling of the land, or at best, with minimum tillage, are rapidly gaining ground. Recent surveys in Iowa, for instance, indicate that conservation tillage of one kind or another is used on 43 percent of the row-crop land.(1)

Plowing the land prior to planting dates as far back as recorded history, and has taken many forms. In the United States about fifty years ago, a corn grower in the mid-west would probably make 10 to 12 trips over the same field. The field was first plowed and then harrowed to break up the clods to make a fine seed bed. After planting, the land would be cultivated lightly to control weed growth. During the growth of the corn, 3 to 4 more cultivations would be required, primarily to control weeds, but also to conserve moisture. The corn plants themselves eventually grow high enough to inhibit the growth of weeds, but often one more cultivation using a small cultivator drawn by a horse or mule was necessary. In addition, hand labor or hoeing to eliminate the surviving weeds was often necessary. The production of cotton was similar, but oats, wheat, rye and barley required fewer operations because the seeds are sown closer together and there is no room for cultivation.

The same techniques of plowing and cultivation lasted long after the demise of the horse drawn implements due to the introduction of ever-bigger tractors. The easy availability of cheap energy in the form of petroleum made this type of operation very efficient in terms of man hours. It was estimated that in 1970, an acre of corn required only 9 man hours of labor.(2) The operation may be efficient in terms of human labor, but it did require large energy inputs (the energy equivalent of 80 gal. gasoline/acre) and there were other serious problems, such as soil erosion and soil compaction. The cost of diesel fuel alone will probably guarantee that this type of agriculture will have to change. Fortunately, there are good alternatives.

There are alternatives to the conventional system of agriculture described above. Probably the best known one was devised by Edward H. Faulkner in Ohio, about forty years ago. His book entitled, "Plowmans Folly" was a classic. Faulkner's system involved discing, not plowing the soil, and leaving crop residues on the surface of the soil. His system was devised primarily to control soil erosion, but the weed problem still remained and much hand labor was required. Other methods of controlling weeds, such as the mulch culture, defended so staunchly by the organic gardeners, are effective in controlling weeds after the crop is established. Unfortunately, the amount of mulch required for commercial agriculture is just not available and the labor to apply it is a drawback.

Many combinations of plowing, discing and mulching have been developed, but none are completely satisfactory due to the weed problem. The solution to the weed problem came with the development of selective herbicide chemicals, which would kill the competing weeds and not interfere with the growth of the crop. The development of suitable weed-killing chemicals has been studied very extensively by Drs. Glover B. Triplett and David M. Van Doren and co-workers in Ohio.(3) The first successful herbicides developed to kill broadleaved weeds was 2,4—D, introduced in the late 1940's. Since then, over 100 selective weed killers have been developed. No one chemical is effective against all weeds and specific combinations and schedules have been developed for most of the major crops. One major advantage of these herbicides is that they could inhibit the weeds within the rows, which could not be reached by the cultivators. They effectively eliminated hand hoeing and soon became well entrenched in the American agriculture scene. The development of the herbicides made Faulkners system practical for large scale agriculture. The trend towards less and less tillage began to pick up momentum, and the recent quadrupling of oil prices accelerated the trend.

The ultimate extension of the trend towards reduction in tillage is no tillage at all. No-tillage systems were first introduced to improve pastures and have spread rapidly to other areas of agriculture. In a typical no-tillage operation, the grower first sprays herbicides on the soil to kill any growing weeds and to prevent existing seeds from germination. In the next operation, liquid or solid fertilizers, are placed in a band in the soil. The seeds are then planted by a machine which cuts a slit through the plant residue on the surface and covers the seed in one operation. The application of fertilizer, opening the soil, positioning the seed and covering the seed, can all be done in one operation. The soil is undisturbed except for a band 2–3 inches wide. Thus, in two passes—herbicide spraying and planting—the land is prepared and the crop planted. Often, no other operations are necessary until harvest.

TABLE 1. Energy Costs of Several Types of Soil Operations

Type	Gallons of Fuel Per 100 Acres Using a 100 Horsepower Diesel Tractor
Moldboard Plowing	180
Chisel Plowing	115
One-Time Discing	70
Conventional Planting	65
One-Time Cultivation	48
No-Till Planting	40

Adapted from Triplett and Van Doren(3)

The application of no-tillage concepts to production of corn has resulted in amazing savings in energy utilization alone, (Table 1) and this, in itself, will ensure rapid adoption. Conventional mold board plowing alone used four times as much gasoline as no-tillage planting. Yet, there are some drawbacks. Continuous no-tillage agriculture causes some types of soil to become more dense.(1) It may be necessarty to resort to conventional plowing every four or five years, primarily to aerate the soil. Some heavy, poorly drained soils are not suitable for no-tillage planting, because a reduction in crop yield occurs when compared with conventional tillage. Researchers suspected that the lower yields were related to unfavorable growing conditions for very young plants. A recent breakthrough by Dr. R.J. Cook at the Northwest Cereal Disease Laboratory in Pullman, Washington has confirmed this.(6) He discovered that a fungus, *Pythium,* grows in plant residue left on the soil surface and causes the seeds and roots of young wheat plants to rot. The fungus grows well in cold, wet soil whereas other fungi, which would normally outgrow Pythium and are beneficial to wheat plants, grow much slower. Dr. Cook discovered a fungicide which prevents the growth of Pythium, thus allowing normal yields of what under conditions previously unfavorable to no-tillage agriculture.

The energy savings in no-tillage agriculture will probably be the most immediate short-term advantage of no-tillage agriculture. Yet, long term, there is another advantage which eventually is bound to be more important. This advantage is the control of soil losses due to erosion. The layer of plant debris left on the surface of the soil protects the soil from both wind and water erosion. Soil erosion is a slow, insidious loss which is difficult to perceive year by year, but it is none-the-less very real. The "Okies" portrayed so vividly in John Steinbeck's "Grapes of Wrath" are believers. The dust storms in the 1930's in the United States are reminders of the terrible erosion effects of unprotected land in a dry cycle. The lessons of the dust bowl in the 1930's reinforced the measures advocated by the Soil Conservation Service to protect the land. One of the measures was to plant trees to provide windbreaks in susceptible areas. Unfortunately, the windbreaks were incompatible with the huge circular irrigation systems recently introduced, so the trees began to be removed. It is inevitable that we will have more dry cycles and the process may repeat itself. The introduction of no-tillage agriculture will certainly help to reduce the erosion problems.

The problems in soil erosion are hard to imagine on casual observation. For example, the 8½ million acres in the Palouse region of the United States Pacific Northwest (parts of Washington, Idaho and Oregon) contains some of the worlds most fertile and productive topsoil.(7) Each year more than 110 million tons of topsoil are lost to erosion. During the last 100 years, 40 percent of the original topsoil has been lost. Topsoil is built by nature at the rate of one inch in 800 years and is being lost by erosion at the rate of one inch in 15 years. "For every bushel (60 lbs.) of wheat grown in the Palouse, 1200 lbs. of topsoil are lost."(7) Eventually unless soil erosion is controlled, food production will be drastically reduced.

The main culpit in soil erosion is the conventional practice of summer fallow, in which land is left idle for a year. The land is tilled constantly to provide a soil texture with very fine particles in order to conserve moisture and control weeds. The land with a two year accumulation of moisture does provide a good crop, but the unprotected land is subject to water and wind erosion. Yarris describes the process as "on a short term basis, summer fallowing may be an agricultural and economic boom, but all evidence indicates that for this region in the long run, its a bankrupt policy." (7) The introduction of no-tillage practices or even partial tillage practices could immediately reduce the erosion losses by 70–80 percent.

There is even another advantage to no-tillage agriculture that may be very important. Slopes that are too steep for cultivation by conventional means are usually left in permanent pasture. They can be made more productive by using herbicides to kill strips of grass with subsequent planting to cereals or even some row crops. Previously erosion problems would have made this practice impractical. Another advantage of growing crops through a soil cover of plant residue is the reduced run-off of pesticide chemicals and fertilizers. The organic gardeners have known for many years that yields could be increased by as much as three times with a proper mulch cover. The increased yield is due mainly to better water holding capacity, weed control, soil temperature, and in subsequent years, to better soil texture. The plant residue in no-tillage agriculture does provide better water retention in the soil, thus reducing fertilizer and pesticide input into the streams and rivers. Another advantage of no-tillage agriculture is the possibility of multiple cropping in the same year. For example, a spring grain crop followed by a soybean crop is possible in Ohio.(4, 5) Multiple cropping usually involves very careful timing in order to get the second crop established early enough to provide a crop. The lighter equipment required for no-tillage methods allows the grower to proceed in situations where the land might be too wet for conventional agricultural equipment. In the tropical areas where systems are being introduced to produce as many as five crops per year from the same land, the timing of each operation is critical. The use of selective herbicides provides yet another tool in these sophisticated systems for food production.

The above paragraphs provide ample reason why the concept of conventional agriculture should change. And it will!

REFERENCES

1. Dull, S., 1979. "Tillage: More Interest in Less." *The Furrow*, 84 (8) 2–5.
2. Pimentel, D., L.E. Hurd, A.C. Belotti, M.J. Forster, I.N. Oka, O.D. Sholes, and R.J. Whitman, 1973. "Food Production and the Energy Crisis." *Science*, 182: 443–449
3. Triplett, G.B. and D.M. Van Doren, 1977. "Agriculture without Tillage." *Scientific American*, 236 (1) 28–33.
4. Triplett, G.B., 1978. "Weed control for double crop soybeans planted with the no-tillage method following small grain harvest." *Agronomy Journal*, 70 (4) 577–581.
5. Van Doren, D.M., G.B. Triplett, Jr., and J.E. Henry, 1976. "Influence of long term tillage, crop rotation, and soil type combinations on corn yield." *Soil Science Soc. America Journal*, 40 (1): 100–105, 1976.
6. Yarris, L.C., 1979. "Breakthrough discovery in wheat." *Agricultural Research*, 28 (2) 7.
7. Yarris, L.C., 1979. "Learning from the past." *Agricultural Research*, 28 (4) 4–9.